Market Expectations and Option Prices

Contributions to Economics

http://www.springer.de/cgi-bin/search_book.pl?series=1262

Further volumes of this series can be found at our homepage.

Kirstin Hubrich
Cointegration Analysis in a German Monetary System
2001. ISBN 3-7908-1352-4

Nico Heerink et al. (Eds.)
Economic Policy and Sustainable Land Use
2001. ISBN 3-7908-1351-6

Friedel Bolle/Michael Carlberg (Eds.)
Advances in Behavioral Economics
2001. ISBN 3-7908-1358-3

Volker Grossmann
Inequality, Economic Growth, and Technological Change
2001. ISBN 3-7908-1364-8

Thomas Riechmann
Learning in Economics
2001. ISBN 3-7908-1384-2

Miriam Beblo
Bargaining over Time Allocation
2001. ISBN 3-7908-1391-5

Peter Meusburger/Heike Jöns (Eds.)
Transformations in Hungary
2001. ISBN 3-7908-1412-1

Claus Brand
Money Stock Control and Inflation Targeting in Germany
2001. ISBN 3-7908-1393-1

Erik Lüth
Private Intergenerational Transfers and Population Aging
2001. ISBN 3-7908-1402-4

Nicole Pohl
Mobility in Space and Time
2001. ISBN 3-7908-1380-X

Pablo Coto-Millán (Ed.)
Essays on Microeconomics and Industrial Organisation
2002. ISBN 3-7908-1390-7

Mario A. Maggioni
Clustering Dynamics and the Locations of High-Tech-Firms
2002. ISBN 3-7908-1431-8

Ludwig Schätzl/Javier Revilla Diez (Eds.)
Technological Change and Regional Development in Europe
2002. ISBN 3-7908-1460-1

Alberto Quadrio Curzio/Marco Fortis (Eds.)
Complexity and Industrial Clusters
2002. ISBN 3-7908-1471-7

Friedel Bolle/Marco Lehmann-Waffenschmidt (Eds.)
Surveys in Experimental Economics
2002. ISBN 3-7908-1472-5

Pablo Coto-Millán
General Equilibrium and Welfare
2002. ISBN 7908-1491-1

Wojciech W. Charemza/Krystyna Strzala (Eds.)
East European Transition and EU Enlargement
2002. ISBN 3-7908-1501-2

Natalja von Westernhagen
Systemic Transformation, Trade and Economic Growth
2002. ISBN 3-7908-1521-7

Josef Falkinger
A Theory of Employment in Firms
2002. ISBN 3-7908-1520-9

Engelbert Plassmann
Econometric Modelling of European Money Demand
2003. ISBN 3-7908-1522-5

Reginald Loyen/Erik Buyst/Greta Devos (Eds.)
Struggeling for Leadership: Antwerp-Rotterdam Port Competition between 1870–2000
2003. ISBN 3-7908-1524-1

Pablo Coto-Millán
Utility and Production, 2nd Edition
2003. ISBN 3-7908-1423-7

Emilio Colombo/John Driffill (Eds.)
The Role of Financial Markets in the Transition Process
2003. ISBN 3-7908-0004-X

Guido S. Merzoni
Strategic Delegation in Firms and in the Trade Union
2003. ISBN 3-7908-1432-6

Jan B. Kuné
On Global Aging
2003. ISBN 3-7908-0030-9

Sugata Marjit, Rajat Acharyya
International Trade, Wage Inequality and the Developing Economy
2003. ISBN 3-7908-0031-7

Francesco C. Billari, Alexia Prskawetz (Eds.)
Agent-Based Computational Demography
2003. ISBN 3-7908-1550-0

Martin Mandler

Market Expectations and Option Prices

Techniques and Applications

With 64 Figures
and 13 Tables

Physica-Verlag
A Springer-Verlag Company

Series Editors
Werner A. Müller
Martina Bihn

Author

Dr. Martin Mandler
Department of Economics and Business Administration
University of Gießen
Licher Straße 62
35394 Gießen
Germany

This book was submitted as a doctoral dissertation to the Department of Economics and Business Administration of the Justus-Liebig-University Gießen, Germany, in 2002.

ISSN 1431-1933
ISBN 3-7908-0049-X Physica-Verlag Heidelberg New York

Cataloging-in-Publication Data applied for
A catalog record for this book is available from the Library of Congress.
Bibliographic information published by Die Deutsche Bibliothek
Die Deutsche Bibliothek lists this publication in the Deutsche Nationalbibliografie; detailed bibliographic data is available in the Internet at <http://dnb.ddb.de>.

Physica-Verlag Heidelberg New York
a member of BertelsmannSpringer Science+Business Media GmbH

Softcover Design: Erich Kirchner, Heidelberg

SPIN 10920152 88/3130/DK-5 4 3 2 1 0 – Printed on acid-free and non-aging paper

Preface

This book is a slightly revised version of my doctoral dissertation which has been accepted by the Department of Economics and Business Administration of the Justus-Liebig-Universität Giessen in July 2002.

I am indebted to my advisor Prof. Dr. Volbert Alexander for encouraging and supporting my research. I am also grateful to the second member of the doctoral committee, Prof. Dr. Horst Rinne.

Special thanks go to Dr. Ralf Ahrens for providing part of the data and to my colleague Carsten Lang, who spent much time reading the complete first draft.

Wetzlar, January 2003 Martin Mandler

Contents

1

Introduction

Expectations about future realizations of economic variables play an important role in the analysis of economic problems. Nearly every complete dynamic framework must include expectation formation processes.
In particular, expectations are important in the determination of asset prices because these are primarily based on expectations about what the asset's value will be in the future. For risk-averse investors not only does the level of expected asset prices or asset returns matter but also the degree of uncertainty associated with these expectations. Their portfolio decisions are not only based on expected returns but statistics like the standard deviation of the probability distribution of expected returns have to be taken into account as well. For example, Tobin (1958) in his seminal contribution to the theory of money demand explicitly accounts for the expected uncertainty in bond returns. Nevertheless, the bulk of commonly used stochastic macro-models is based on linear-quadratic frameworks containing only first moments. A few more complex models incorporate moments of higher order.

Within theoretical models, the probability distributions of future realizations of economic variables usually follow from the model's specified stochastic properties. A well known example is the famous Black-Scholes model where the probability distribution of future stock prices is lognormal. This raises the question of whether it is possible to determine the probability distributions associated with agents' expectations empirically. Again, this discussion is focussed on asset markets, because there - as mentioned above - price or return expectations play a particularly important role. Changes in the market participants' expectations cause portfolio adjustments that, in turn, affect asset prices. This suggests that information on market expectations can be extracted from observed asset prices. Most research on this issue is focussed on financial assets because appropriate data can be found only in the highly differentiated financial markets with high liquidity. Therefore, interest has been centered on developing techniques that extract information on market expectations from financial derivative prices. Since financial derivatives are nothing other than more or less complex 'bets' on future outcomes this strategy is immediatly comprehensible.

The first stage in this process is represented by empirical approaches based on the interpretation of forward and futures prices as expectations of future prices of the underlying asset (e.g. Fama (1984a,b)). Before that, empirical estimates for expectations either were obtained from surveys or were derived from historical data, for example, by estimating a time series model and treating its forecasts for future variables as representing the economic agents' expectations.[1] In contrast, from derivative prices information on expectations can be extracted that refers explicitly to the future. Later, researchers also began to study option markets and it became clear that these types of derivatives could potentially provide much richer information on market expectations. In fact, it is possible to extract complete probability density functions with respect to future outcomes from observed option prices. These techniques, their presentation, critical discussion and application are the focus of this book.

Many interesting applications are possible based on these approaches. To date only a subset of these areas has been worked out. For example, information on expectations extracted from market prices can be useful for portfolio decisions by investors in international capital markets, in particular if issues related to the risk of various assets are concerned. In the field of risk management probability distributions implied by option prices can be used to provide market based risk assessments explicitly referring to the future and supplementing the currently used risk measures derived from historical data. In addition, probability distributions constructed from option prices might be helpful for investigating the behaviour of risk premia. Other potential applications can be found outside the field of financial economics: information on market expectations extracted from option prices can be applied to analyse issues of policy credibility. Examples can be found in the papers by Campa and Chang (1998b) or Campa, Chang and Reider (1997). They derive from option prices market-based assessments of the credibility of fixed exchange-rate regimes. Bahra (1997) uses probability distributions implicit in option prices to study how central bank policy is perceived by financial markets. In fact, the second part of this book contains some empirical applications related to this issue. Finally, interesting empirical applications to the theories of economic learning and expectation formation are conceivable.[2]

Empirical studies of the uncertainty in expectations are a consequent step in applied economics. After a time period during which economic models were almost exclusively constructed in terms of actual realizations of variables, the rational-expectations revolution following the seminal papers of Lucas (1972,

[1] Examples for this approach can be found in the empirical literature on the effects of unanticipated vs. anticipated monetary policy, e.g. Barro (1977).

[2] A good introduction to theoretical learning models is the book by Evans and Honkapohja (2001).

1973) made the consideration of expectations an integral part of economic theory and its applications.[3] The empirical counterpart to this development was an extended literature testing the validity of the rational-expectations hypothesis.[4] Another strand of the literature investigated the predictive content of futures and forward prices, that under risk neutrality should be unbiased forecasts of future spot prices.
However, there is no comparable literature on uncertainty in expectations. Applied work has mainly focussed on actual uncertainty, particularly in financial markets, as opposed to uncertainty in expectations. In most of these papers researchers have looked at the volatility of financial asset prices, relying on applications of ARCH or GARCH techniques introduced by Engle (1982) and Bollerslev (1986).[5] In this book we will study explicitly uncertainties in expectations and in this way we will make a contribution to close the gap pointed out above.

In the first part of the book the theoretical and technical foundations for the extraction of market expectations from option prices are laid and discussed. In Chapter 2 we start by reviewing some principles of arbitrage pricing of derivatives. Within the very simple framework of the Black/Scholes-Merton model we consider the representation of the derivative price as conditional expectation and discuss how this representation relates to the concept of risk-neutral valuation. Chapter 3 presents an overview of the related literature. Studies on the forecasting ability of forward and futures prices are considered as well as studies investigating the information content of implied volatilities and of the "skewness premium" implicit in option prices. In Chapter 4 issues related to the presentation and interpretation of implicit probability distributions extracted from option prices are discussed. Chapter 5 presents the most important techniques used to extract market expectations from option prices in some detail. We have tried to make the discussion as comprehensive as possible so that the reader should be able to implement any of the techniques explained with appropriate software. Furthermore, we consider some important issues related to data selection and data preparation. Based on Chapter 5, Chapter 6 summarizes the results from studies comparing various methods for the construction of implicit probability distributions from option prices. Two aspects are of crucial importance: First, do the various approaches yield similar results for the implied probability density functions or are the results dependent on the choice of method? Second, how sensitive are the different

---

[3] An example for an economic model that does not consider expectation formation is the textbook IS-LM model.

[4] See, for example, the research on the *Livingston* data by Pesando (1975), Carlson (1977), or DeBondt and Bange (1992), on interest-rate expectations (Friedman (1980)) or on exchange-rate expectations (Dominguez (1986), Frankel and Froot (1987)).

[5] See, for example, the surveys in Bollerslev, Engle, and Nelson (1994) and Cuthbertson (1996).

techniques with respect to measurement errors and distorted data? The selection of the method used in the empirical applications in the second part of this book is based on these considerations.

The second part mainly contains our own empirical applications of the techniques outlined before. In Chapter 7 we review various examples of empirical analyses based on risk-neutral probabilities. In Chapter 8 we use one of the techniques described in Chapter 5 to extract implicit probabilities from options on interest-rate futures. We then investigate the effects of central bank council meetings on the uncertainty in market expectations.[6] While the approach considered in Chapter 8 is focused on general characteristics of this relationship, Chapter 9 turns to event studies. We look at specific central bank meetings in small time windows and study how market expectations reacted to them. Chapter 10 contains a summary of the most important results.

[6] The effects of central-bank policy on market volatility are the subject of an extensive theoretical literature. However, a much smaller number of empirical studies of the relationship between monetary policy decisions and uncertainty on financial markets measured by observed volatilities can be found, e.g. Alexander (1998), Ball and Torous (1999). To date the issue of how central-bank policy affects uncertainty in expectations has been neglected.

Part I

Theoretical Foundations

2

Arbitrage Pricing and Risk-Neutral Probabilities

This Chapter reviews some basic elements from asset-pricing theory thus establishing the theoretical foundations of the techniques presented in this book. First, we explain the principles of arbitrage pricing of financial derivatives.[1] The most important implication for our purpose is that derivative prices can be expressed as conditional expectations by transforming the probability measure for the stochastic process of the underlying asset prices. This result can be derived by a replication argument that shows how the pay-off function of the derivative can be replicated by an appropriate portfolio of stocks and bonds.

We then discuss the relationship between the transformed probability measure and the representative agent's expectations about future prices of the underlying asset. It will be shown that under some specific conditions the transformed probability measure can be interpreted as representing the expectations of a risk-neutral agent. The third section shows how this probability measure can be extracted from observed option prices and offers a basic categorization of the techniques applied to this problem. The final section summarizes and concludes.

2.1 Arbitrage Pricing in the Black/Scholes-Merton Model

Valuation of derivatives is centered on the search for a valuation function that gives the value of the derivative in question as a function of various known parameters. The first step to this goal is to construct a market model. The market model specifies the number, type and properties of all assets relevant

[1] Introductory textbooks on derivative pricing are e.g. Neftci (1996), Baxter and Rennie (1996) or Bjørk (1998). More advanced presentations are Duffie (1988, 1996).

for the problem. The complexity of the resulting valuation function depends on both the properties of the derivative and on the specification of the market model. In many cases it is not possible to get a closed-form solution, so that numerical or simulation methods have to be applied.[2]
Since our goal is to illustrate the relationship between risk-neutral probability distributions and derivative prices we only review some very basic principles of arbitrage pricing. We focus on simple European-type call and put options and forward contracts and discuss the valuation problem using one of the most basic models, the Black/Scholes-Merton model.[3] In the following we only sketch the derivation of the valuation function. A more comprehensive presentation can be found in Appendix 2A.

The market model comprises only two different assets, a stock (the underlying) and a bond. The stock price process S_t is described by the stochastic differential equation

$$dS_t = \mu(S_t, t)\, dt + \sigma(S_t, t)\, dB_t. \tag{2.1}$$

on the probability space $(\Omega, \mathcal{F}, P)$.[4] $\mu(S_t, t) > 0$ and $\sigma(S_t, t) > 0$ are processes representing local drift and volatility of S_t. B_t is a standard Brownian motion. The bond price process is

$$d\beta_t = \beta_t r_t dt. \tag{2.2}$$

To complete the model Black und Scholes (1973) make some additional assumptions:

1. The instantaneous rate of return of the bond r is constant.
2. The stock price follows (2.1) with $\mu(S_t, t) = S_t\, \mu$ and $\sigma(S_t, t) = S_t\, \sigma$ where μ and σ are constants.
3. There are no dividends.
4. There are no market imperfections such as taxes and transaction costs. Short sales are not restricted and trading is continuous and frictionless.

With these assumptions (2.1) and (2.2) can be rewritten as

[2] For further information, see Neftci (1996, p. 266), Campbell, Lo, and MacKinlay (1997, p. 382), or Duffie (1996, Ch. 11.)

[3] A European-type option can only be exercised at the expiration date whereas an American type option can be exercised at any time up to the expiration date. The original presentation of this framework is given in Black and Scholes (1973) and Merton (1973). A thorough discussion is offered by Duffie (1988, 1996).

[4] The stochastic differential equation (2.1) is a less rigorous representation for the Itô-Prozeß $S_t = S_0 + \int_0^t \mu(S_s, s)\, ds + \int_0^t \sigma(S_s, s)\, dB_s,\ t \geq 0$. For this process to be well defined the functions μ and σ must satisfy certain regularity conditions, see Duffie (1988, p. 224).

$$dS_t = S_t \, \mu \, dt + S_t \, \sigma d B_t, \tag{2.3}$$
$$d\beta_t = \beta_t \, r \, dt. \tag{2.4}$$

Our problem is to find the value of a European-type call option $C(S_t, t)$ with exercise price K and expiration in $T > t$.

The most important element in the valuation of this option via arbitrage pricing is a replication argument. We construct a self-financing portfolio with exactly the same payoff in T as the option. It follows that to rule out arbitrage opportunities the price of the option has to be equal to the price of the portfolio.[5]

First, the market model (2.3) and (2.4) is discounted with the bond price process: the discounted bond price process is constant and equal to one and the discounted stock price process $Z_t = (S_t/\beta_t), t \in [0, \infty)$ is computed by applying Itô's Lemma,

$$dZ_t = Z_t \, (\mu - r) \, dt + Z_t \sigma \, dB_t, \tag{2.5}$$

on $(\Omega, \mathcal{F}, P)$. The absence of arbitrage opportunities requires that there exists a martingale measure Q that is equivalent to P for Z_t.[6] A probability measure Q on $(\Omega, \mathcal{F})$ is said to be equivalent to P if, for any event $A \in \mathcal{F}$ we have $Q(A) > 0$ if and only if $P(A) > 0$. An equivalent probability measure Q is an equivalent martingale measure for Z if Z is a martingale with respect to Q, and if the Radon-Nikodyn derivative dQ/dP has finite variance (Duffie (1996, p. 108)).
This means that the discounted stock price process will be a martingale under Q. The change of measure from P to Q is performed by applying the Girsanov theorem (see Appendix 2A). Therefore, with respect to Q we have

$$dZ_t = Z_t \, \sigma \, \hat{B}_t, \tag{2.6}$$

where $\hat{B}$ is derived from B by

$$d\hat{B}_t = \frac{\mu - r}{\sigma} \, dt + dB_t. \tag{2.7}$$

In the next step we use the transformed model to construct a dynamic portfolio strategy that replicates the option's payoff at expiration. The portfolio strategy is self financing, i.e. any change in the value of the portfolio is due

[5] This section and the formal argument in Appendix 2A follow Duffie (1996), Baxter and Rennie (1996), and Shreve (1997). Duffie (1988) gives another good exposition and the discussion in Neftci (1996) provides a basic introduction. The seminal papers are Harrison und Kreps (1979) and Harrison und Pliska (1981).

[6] To be more specific, the existence of the equivalent martingale measure follows from the absence of a special form of arbitrage (*approximate arbitrage*) (Duffie (1996, p. 122)).

only to changes in the value of its components (e.g. Baxter and Rennie (1996, p. 40)). This implies that between t and T any portfolio adjustments do not entail cash inflows or outflows. In T the portfolio is cashed in and yields exactly the same pay-off as the call option.
As shown in Appendix 2A the value of portfolio replicating the option can be written as

$$G(S_t, t) = e^{-r(T-t)}\,\mathrm{E}^Q[h(S_T)|\mathfrak{F}_t], \tag{2.8}$$

where $h(S_T)$ is the option's payoff function. In order to eliminate arbitrage opportunities the option's value must be equal to that of the portfolio. Therefore, equation (2.8) states that the option's value is the (conditional) discounted expectation of its payoff. Note that the expectation is taken with respect to the equivalent martingale measure Q as opposed to the true probability measure P.

Consequently, the value of a European call option with exercise price K is[7]

$$\begin{aligned} C(S_t, t) &= e^{-r(T-t)}\,\mathrm{E}^Q\left[\max[S_T - K, 0]|S_t\right] \\ &= e^{-r(T-t)} \int_{-\infty}^{+\infty} \max[S_T - K, 0]\, dQ(S_T|S_t). \end{aligned} \tag{2.9}$$

Evaluating the integral yields the famous Black-Scholes formula,

$$\begin{aligned} C(S_t, t) &= S_t\,\Phi(d_1) - K\,e^{-r(T-t)}\,\Phi(d_2), \\ d_1 &= \frac{\log\frac{S_t}{K} + (r + \frac{1}{2}\sigma^2)(T-t)}{\sigma\sqrt{T-t}}, \\ d_2 &= d_1 - \sigma\sqrt{T-t}, \end{aligned} \tag{2.10}$$

with $\Phi(\bullet)$ representing the cumulative distribution function of the standard normal distribution.

Note that μ, the drift parameter from the stock-price process under P does not appear in the valuation function. This is due to the switch in the probability measure from P to Q. In going from (2.5) to (2.6) the drift parameter of S_t is set equal to r under Q as can be seen from (2.6) in combination with $Z_t = S_t/\beta_t$ and Itô's Lemma.

(2.8) can also be used to value the forward contract on S.[8] By convention the forward price F_t is the exercise price that sets the value of the contract equal to zero,

[7] For notational convenience we only note S_t explicitly as an element of the information set in t.

[8] Since this model features a deterministic interest rate, forward and futures prices are identical, see Bjørk (1998, p. 301).

$$0 = e^{-r(T-t)}\, \mathrm{E}^Q[S_T - F_t | S_t] \tag{2.11}$$
$$\Leftrightarrow F_t = \mathrm{E}^Q[S_T] \tag{2.12}$$
$$\Leftrightarrow F_t = S_t\, e^{r(T-t)}. \tag{2.13}$$

As another illustration consider the valuation of futures options. A European-type option with strike price K expiring in T written on a futures contract expiring in $T' \geq T$ will yield a payoff equal to $h(F_T) = \max[F_T - K, 0] = e^{r(T'-T)} \max[S_T - e^{-r(T'-T)}\, K, 0]$. That means one such futures option is equivalent to $e^{r(T'-T)}$ call options on the stock with strike prices equal to $e^{-r(T'-T)}\, K$. Substituting into (2.10) yields the value of the futures option,

$$C(F_t, t) = e^{r(T'-T)} \left[S_t\, \Phi(d_1) - e^{-r(T-t)}\, e^{-r(T'-T)}\, K\, \Phi(d_2)\right], \tag{2.14}$$

where d_1, d_2 are given by the expressions in (2.10) with K replaced by $e^{-r(T'-T)}\, K$. Substituting $S_t = F_t\, e^{-r(T'-t)}$ we arrive at *Black's formula* (Black (1976a)),

$$C(F_t, t) = e^{-r(T-t)} \left[F_t\, \Phi N(d_1') - K\, \Phi(d_2')\right], \tag{2.15}$$
$$d_1' = \frac{\ln \frac{F_t}{K} + \frac{1}{2}\sigma^2\, (T-t)}{\sigma\sqrt{T-t}},$$
$$d_2' = d_1' - \sigma\sqrt{T-t}.$$

Considering these examples we note the particular difficulty associated with the valuation of American-type options. Whereas the value of a European-type option only depends on the price of the underlying at a single point in time, i.e. at the expiration date, the complete trajectory of the underlying's price matters for the value of American-type options because of their early exercise feature.[9]

2.2 The Equivalent Martingale Measure and Risk-Neutral Valuation

The valuation function (2.8) does not rely on strong assumptions about market participant's preferences. In fact, the only necessary assumption is non-satiation in order to rule out the existence of arbitrage opportunities. More formally, preferences are only assumed to be continuous, convex, and strictly monotonous (Duffie (1988, p. 160)). Since no additional structure has to be

[9] See for example Duffie (1996), Ch. 8 for details. In the special case of an American-type call option on a non-dividend paying stock it can be shown that early exercise will not take place. Therefore, the option can be valued as the corresponding European-type option. See for example Bjørk (1998), p. 94.

imposed on preferences for the results to hold, the valuation is often denoted as "preference free".

Under Q the discounted stock-price process Z_t is a martingale, i.e. the drift parameter of S_t is equal to r. Note, that this drift would also result in a model where all agents are risk-neutral and the expected stock-price change is equal to rS_t in equilibrium. That the derivative is valued as if all agents were risk-neutral was first pointed out by Cox and Ross (1976).[10] Because of this implication the equivalent martingale measure often is called the "risk-neutral probability measure".[11] However, there is a problem with this terminology. Not in every market model does valuation by means of the equivalent martingale measure coincide with risk-neutral valuation (e.g. Cont (1999)). An example of the breakdown of this equivalence is provided by incomplete markets.[12]

To illustrate the problem we extend the model from section 2.1,

$$d\mathbf{S}_t = \mu(\mathbf{S}_t, t)\, dt + \sigma(\mathbf{S}_t, t)\, d\mathbf{B}_t'. \tag{2.16}$$

$\mathbf{S}_t$ is a vector containing $N+1$ price processes with drift vector μ. The first element in $\mathbf{S}_t$ is the bond β_t. σ is a $(N+1) \times d$ matrix that models the dependencies of the price processes on d mutually independent standard Brownian motions in $\mathbf{B}_t$. The market model is complete if the payoff functions of all the tradable assets in $\mathbf{S}_t$ span the space of all possible events (Duffie (1996, p. 8)). That implies that in a complete market model it is always feasible to construct a portfolio from the given tradable assets that replicates any particular state-dependent payoff function (e.g. the payoff of a call option). Therefore, the derivative securities to be valued are redundant and can be priced using arbitrage techniques. The model we used to derive (2.8) is an example of a complete market model.

In contrast, for an incomplete market model the spanning condition is not fulfilled and therefore the equivalent martingale measure is not unique. Arbitrage pricing of the derivative fails because the replicating portfolio cannot

---

[10] However, "risk free" valuation holds only relative to given stock and bond price processes. These price processes themselves are not necessarily the result of arbitrage considerations, for example, if the asset in question is non-redundant. In this case its price can be explained by equilibrium-valuation approaches and preferences affect the price process and, indirectly, also derivative prices.

[11] Other corresponding terminologies are "*state price deflator*", e.g. in Duffie (1996), or "*state price density*", e.g. in Aït-Sahalia und Lo (1998). These notions are based on the fact that in an Arrow-Debreu type general equilibrium model the equivalent martingale measure corresponds to the *state prices*. For further information see Duffie (1998, p. 115), and Cont (1999).

[12] Since the terms "risk-neutral probabilities" or "risk-neutral density" are found almost throughout the literature we shall use them here for the sake of convenience, too.

be constructed.[13]
In cases like this where arbitrage methods are not applicable, equilibrium pricing models can be used to value the derivative. These models implicitly select one equivalent martingale measure from the set of admissible ones. However, the result will depend on the specification of preferences so that the resulting valuation function is not necessarily equal to the risk-neutral solution.

2.3 Extracting Risk-Neutral Probabilities from Option Prices

From (2.8) the value of a European-type call option is given by

$$\begin{aligned} C(S_t, t) &= e^{-r(T-t)}\, \mathbf{E}^Q\left[\max[S_T - K, 0] | S_t\right] \\ &= e^{-r(T-t)} \int_K^{+\infty} (S_T - K)\, q(S_T|S_t)\, dS_T, \end{aligned} \tag{2.17}$$

where $q(S_T|S_t)$ is the conditional density of S_T with respect to Q. Differentiating (2.17) with respect to K yields

$$\begin{aligned} \frac{\partial C(S_t, t)}{\partial K} &= -e^{-r(T-t)} \int_K^{+\infty} q(S_T|S_t) dS_T \\ &= -e^{-r(T-t)} \left(1 - \int_{-\infty}^{K} q(S_T|S_t) dS_T\right). \end{aligned} \tag{2.18}$$

This result shows the close relationship between the first derivative of the European call pricing function with respect to the exercise price and the conditional Q-probability for the underlying being in the money at expiration. The intuition behind this result is as follows: if the option is sufficiently deep in the money it will almost surely finish in the money at expiration. Since it will be exercised with probability one, an increase in the exercise price by one unit will make the owner of the option pay one additional unit of currency for the underlying, thus reducing the call-option value by the present value of one. If, on the other hand, the option is far out of the money and will almost surely expire worthless, a small increase in the exercise price should have no effect on the option value. The option will not be exercised anyway. Finally, if an option is almost certain to end up neither in nor out of the money, an increase in the strike price by one unit reduces the call option value by the

[13] More formally, in an incomplete market model the system of equations $\sigma(\mathbf{S}_t, t)\,\eta_t = \mu_t(\mathbf{S}_t, t)$ from Appendix 2A has no unique solution for the vector η_t of dimension d. As can be seen from the Girsanov theorem the equivalent martingale measure can only be uniquely determined if there exists a unique solution for η_t. This requires $\text{rank}(\sigma) = d$, i.e. the market model must be complete (Duffie (1996), Ch. 6).

present value of an amount between zero and one depending on the likelihood of the option being in the money at expiration.[14]

Differentiating once again with respect to K leads to

$$\frac{\partial^2 G(S_t,t)}{\partial K^2} = e^{-r(T-t)}\, q(K|S_t). \tag{2.19}$$

The second derivative of the European call-option value with respect to the strike price is equal to the discounted risk-neutral probability density of S_T![15] This result was first derived by Breeden and Litzenberger (1978). They show that the payoff functions of pure Arrow-Debreu securities can be replicated by portfolios of call options.[16] The payoff of a pure Arrow-Debreu security is one if a specific state of the world (in our case a specific realization of the stock price) occurs and zero elsewhere. In a risk-neutral world the prices of pure Arrow-Debreu securities have an interpretation as discounted probabilities for these specific events. For an Arrow-Debreu security the value of the replicating options portfolio can be written as a second-order difference quotient that in the limit tends to the second derivative of the call-option pricing function.[17]

Since the conditional density function (2.19) might embody important information about market participants' expectations concerning future prices of the underlying asset, techniques have been developed to extract the risk-neutral density q from observed option prices. Computing the risk-neutral density by equation (2.19) requires call prices being available for continuous strike prices. However, in reality we are usually limited to just a few discretely spaced observations. Therefore, all these techniques directly or indirectly entail the construction of a continuous option pricing function from observed prices. As suggested by Chang and Melick (1999) the different approaches can be divided into three categories:

Approaches in the first category are directly based on (2.17). Using some assumptions about the shape of the conditional density $q(\bullet)$ a parametric representation for option prices is derived and the free parameters are estimated to fit observed option prices.

---

[14] "Almost surely" or similar expressions refer to the equivalent martingale measure Q and therefore cannot be directly interpreted as statements about the realization of the stochastic process under the 'true' density P.

[15] The same result can be derived using European put options.

[16] These portfolios are *butterfly spreads* that are composed of two long and two short call options. The exercise price of both short calls is halfway in between the exercise prices of the two long call options. In the limit as the difference between the exercise prices goes to zero the butterfly spread's payoff becomes a Dirac-Delta function, e.g. Merton (1999, p. 447).

[17] Ross (1976) already demonstrated that portfolios of simple options with different exercise prices replicate any future payoff conditional on the option's underlying. Further important contributions are from Banz and Miller (1978) who independently derive a result similar to Breeden and Litzenberger (1978) and Bick (1982).

The second important group of techniques more or less directly constructs a continuous option-pricing function from observed option prices. Then, the option-pricing function is differentiated analytically or numerically in order to arrive at the conditional density.
Finally, approaches from the third category assume a specific stochastic process for the price of the underlying asset and its parameters are chosen to match theoretical with observed option prices. This strategy is similar to that applied within the first category because the choice of a stochastic process implicitly specifies a conditional density for the underlying's price. However, the process-oriented approach is much more restrictive than directly modelling the conditional density. A given density can result from many different price processes whereas a given price process implies a particular density function (e.g. Melick und Thomas (1997) p. 93).

The selected technique can exert a considerable influence on the shape of the extracted density function. One reason is the indeterminacy of the equivalent martingale measure in incomplete markets. In addition, the comparatively few observed option prices constitute only relatively weak restrictions on the shape of the conditional density. This problem becomes worse in face of measurement errors in option prices or in the presence of bid-ask spreads. Therefore, it is not possible to extract the 'correct' risk-neutral probability density function and the selection of the technique to be applied in a particular study should be made with respect to such criteria as stability, computing resources, or issues concerning the economic interpretaton of the results.

2.4 Summary

Using the simple Black-Scholes/Merton market model it was shown by a replication argument that derivative prices can be written as discounted expectations of their payoff functions. However, the expectation is taken with respect to the equivalent martingale measure resulting from a transformation of the original 'true' probability measure associated with the underlying's price process. Under the equivalent martingale measure the underlying's drift is equal to the risk-free rate of interest. Arbitrage pricing yields the same valuation for the derivative as would be assigned by a risk-neutral agent. Therefore, the conditional distribution of the underlying's price under the equivalent martingale measure is often called "risk-neutral" distribution. "Risk-neutral" probabilities can be interpreted as representing the expectations a risk-neutral market participant holds for future prices of the underlying asset. However, if markets are incomplete and derivatives are non-redundant, arbitrage pricing might be impossible. In these cases risk-preferences matter for derivatives prices. That derivative prices indeed contain useful information about market expectations will be shown in Chapter 3 where the extensive literature on the information content of derivative prices is reviewed.

The first derivative of the call-pricing function with respect to the strike price is closely related to the risk-neutral cumulative probability distribution function and the second derivative is equal to the discounted risk-neutral probability density function of the underlying's price. Using these relationships it is possible to extract risk-neutral probabilities from observed option prices. Alternative approaches either rely on imposing restrictions on the risk-neutral density's shape, on the interpolation of observed option prices, or on the specification of the stochastic process of the underlying's price. The various techniques will be thoroughly discussed and presented in some detail in Chapter 5. The shape of the risk-neutral density function extracted from option prices might be affected by the choice of technique. Therefore, in Chapter 6 we discuss whether different techniques lead to similar oder very different results.

Appendix 2A: The Valuation Function in the Black/Scholes-Merton Model

Prior to discussing how to derive the valuation function, two theoretical concepts must be introduced in order to describe the market participant's information set.

The concept of a filtration F is used to model the evolution of the economic agents' information set over time. A filtration is a collection $F = \{\mathfrak{F}_t : t \in [0, \infty)\}$ of σ-subfields of events in a complete probability space $(\Omega, \mathfrak{F}, P)$ with the property $\mathfrak{F}_s \subseteq \mathfrak{F}_t$ for $s \leq t$, e.g. Davidson (1995, p. 500). This implies that no information is lost through time. For our purpose it is important that an economic agent only knows of the occurence of event $A \subseteq \Omega$ if $A \in \mathfrak{F}_t$. Consequently, a filtration is a model that describes how information is revealed to the agents over time.

The notion of an "adapted process" relates to the evolution of the information set with respect to the stochastic process $S_t, t \in [0, \infty)$. A stochastic process X_t, $t \in [0, \infty)$ is said to be adapted to a filtration $F = \{\mathfrak{F}_t : t \in [0, \infty)\}$ if X_t is $\mathfrak{F}_t$ measurable for all $t \in [0, \infty)$. Put simply, this states that X_t is a random variable with respect to $(\Omega, \mathfrak{F}_t)$. The realization of an F-adapted stochastic process X_t is known to the agent at time t. Since any action d_t taken by the agent can only depend on the information set at time t, the stochastic process $D = \{d_t : t \in [0, \infty)\}$ must also be F-adapted (Duffie (1988, p. 130) and Davidson (1994, p. 500)). In the market model (2.1) and (2.2) $\mu(\bullet), \sigma(\bullet), B_t, S_t$ and β_t are all F-adapted processes.

The stochastic component of the stock-price process (2.1) is given by a standard Brownian motion. A standard Brownian motion defined on the probability space $(\Omega, \mathfrak{F}, P)$ is a continuous adapted process $B = \{B_t, \mathfrak{F}_t; t \in [0, \infty)\}$ that has the following properties:[18]

1. For each s and t, $0 \leq s < t$, $(B_t - B_s)$ is normally distributed with mean zero and variance $t - s$.
2. For s and t, $0 \leq s < t$, the increment $(B_t - B_s)$ is independent of $\mathfrak{F}_s$.
3. $P(\{B_0 = 0\}) = 1$.[19]

It follows that B is a martingale on the probability space $(\Omega, \mathfrak{F}, P)$ and with respect to the filtration F, i.e. $\mathbf{E}^P(B_t | \mathfrak{F}_s) = B_s$.

Now we derive the valuation function. First, the market model given by

$$dS_t = S_t \, \mu \, dt + S_t \sigma \, dB_t, \tag{2A.1}$$
$$d\beta_t = \beta_t \, r \, dt \tag{2A.2}$$

is discounted with the bond-price process: $Z_t = (S_t / \beta_t), t \in [0, \infty)$ and

$$dZ_t = Z_t \, (\mu - r) \, dt + Z_t \, \sigma d \, B_t \tag{2A.3}$$

on $(\Omega, \mathfrak{F}, P)$. The absence of arbitrage opportunities implies the existence of a martingale measure Q equivalent to P for Z. The relationship between the discounted stock price processes under P and Q is described by the Girsanov theorem.[20]

Theorem 1 (Girsanov-Theorem). *Let Y be an Itô process of the form*

$$dY_t = \mu_Y(Y_t, t) \, dt + \sigma_Y(Y_t, t) \, dB_t, \qquad t \in [0, T), \tag{2A.4}$$

where $T \leq \infty$ is a given constant and B_t is a standard Brownian motion on $(\Omega, \mathfrak{F}, P)$, $\eta(Y_t, t)$ and $\alpha(Y_t, t)$ are F-adapted with $P\big[\int_S^T \eta(Y_s, s)^2 \, ds < \infty\big] = 1$ and $P\big[\int_S^T \alpha(Y_s, s)^2 \, ds < \infty\big] = 1$, such that

$$\sigma_Y(Y_t, t) \, \eta(Y_t, t) = \mu_Y(Y_t, t) - \alpha(Y_t, t). \tag{2A.5}$$

Assume that $\eta(\bullet)$ satisfies Novikov's condition,

$$\mathbf{E}\left[\exp\left(\frac{1}{2}\int_0^T \eta(Y_s, s)^2 \, ds\right)\right] < \infty. \tag{2A.6}$$

[18] See Karatzas und Shreve (1991, p. 47). A lucid discussion of the economic interpretation of standard Brownian motion is provided by Merton (1990), Ch. 3.

[19] In particular, property (2.) implies independence of $(B_t - B_s)$ from S_s and B_s.

[20] For a complete presentation, see Øksendal (1998, pp. 153). The version stated here is slightly less general, since we restrict the coefficients to depending only on the realizations of the Itô process and on time.

Put[21]

$$M_t = \exp\Big(-\int_0^t \eta(Y_s,s)\,dB_s - \frac{1}{2}\int_0^t \eta^2(Y_s,s)\,ds\Big), \qquad t \in [0,T)$$
$$dQ = M_T\,dP \text{ on } \mathcal{F}_T. \tag{2A.7}$$

Then

$$\hat{B}_t := \int_0^t \eta(Y_s,s)\,ds + B_t; \quad t \in [0,T) \tag{2A.8}$$

is a standard Brownian motion with respect to Q and Y_t has the representation,

$$dY_t = \alpha(Y_t,t)\,dt + \sigma_Y(Y_t,t)\,d\hat{B}_t. \quad \square \tag{2A.9}$$

The Girsanov theorem shows how to transform the standard Brownian motion B_t with respect to P into $\hat{B}_t$, a standard Brownian motion with respect to Q. As stated in (2A.8), $\hat{B}_t$ has drift $\eta(Y_t,t)$ under P,

$$d\hat{B}_t = \eta(Y_t,t)\,dt + dB_t. \tag{2A.10}$$

However, under Q, $\hat{B}_t$ is driftless. Furthermore, we note that the drift of the process Y_t changes in switching from P to Q but that its volatility is unaffected (compare (2.A4) and (2A.9)). This demonstrates that under the conditions stated in theorem 2A it is possible to change the drift of an Itô process by appropriately transforming the probability measure. Now, this result is applied to transform the discounted stock-price process (2A.3) into a martingale with respect to Q. Using the notation in theorem 2A we have $\mu_Z(Z_t,t) = Z_t\,(\mu - r)$ and $\sigma_Z(Z_t,t) = Z_t\sigma$. Since Z_t should be a martingale with respect to Q, $\alpha(Z_t,t) = 0$. Equation (2A.5) shows that the following process for $\eta(\bullet)$ should be selected[22]

$$\eta(Z_t,t) = \frac{\mu_Z(Z_t,t)}{\sigma_Z(Z_t,t)} \tag{2A.11}$$
$$= \frac{\mu - r}{\sigma}. \tag{2A.12}$$

So that (under Q),

$$dZ_t = Z_t\,\sigma\,\hat{B}_t, \tag{2A.13}$$

where

[21] M_T in (2A.7) is the *Radon-Nikodym* derivative of Q with respect to P, that transforms the probability measure P into Q. M_t ist a martingale on $(\Omega, \mathcal{F}, P)$, $dM_t = -\eta(Y_t,t)\,M_t\,dB_t$ by Itô's Lemma.

[22] It is easy to check that $\eta(\bullet)$ is F-adapted and satisfies Novikov's condition.

$$d\hat{B}_t = \frac{\mu - r}{\sigma}\, dt + dB_t. \tag{2A.14}$$

Next, the portfolio replicating the derivative's payoff is constructed. This implies specifying a portfolio process Δ_t representing the number of stocks in the portfolio. Let X_t be the value of the portfolio. Since portfolio-adjustment decisions are based on the agent's information set, the portfolio process will be F-adapted. Note that the discussion still refers to the discounted market model. The discounted value of the portfolio obeys

$$d\left(\frac{X_t}{\beta_t}\right) = \Delta_t\, dZ_t = \Delta_t\, Z_t\, \sigma\, d\hat{B}_t, \text{ i.e.} \tag{2A.15}$$

$$\frac{X_t}{\beta_t} = X_0 + \int_0^t \Delta_s\, Z_s\, \sigma\, d\hat{B}_s. \tag{2A.16}$$

In order to replicate the European-type call option, an adapted process Δ_t and a value X_0 have to be chosen such that the value of the portfolio in T coincides with the option's payoff. The solution to this problem is provided by the martingale representation theorem.[23]

Theorem 2 (Martingale Representation Theorem). *Suppose Y_t is a martingale with respect to Q and $Y_t \in L^2(P), t \geq 0$. Let $\hat{B}_t$ be a standard Brownian motion with respect to Q. Then there exists a unique adapted stochastic process $\delta_t, t \geq 0$, such that, $\mathbf{E}^Q \int_S^T \delta_t^2\, dt < \infty$ for all $t \geq 0$, and,*

$$Y_t = Y_0 + \int_0^t \delta_s\, d\hat{B}_s, \qquad \textit{almost surely, for all} \quad t \geq 0. \quad \Box \tag{2A.17}$$

Define the Q-martingale

$$Y_t = \mathbf{E}^Q\left[\frac{h(S_T)}{\beta_T}\,\middle|\, \mathcal{F}_t\right], \quad 0 \leq t \leq T. \tag{2A.18}$$

Theorem A2 states that there exists an adapted process δ_t, such that

$$Y_t = Y_0 + \int_0^t \delta_s\, d\hat{B}_s, \quad 0 \leq t \leq T. \tag{2A.19}$$

From (2A.16), setting $X_0 = Y_0$ and $\Delta_t\, Z_t\, \sigma = \delta_t$ yields

$$\frac{X_t}{\beta_t} = Y_t = \mathbf{E}^Q\left[\frac{h(S_T)}{\beta_T}\,\middle|\, \mathcal{F}_t\right], \quad 0 \leq t \leq T. \tag{2A.20}$$

Particularly, for $t = T$ we have

[23] For a more general statement see Øksendal (1998, p. 53).

$$\frac{X_T}{\beta_T} = \mathbf{E}^Q\left[\frac{h(S_T)}{\beta_T}\,\middle|\,\mathcal{F}_T\right] = \frac{h(S_T)}{\beta_T} \tag{2A.21}$$

$$\Leftrightarrow X_T = h(S_T). \tag{2A.22}$$

The argument shows, that the option's payoff in T indeed can be replicated by the dynamic portfolio strategy (2A.15). This is due to the definition of Y_t as the conditional expectation of the option's payoff.[24] To rule out arbitrage opportunities the option price must be equal to the portfolio value at each point in time,

$$G(S_t, t) = X_t = \beta_t \,\mathbf{E}^Q\left[\frac{h(S_T)}{\beta_T}\,\middle|\,\mathcal{F}_t\right]. \tag{2A.23}$$

Since r is nonstochastic β_T can be moved in front of the brackets. Furthermore, r is a constant and therefore,

$$G(S_t, t) = \frac{\beta_t}{\beta_T}\,\mathbf{E}^Q[h(S_T)|\mathcal{F}_t] = e^{-r(T-t)}\,\mathbf{E}^Q[h(S_T)|\mathcal{F}_t]. \tag{2A.24}$$

Accordingly, the value of a European-type call option is

$$\begin{aligned} C(S_t, t) &= e^{-r(T-t)}\,\mathbf{E}^Q\left[\max[S_T - K, 0]|S_t\right] \\ &= e^{-r(T-t)} \int_{-\infty}^{+\infty} \max[S_T - K, 0]\, dQ(S_T|S_t). \end{aligned} \tag{2A.25}$$

In order to evaluate this expression we require the conditional density of S_T with respect to Q. From (2A.13) and Itô's Lemma together with $Z_t = S_t/\beta_t$ it follows that

$$Z_t = Z_0 \exp\left[-\frac{1}{2}\sigma^2\, t + \sigma\, \hat{B}_t\right] \tag{2A.26}$$

$$\Rightarrow S_t = S_0 \exp\left[\left(r - \frac{1}{2}\sigma^2\right) t + \sigma\, \hat{B}_t\right] \tag{2A.27}$$

$$\Rightarrow S_T = S_t \exp\left[\left(r - \frac{1}{2}\sigma^2\right)(T-t) + \sigma\,(\hat{B}_T - \hat{B}_t)\right]. \tag{2A.28}$$

Rewrite $S_T = S_t\, e^{Y_T}$, where $Y_T = \left[\left(r - \frac{1}{2}\sigma^2\right)(T-t) + \sigma\,(\hat{B}_T - \hat{B}_t)\right]$. Y_T is a normally distributed random variable under Q,

$$Y_T \sim No\left(\left(r - \frac{1}{2}\sigma^2\right)(T-t), \sigma^2\,(T-t)\right). \tag{2A.29}$$

(2A.25) becomes

[24] Appendix 2B shows an alternative discussion of the hedging strategy.

$$C(S_t, t) = e^{-r(T-t)} \int_{-\infty}^{+\infty} \max[S_t\, e^{Y_T} - K, 0] \frac{1}{\sqrt{2\,\pi\,\sigma^2\,(T-t)}} \tag{2A.30}$$
$$\cdot e^{-\frac{1}{2\sigma^2 (T-t)} (Y_T - (r - \frac{1}{2}\sigma^2)\,(T-t))^2}\, dY_T.$$

Evaluating the integral expression yields the Black-Scholes formula (2.10).[25]

Appendix 2B: Some Further Details on the Replication Strategy

We shall now demonstrate that the replication argument shown in Appendix 2A for the discounted market model also applies to the original undiscounted model. In this we follow the discussion in Baxter and Rennie (1996, p. 87).

The portfolio at each t, $0 \leq t \leq T$, consists of Δ_t stocks and $\psi_t = Y_t - \Delta_t\, Z_t$ bonds, $Z_t = S_t/\beta_t$ and $Y_t = \mathbf{E}^Q\left[h(S_T)/\beta_T \,\middle|\, \mathfrak{F}_t\right]$. At T the portfolio value is

$$X_T = \Delta_T\, S_T + \psi_T\, \beta_T = \Delta_T\, S_T + (Y_T - \Delta_T\, Z_T)\, \beta_T = Y_T\, \beta_T = h(S_T), \tag{2B.1}$$

This proves that the portfolio replicates the option's payoff in T.

It can be shown that the portfolio is self-financing: From $X_t = \Delta_t\, S_t + \psi_t\, \beta_t = \beta_t\, Y_t$ it follows that

$$dX_t = \beta_t\, dY_t + Y_t\, d\beta_t, \tag{2B.2}$$

(β_t is nonstochastic) and from the martingale representation theorem we have

$$dY_t = \delta_t\, d\hat{B}_t. \tag{2B.3}$$

Using (2B.3) $\Delta_t\, Z_t\, \sigma_t = \delta_t$ (2B.3) can be rewritten as

$$dY_t = \Delta_t\, Z_t\, \sigma_t\, \hat{B}_t = \Delta_t\, dZ_t. \tag{2B.4}$$

Substitution into the portfolio value process yields

$$dX_t = \Delta_t\, \beta_t\, dZ_t + Y_t\, d\beta_t. \tag{2B.5}$$

Since $Y_t = \Delta_t\, Z_t + \psi_t$

$$dX_t = \Delta_t\, \beta_t\, dZ_t + (\Delta_t\, Z_t + \psi_t)\, d\beta_t = \Delta_t\, (\beta_t\, dZ_t + Z_t\, d\beta_t) + \psi_t\, d\beta_t. \tag{2B.6}$$

[25] The evaluation of (2A.30) is rather tedious and is not shown here. For more details see e.g. Neftci (1996), 307-10.

However, $\beta_t \, dZ_t + Z_t \, d\beta_t = d(\beta_t \, Z_t) = dS_t$, so that

$$dX_t = \Delta_t \, dS_t + \psi_t \, d\beta_t. \tag{2B.7}$$

This proves that the portfolio is self financing because any change in its value is due to changes in the value of its individual components. Consequently, the dynamic portfolio strategy (Δ_t, ψ_t) does not entail any cash inflows or outflows after the portfolio has been set up. Finally, when sold in T the portfolio yields a payoff of $h(S_T)$.

3

Survey of the Related Literature

There is an extensive body of empirical work on the information content of derivative prices. However, the literature reviewed in this Chapter does not attempt to extract complete probability density functions from option prices and has a narrower focus. First, there are studies investigating the forecasting abilities of forward and futures prices with respect to future spot prices. Since a number of excellent surveys on this topic are available (e.g. Cuthbertson (1996)) the discussion in section 3.1 will be very brief. Section 3.2 surveys empirical contributions on the information content of implied volatilities that are computed from observed option prices by inverting an appropriate option valuation formula. It will be shown that implied volatility can be interpreted as the average volatility of the underlying's price market participants expect to prevail until the option expires. Empirically, implied volatilities vary with the exercise price and with the option's time to expiration. The relationship between implied volatility and the exercise price provides some basic information about the shape of the risk-neutral density (section 3.2.1). The information content of the term structure of implied volatility is discussed in section 3.2.2.

A central part of this Chapter is section 3.2.3 where we survey the literature on the forecasting ability of implied volatilities. We consider whether or not implied volatilities predict future observed volatilities. Section 3.2.4 reviews some evidence on the forecasting ability of implied correlations - an extension of the literature on implied volatilities to foreign-exchange options. In section 3.2.4 we discuss approaches to construct from observed option prices a measure of asymmetry in the risk-neutral probability density function. Finally, section 3.3 summarizes and concludes.

3.1 The Information Content of Forward and Futures Prices

As shown in Chapter 2 (equation (2.12)) the forward price of a financial asset is equal to the expected value of the underlying's price at expiration under the "risk-neutral" probability measure Q ($F_t = \mathbf{E}_Q[S_T|S_t]$). Thus, the forward price can be interpreted as the risk-neutral expectation of the underlying's price in T. This is the starting point for many studies that investigate if the forward price embodies information on future (spot) prices.

Assuming risk-neutral economic agents and rational expectations, the forward price should be an unbiased forecast of the future spot price (unbiasedness hypothesis). For interest rates this hypothesis is tested, for example, by Fama (1984a), Fama and Bliss (1987), Mishkin (1988), Hardouvelis (1988) and Shiller, Campbell, and Schoenholtz (1983). In particular, they analyze whether implied forward rates, computed from the term structure of interest rates, are unbiased forecasts of future spot rates. Fama (1984a), Fama and Bliss (1987), Hardouvelis (1988) and Mishkin (1988) reject the unbiasedness hypothesis. Nevertheless, their results indicate that forward rates contain some information about future spot rates. In contrast, Shiller, Campbell, and Schoenholtz (1983) do not find any evidence indicating that that implied forward rates aid in forecasting future spot rates.
Howard (1982) and Hegde and McDonald (1986) consider the forecasting ability of treasury bill futures.[1] Howard (1982) concludes that both forward and futures rates contain information on future spot rates but that for short forecasting horizons these are inferior to naive forecasts. In contrast, Hegde and

[1] Futures and forward prices can differ because of various reasons. Futures contracts are "marked to the market" on a daily basis so that money is transferred for gains and losses between both sides of the contract before expiration. In contrast, a forward contracts' gains and losses are settled at expiration (see Cox, Ingersoll, and Ross (1981) and Jarrow and Oldfield (1981)). Additional reasons for differences between futures and forward prices are, for example, the option implicit in the futures contract allowing some choice with respect to the delivery of the underlying asset (Gay and Manaster (1984)), limits to maximum daily price movements imposed by exchanges, differential tax treatment of futures and forwards, transaction costs (e.g. Capozza and Cornell (1979)) and other market imperfections.
The empirical relevance of differences between forward and futures prices is subject to debate. Most researchers find significant differences for treasury-bill forwards and futures (e.g. Capozza und Cornell (1979) and Rendleman and Carabini (1979)) but not for foreign-exchange forwards and futures (Cornell and Reinganum (1981) and Chang and Chang (1990)). The latter studies are criticized by Dezhbakhsh (1994) and Polakoff and Grier (1991), who provide some evidence for significant discrepancies between foreign-exchange forward and futures prices. Furthermore, French (1983) points out significant differences between forward and futures prices for copper and silver.

McDonald (1986) provide some evidence that favours forward and futures prices over naive no-change forecasts for short forecasting horizons. Moreover, they fail to reject the hypothesis that forward rates do not contain any information on future spot rates independent from that in futures prices. For forecasting horizons up to 91 days, MacDonald and Hein (1989) find evidence for a superior forecasting performance of futures relative to forward prices.[2]

Studies of the unbiasedness hypothesis for exchange rates also arrive at conflicting conclusions.[3] For example, Frankel (1980) cannot reject the unbiasedness hypothesis whereas MacDonald (1983) shows rejection for four out of six exchange rates against the US dollar. Furthermore, Fama (1984b), Meese and Rogoff (1983), and Scott (1992) present some evidence for a negative correlation of the forward-spot premium with future exchange-rate changes.

Interpretation of the forward rate as the expectation of the future spot rate is based on risk-neutrality of the economic agents. If agents are in fact risk averse a risk premium must be considered. The literature provides some evidence that risk premia might be highly variable over time. As a consequence, even if forward rates contain important information about future spot rates their forecasting power might be diminished in the presence of a very volatile risk premium.[4]

3.2 The Information Content of Implied Volatilities

Among the parameters entering the Black-Scholes formula (2.10) only the volatility σ cannot be observed. However, using an observed option price an implied volatility (σ_{IV}) can be computed by inverting the option pricing formula.[5] The Black/Scholes-Merton model assumes the volatility parameter to

[2] Kumar (1992) provides a similar exercise for commodity markets. He investigates the forecasting ability of crude-oil futures and finds futures prices to outperform random walk forecasts and forecasts derived from time-series models.

[3] Cuthbertson (1996), Ch. 12 and Hodrick (1987) provide comprehensive surveys on this topic.

[4] For the term structure of interest rates, see e.g. Fama (1984a), Hardouvelis (1988), and Mankiw and Summers (1984). For exchange rates, see e.g. Fama (1984b), the surveys in Hodrick (1987), Ch. 5, and Lewis (1995).

[5] Often σ_{IV} is called the *Black-Scholes implied volatility*, thus making explicit from which valuation function implied volatility is derived. Note that the Black-Scholes formula does not allow an analytical solution for implied volatility so that it has to be computed numerically. Option-pricing models assume all parameters to be known to the agents with certainty. Therefore, the computation of implied parameters is not a problem of estimation but of inversion (see Bates (1996a, p. 586)). Note that estimating parameters in the valuation function also ignores deterministic arbitrage-based relationships between option prices for different maturities and different strike prices (see Clement et. al. (2000)).

be constant. However, empirically observed implied volatilities are at odds with this assumption:[6]

- Implied volatilities of options with the same time to expiration but with different strike prices are not identical. This observation is called the *volatility smile.*
- Implied volatilities of options with the same strike price but with different time to expiration are not identical. There exists a *term structure* of implied volatilities.

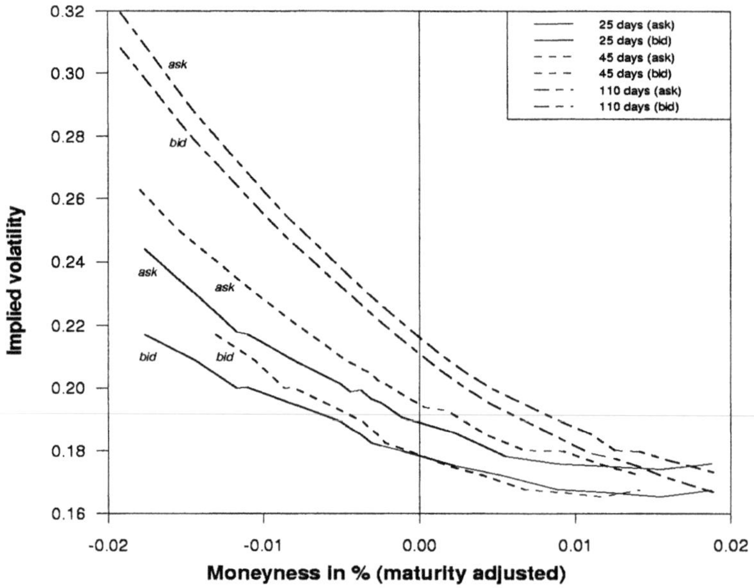

Fig. 3.1. Implied volatilities (annualized) from SPX options (CBOE) 14.07.2000

Figure 3.1 illustrates the relationship between implied volatilities and strike prices typically found for S&P 500 index options.[7]. Before the October crash in 1987 implied volatilities exhibited a so called "*smile effect*". Implied volatilities at the money were below those far out of the money or far in the money.

[6] Since the Black/Scholes-Merton model assumes σ to be constant, the volatility parameter is already exactly identified by a single observed option price. For more observed option prices the volatility parameter is overidentified (see Bates (1996a, p. 586)).

[7] *Moneyness* is computed as $\left(\frac{K}{S_t} - 1\right)/\sqrt{T-t}$. See, for example, Bates (2000), Rubinstein (1994), Derman (1999), Dumas, Fleming and Whaley (1998), and Rosenberg (2000) for studies showing the typical shape of the volatility smile.

After the crash, the pattern in figure 3.1 became prevalent: implied volatilities decrease with increasing strike price, a result sometimes referred to as the "*volatility sneer*". Typically, this relationship is less pronounced for options with a short time to expiration. The differences between implied volatilities in many cases are sufficiently large to generate arbitrage profits in theory. For example, in figure 3.1, the bid-volatility of a 25-days in the money call option is greater than the corresponding at the money ask-volatility.[8] This difference can be exploited profitably by selling the in the money call, buying the at the call and appropriately adjusting the portfolio as time evolves. In general, the observed differences are greater than the transaction costs from rebalancing the arbitrage portfolio (Dumas, Fleming and Whaley (1998)).

3.2.1 Implied Volatilities and the Risk-Neutral Probability Density

The observed deviations of implied volatilities from the Black-Scholes assumption of a constant provide some information about the shape of the risk-neutral probability density function implied by option prices. Since the Black-Scholes price is monotonously increasing in volatility, deviations of implied volatilities from a constant are related to the pricing errors of the Black-Scholes formula. Options with implied volatility above (below) the constant volatility of the Black/Scholes-Merton model are underpriced (overpriced) by the Black-Scholes formula.[9] These pricing errors, in turn, can be related to deviations of the risk-neutral from the lognormal density (see Ch. 2).

For example, consider a risk-neutral density that exhibits higher kurtosis relative to the lognormal distribution. This leads to far out of the money calls and puts being underpriced by the Black-Scholes formula. The reason is that far out of the money option prices only depend on the probability of extreme realizations for the underlying's price process and that these are understated by the lognormal density. Therefore, higher kurtosis compared to the lognormal density leads to a volatility smile effect. Skewness in the risk-neutral density

[8] The size of the difference between bid and ask implied volatilities depends on two factors (Dumas, Fleming and Whaley (1998)): first, the bid-ask spread in option prices varies with the exercise price. In particular, the maximum bid-ask spread allowed at CBOE increases with the option price, i.e. declines with moneyness. Second, the sensitivity of the option price with respect to volatility (*vega*) is largest at the money. Hence, the difference between bid- and ask-implied volatilities ceteris paribus is smallest at the money.

[9] In order to identify these differences, first the Black-Scholes constant volatility has to be determined. However, the problem of overidentification explained above requires the aggregation of a number of different implied volatilities into a single volatility measure. Most often a weighted average of implied volatilities for different strike prices is used or the implied volatility of the at the money option is selected. Bates (1996a, p. 589) surveys various methods encountered in applied work.

different from that of the lognormal 'tilts' the volatility smile. A more positively skewed (negatively skewed) risk-neutral density causes implied volatilities of out of the money calls to rise (decline) relative to those of out of the money puts because extremely positive returns become more likely than extremely negative returns.[10]

There is a number of empirical studies relating Black-Scholes pricing errors to deviations of the risk-neutral density from the lognormal benchmark. Using options on 30 different stocks Rubinstein (1985) finds evidence for a more positively skewed risk-neutral density from August 1976 to October 1977 but for a more negatively skewed density from October 1977 to August 1978. MacBeth and Merville (1979) consider options on six individual stocks. Their results indicate a more positively skewed risk-neutral density from December 1975 to December 1976. Emanuel and MacBeth (1982) provide similar conclusions for 1976. For 1978 they find evidence for a more negatively skewed risk-neutral density. Sheikh (1991) presents results that show the risk-neutral density of the S&P 500 to be more positively skewed in 1985 and more leptokurtic relative to the lognormal distribution in 1986. The results in Whaley (1986) indicate for 1983 a relatively more positively skewed risk-neutral density of the S&P 500. Bates (1991) considers S&P 500 index option data from 1985-93. He illustrates how the properties of the risk-neutral density changed from an almost symmetrical density in 1986 to a significantly more positively skewed density – in particular at the end of 1986, in the middle of 1987 and after the crash in October 1987. A pronounced positive skewness has prevailed ever since (Bates (2000)).

One possible reason for a strongly positively skewed density is a negative correlation of volatility and the underlying's price. Such a correlation was documented by Black (1976b) for individual stocks and by Nelson (1991) for stock indices. Negative correlation of volatility and stock prices can be motivated by the *leverage* effect (Black (1976b)): a decline in the company value causes volatility to rise. Another reason might be *volatility feedback* (Poterba and Summers (1986)), where higher volatility leads to stronger discounting of future earnings and depresses stock prices.[11] Other theories emphasize feedback effects from portfolio insurance strategies that can also cause positively skewed risk-neutral density functions (Grossman (1988), Grossman and Zhou (1996), and Platen and Schweizer (1994)).[12]

[10] See Bates (1996a, p. 596). In the context of a stochastic equilibrium asset-pricing model Garćia and Renault (1998) show how an asymmetric volatility smile is related to a specific type of asymmetry in the equivalent martingale measure. In their model, this asymmetry coincides with *preference dependent* option valuation due to a risk premium for changes in interest rates and the existence of a general leverage effect.

[11] Empirical studies of the leverage effect are e.g. Christie (1982) and, focussing specifically on option markets, Toft and Prucyk (1997).

[12] For other possible explanations, see Jackwerth and Rubinstein (1998).

For foreign-exchange options Bodurtha and Courtadon (1987) study data on four different exchange rates from 1983-85 and find the risk-neutral density to be more positively skewed than the lognormal benchmark. Using futures options, Bates (1996b) presents results that indicate a strong negative skew in the risk-neutral density of the US dollar/D-Mark exchange rate in 1984-86. After that, from 1986 to 1992 skewness exhibits pronounced changes from positive to negative values. A similar result is shown for the US dollar/Japanese yen exchange rate.

Some authors investigate whether observed patterns of implied volatilities can be explained by alternative option pricing models, i.e. by departing from the Black-Scholes formula. Their general result is that no option-pricing model is capable of adequately accounting for all observed characteristics of implied volatilities.[13]

3.2.2 The Term Structure of Implied Volatilities

Figure 3.1 clearly shows that implied volatilities vary with time to expiration, i.e. that there is a term structure of implied volatilities.[14] Again, implied volatilities varying with time to expiration are in conflict with the constant volatility assumption in the Black/Scholes-Merton model where the volatility parameter is assumed to be the same for all maturities. Therefore, the term structure of implied volatilities provides information about how pricing biases of the Black-Scholes formula are related to the option's time to expiration.

Generally, the term structure of implied volatilities indicates the presence of mean reversion, i.e. the term structure is upward (downward) sloping if short-term volatilities are low (high).[15] Stein (1989) considers whether the term structure observed from December 1983 to September 1987 is consistent with the time-series properties of implied volatilities. He shows the persistence of shocks to implied volatility to be significantly higher in the term structure than indicated by the estimates of an AR(1) model. This result is interpreted as evidence for 'overreaction' of longer-term implied volatilities to volatility shocks. Using another approach that does not rely on the AR(1) model, Stein (1989) rejects the hypothesis that the difference between implied volatilities with maturities of two months and one month is an unbiased fore-

[13] See, for example, Das and Sundaram (1999), Heynen (1994), Rubinstein (1985), and Sheikh (1991).

[14] Studies finding evidence of a term structure of implied volatilities are, for example, Bodurtha and Courtadon (1987), Rubinstein (1994), Stein (1989), and Xu and Taylor (1994).

[15] See, for example, Xu and Taylor (1995) for foreign-exchange options and Stein (1989) for S&P 500 index options.

cast of changes in the one-month implied volatility.[16] The empirical approach employed by Stein (1989) is criticized by Diz and Finucane (1993). Using data from 1985 to 1988 they do not find any evidence for overreaction.
Heynen, Kemna, and Vorst (1994) consider index and individual stock options from the European Stock Exchange (EOE) and the Amsterdam Stock Exchange (sample period January 1988 - January 1989). Apart from a mean-reverting specification they also consider a GARCH(1,1) and an EGARCH(1,1) model of implied volatility. Evidence for overreaction can be found for the GARCH(1,1) model and the mean-reverting specification but not for the EGARCH(1,1) model.

For foreign-exchange rate options more studies tend to find the term structure of implied volatilities to be consistent with the implied volatilities' time-series properties. Xu and Taylor (1994) cannot find evidence for overreaction using options on four different currencies from 1985-89. Campa and Chang (1995, 1998b) study implied volatilities of options on four different currencies from December 1989 to March 1992 and are unable to reject the expectations hypothesis of the term structure of implied volatilities. Furthermore, they cannot find any evidence for overreaction.[17]

Obviously, the Black/Scholes-Merton model is misspecified. This raises the question of whether there are other option-pricing models that can explain the empirically observed term structure of implied volatilities. Das and Sundaresan (1999) show that a jump-diffusion model leads to an upward sloping term structure of at-the-money implied volatilities. However, empirically the term structure is not always increasing. Furthermore, the jump-diffusion model's theoretical term structure is too flat to be consistent with the empirical evidence. The authors also consider a model with stochastic volatility as an alternative specification. This model is consistent with a wide range of shapes of the volatility term structure. However, theoretically derived differences between the implied volatilities of different maturities turn out to be too small compared to empirical observations.

3.2.3 The Forecasting Information in Implied Volatilities

Obviously, implied volatilities that vary from day to day are inconsistent with the Black-Scholes assumption of a constant volatility parameter. If volatility is indeed subject to random shocks, this fact must be accounted for by appropriate modifications of the option-pricing model. This is the rationale behind

[16] This approach is equivalent to standard tests of the expectations hypothesis of the term structure of interest rates, e.g. Campbell and Shiller (1984).

[17] Only Campa and Chang (1995,1998) and Heynen, Kemna, and Vorst (1994) consider explicitly that implied volatilities should be interpreted as the expected average volatility until the option's expiration.

the development of stochatic volatility models, e.g. the models by Hull and White (1987), Scott (1987), and Heston (1993).

Modifying the market model from Chapter 2, Hull and White (1987) assume that the volatility parameter follows a stochastic process that is driven by a second standard Brownian motion,[18]

$$dS_t = \mu_1 S_t \, dt + \sigma_t S_t \, dB_{1t}, \tag{3.1}$$
$$d\sigma_t^2 = \mu_2(\sigma_t^2) \, dt + \gamma(\sigma_t^2) \, dB_{2t}. \tag{3.2}$$

This model cannot be solved by arbitrage pricing. Application of equilibrium pricing techniques leads to the following valuation function for a European-type call option (see, for example, Cox, Ingersoll, and Ross (1985))

$$C(S_t, \sigma_t, t) = \hat{\mathrm{E}}_t\left[e^{-r(T-t)} \max[S_T - K, 0]\right], \tag{3.3}$$

where the expectation is taken with respect to the risk-neutral processes

$$dS_t = rS_t \, dt + \sigma_t S_t \, dB_{1t}, \tag{3.4}$$
$$d\sigma_t^2 = [\mu_2(\sigma_t^2) - \lambda(\sigma_t^2)] \, dt + \gamma(\sigma_t^2) \, dB_{2t}, \tag{3.5}$$

with $\lambda(\sigma_t^2)$ representing a risk premium. Since there is no closed-form solution for the valuation function, numerical techniques have to be applied.
Here, we focus on the special of B_{1t} and B_{2t} being uncorrelated. Using this assumption the call pricing function can be solved analytically,

$$C(S_t, \sigma_t, t) = \int_0^\infty \left\{S_t \, \Phi(d_1) - e^{-r(T-t)} K \, \Phi(d_2)\right\} dF(V|\sigma_t^2, t), \tag{3.6}$$
$$d_1 = \frac{\ln(\frac{S_t}{K}) + r(T-t) + \frac{1}{2}V^2(T-t)}{V\sqrt{T-t}}, \tag{3.7}$$
$$d_2 = d_1 - \sqrt{V(T-t)}, \tag{3.8}$$
$$V = \sqrt{\frac{1}{T-t}\int_t^T \sigma_u^2 \, du}. \tag{3.9}$$

Here, $F(V|\sigma_t^2, t)$ is the conditional distribution function of V, where V represents the average volatility of the underlying's price until the option's expiration. The valuation function (3.6) is of the same structure as the Black-Scholes formula with σ replaced by V.

Using the definition

$$C^{BS}(S_t, V, t) = S_t \, \Phi(d_1) - e^{-r(T-t)} K \, \Phi(d_2), \tag{3.10}$$

(3.6) can be expanded by Taylor-approximation as

---

[18] This discussion follows Fleming (1998, p. 319) and Scott (1998, p. 51).

$$C(S_t,\sigma_t,t) = C^{BS}(S_t,\mathbf{E}_t[V],t) + \frac{1}{2}\frac{\partial^2 C^{BS}(S_t,\mathbf{E}_t[V],t)}{\partial V^2}\mathbf{E}_t(V-\mathbf{E}_t[V])^2 + ... \quad . \tag{3.11}$$

The first expression on the right hand side of (3.11) is the Black-Scholes formula with the $\mathbf{E}_t[V]$ in place of σ. The second expression is proportional to the variance of volatility and its sign only depends on the sign of the derivative of the Black-Scholes formula with respect to V. Hence, truncating the approximation after the second term, it is obvious that $C(S_T,\sigma_t,t) < C^{BS}(S_t,\hat{\mathbf{E}}_t[V],t)$ for regions in which the Black-Scholes formula is concave in V. This implies that the Black-Scholes implied volatility is a downward biased estimator for $\hat{\mathbf{E}}_t[V]$.
For at-the-money options the Black-Scholes formula is almost linear in volatility (Feinstein (1989)). Therefore, at the money, the Black-Scholes price with the expectation of V appears to be a good approximation of the Hull-White option price, i.e.

$$C(S_t,\sigma_t,t) \approx C^{BS}(S_t,\hat{\mathbf{E}}_t[V],t). \tag{3.12}$$

If this relationship were to hold exactly, we should have

$$\sigma_{IV,t} = \hat{\mathbf{E}}_t[V]. \tag{3.13}$$

With these assumptions the Black-Scholes implied volatility is an unbiased forecast of the (risk-adjusted) expected average volatility of the underlying's price until the option's expiration. The accuracy of this approximation is studied by Scott (1998). His benchmark model features stochastic volatility, a stochastic interest rate and discrete jumps in the price process. He concludes that the Black-Scholes implied volatility is a good approximation of the expected average volatility if the effects of discrete jumps are small, the correlation between volatility and the underlying's price is low and the variability of volatility is not too large.[19]

Nevertheless, some important limitations should be kept in mind: first, the result holds only for European-type but not for American-type options. Second, in deriving (3.6)-(3.9) it is assumed that the correlation between S_t and σ_t is zero (B_{1t} and B_{2t} are uncorrelated). However, negative correlation between volatility and stock prices or stock index levels has been documented extensively (see the discussion in section 3.2.1). Third, (3.9) and (3.13) refer to the risk-adjusted volatility process (3.5) instead of actual volatility (3.2). The risk premium $\lambda(\sigma_t^2)$ can cause large differences between risk-adjusted and true volatility so that the Black-Scholes implied volatility might be a biased

[19] Similar results are documented by Lamoureux and Lastrapes (1993).

forecast of $\mathbf{E}_t[V]$.[20] On the other hand, since both volatility processes start at the same level σ_t^2 they should be highly correlated (Scott (1998, p. 54)).[21]

Most empirical studies of the information content of implied volatilities are based on regression analyses. Actual ex-post volatilities are observed over a time period of length h, ($\hat{\sigma}_{t+h}$) and then regressed on period t implied volatilities,

$$\hat{\sigma}_{t+h} = \alpha + \beta\sigma_{IV,t} + \epsilon_t. \tag{3.14}$$

Implied volatilities contain forecasting information on future actual volatilities if β is significantly different from zero. The unbiasedness of volatility forecasts is examined by testing for $\alpha = 0$ and $\beta = 1$.

Often the forecasting performance of implied volatilities relative to other volatility forecasts is studied by comparing root mean squared errors (RMSE). First, equation (3.14) is estimated using implied volatility and then a similar regression is estimated with σ_{IV} replaced by, for example, historical volatility (i.e. lagged ex-post volatility). The regressor yielding the lowest RMSE is considered to be superior in predicting future actual volatility. However, Fair and Shiller (1990) note the ambiguity of RMSE comparisons und suggest another approach to evaluate relative forecasting performance. They recommend regressing actual ex-post volatilities on lagged implied volatilities as well as on other measures that might contain useful forecasting information (e.g. historical volatilities σ_{HV}, lagged stock prices etc.),

$$\hat{\sigma}_{t+h} = \alpha + \beta_1\sigma_{IV,t} + \beta_2\sigma_{HV,t} + \epsilon_t. \tag{3.15}$$

Regression (3.15) can be used to test for the relative efficiency of implied volatilities in forecasting future actual volatilities, i.e. it is tested if implied volatilities contain all information helpful to forecast future volatilities (Bates (1996a, p. 593)).

If neither β_1 nor β_2 are significantly different from zero, neither implied nor historical volatilities are useful for volatility forecasts (R^2 is small), or both variables contain all important forecasting information and thus are perfectly correlated (R^2 is large). If β_1 and β_2 are significantly different from zero, both implied and historical volatilities carry independent forecasting information for future volatility . Finally, if the forecasting information in historical volatilities is a subset of the information contained in implied volatilities, β_1 is significantly different from zero but not β_2 and vice versa (Fair and Shiller (1990), Bank of Japan (1995)).

[20] Scott (1992, p. 53) presents an example in which the actual volatility is stationary but the risk-adjusted process is nonstationary.

[21] Bates (1991) estimates the parameters of a model with jumps in the underlying's price process. He shows the relative difference between the 'true' implied volatilities and those computed with a variant of the Black-Scholes formula to be less than 1% as long as the density function is not strongly skewed.

An early investigation into the information content of implied volatilities is Black and Scholes (1972). They observe that predicted option prices differ less from ex-post observed option prices if the actual ex-post volatility is inserted into the Black-Scholes formula instead of the historical volatility.
Latané and Rendleman (1976) compute the squared implied volatility as a weighted average. The implied variance for alternative strike prices is weighted by the square of *vega*, the derivative of the Black-Scholes formula with respect to σ.[22] Their data set consists of daily observations on 24 individual stock options from 1973-74. They find future actual volatility to be more strongly correlated with implied than with historical volatility. Schmalensee and Trippi (1979) construct an implied volatility variable from equally-weighted implied volatilities of stock options with different exercise prices. Options very far out of and far in the money have been eliminated from their sample as well as options with extremely short time to expiration. They show implied volatility to be uncorrelated with proxy variables for historical volatilities like actual changes in the stock prices, the difference of weekly high and low etc. The authors conclude that market expectations are based on a much richer information set than only on historical volatilities. However, the variables considered by Schmalensee and Trippi (1979) have been criticized for being inadequate proxies for historical volatilities (Scott (1998), p. 81).

Chiras and Manaster (1978) examine directly the forecasting performance of implied volatilities. They consider a cross section of individual stock options from 1973-75. Implied volatilities for different strike prices are weighted by the elasticity of the Black-Scholes price with respect to σ, so that implied volatilities of far-out-of-the-money options receive the largest weights (Bates (1996a, p. 81)).[23] They focus on a forecasting horizon of one month and obtain mixed results. Implied volatilities tend to be superior to historical volatilities in the second half of their observation period (higher R^2) but the results for the first nine months are inconclusive. For the final 14 months implied historical volatilities do not contain more forecasting information than implied volatilities (i.e. $\beta_2 = 0$ in (3.15) cannot be rejected).
Beckers (1981) studies the forecasting ability of implied volatilities computed from various individual stock options in 1975-76. He compares a range of alternative schemes to construct implied volatilities: the weighting scheme of Latané and Rendleman (1976), the minimium of the sum of *vega* weighted

[22] $\sigma_{IV,t} = \frac{\sum_i w_i^2 \sigma_{i,t}^2}{(\sum_i w_i)^2}, w_i = \frac{\partial C^{BS}}{\partial \sigma}|_{\sigma_{i,t}}$. Since the weights do not sum to unity this weighting scheme produces a biased estimate of implied volatility (Bates (1996a, p. 588)). *Vega* weighting gives more weight to at the money options because the value of *vega* is largest at the money. Bates (1996a) points out that alternative weighting schemes imply different assumptions about the nature of measurement errors in option prices. However, on this subject there are no detailed studies available yet (Bates (1996a, p. 588)).

[23] $\sigma_{IV,t} = \frac{\sum_i w_i \sigma_{i,t}}{\sum_i w_i}, w_i = \frac{\partial C^{BS}}{\partial \sigma} \frac{\sigma}{C^{BS}}|_{\sigma_{i,t}}$.

quadratic deviations of Black-Scholes prices from observed option prices, and using the at-the-money implied volatility only. The forecasting horizon is equal to the option's time to expiration. His results indicate a superior forecasting performance of any implied volatility measure compared to historical volatility. However, Beckers (1981) finds these forecasts to be biased. In most cases the at-the-money implied volatility yields the best predictions among the implied volatility-based variables. Nevertheless, the relative efficiency is rejected for implied volatility. Therefore, historical volatility also contributes to volatility forecasts.
A serious problem might be caused by the cross sectional dimension of the regression studies discussed so far. If volatilities of different stocks are subject to common shocks, the error terms will be correlated, standard errors will be underestimated and significance tests will be biased (Scott (1998, p. 61)). In order to avoid this problem, most of the later studies focus on time series of implied volatilities.

The information content of implied volatilities for the Nikkei 225 index, for Japanese government bond futures, for short-term Euro-Yen interest rate futures and for the Yen/US-Dollar exchange rate is examined in Bank of Japan (1995). The study is based on option prices observed from 1990-94, in some cases only from 1993-94. Implied volatility is specified as the at-the-money implied volatility. The regressions of actual ex-post on implied or historical volatility alone produce mixed results. Coefficients on implied volatility significantly different from zero are found in the equations for the Nikkei 225, for the government bond futures and for the one-month yen/US dollar exchange rates futures but not for the Euro-Yen futures and the three months yen/US dollar exchange rates. However, implied volatilities yield efficient volatility forecasts relative to historical volatilities only for the Nikkei 225 and for the one month yen/US dollar exchange rate.[24]

Building upon these results, Neuhaus (1995) studies implied volatilities from German Bund futures options for the time period from June 1989 to November 1994. For forecaseting horizons of 40 and 60 days, he finds implied volatility to be an unbiased predictor of future actual volatility, i.e. α is not significantly different from zero and β is not significantly different from one.[25] For the regressions on implied volatility R^2 tends to be higher than for those on historical volatility. However, the value of R^2 is quite low in all regressions.

[24] The results summarized above are derived from monthly and quarterly data. The results for daily data are slightly different. For example, $\beta = 0$ can only be rejected for the Nikkei 225 and the one-month foreign exchange options. Furthermore, in regression (3.15) the coefficients on historical volatility sometimes turn out to be signficantly different from zero.

[25] Neuhaus (1995) considers various measures of implied volatility: the implied volatility of an at-the-money call or put option, their average implied volatility, an equally weighted average of all implied volatilities of a given option contract, and a *vega*-weighted average.

For shorter forecasting horizons Neuhaus (1995) finds some evidence for an improving forecasting performance of historical volatilities. Regressions like (3.15) yield some evidence that implied volatilities contain forecasting information superior to that in historical volatilities, particularly for longer forecasting horizons. However, over all forecasting horizons historical volatilities also contain some independent information useful for volatility forecasts.[26]

Lamoureux and Lastrapes (1993) compare implied volatility-based forecasts to those from a GARCH(1,1) model. Using daily data on ten individual stocks and stock options from 1982-84 they estimate the following model,

$$\begin{aligned} r_t &= \bar{r} + \epsilon_t, \\ \epsilon_t | \epsilon_{t-1}, \epsilon_{t-2}, \ldots &\sim N(0, h_t), \\ h_t &= C + \alpha\epsilon_{t-1}^2 + \beta h_{t-1} + \gamma\sigma_{IV,t-1}^2, \end{aligned} \tag{3.16}$$

where $\alpha > 0, \beta > 0, \gamma > 0$. r_t is the daily stock return. Implied volatilities are computed from at-the-money options with medium time to expiration. The authors consider whether implied volatilities contribute to the explanation of conditional variance of stock returns by testing for $\gamma = 0$ and reject the null hypothesis. Testing for relative efficiency indicates that GARCH forecasts do also contribute to predicting conditional stock return variance. However, the model (3.16) examines the forecasting ability of implied volatilities with respect to the next day's actual volatility while, theoretically, implied volatility is an estimate of the expected average volatility over the remaining time to expiration (maturity mismatch problem). Therefore, Lamoureux and Lastrapes (1993) generate out of sample forecasts for daily volatilities $h_{t+1}, h_{t+2}, \ldots, h_T$ from the GARCH model by recursive substitution using only information available at date t. Then, in regressions like (3.14), the predictive power of the *average* of the GARCH forecast is compared to implied and historical variances. It turns out that implied volatility is a downward-biased and inferior predictor of future variances compared to historical volatility and GARCH forecasts. In order to test for relative efficiency, they regress the actual ex-post variance over the option's time to expiration simultaneously on the GARCH forecast, the implied variance $\sigma_{IV,t}^2$ and on the historical variance $\sigma_{\epsilon,t}^2$. The results indicate that an optimal forecast of actual volatility should use both implied volatility and historical volatility but not the GARCH forecasts.

Day and Lewis (1992) analyze weekly S&P 100 excess returns er_t. Using observations from 1983 to 1989 they estimate a GARCH-M(1,1) model,

---

[26] The coefficients on both implied and historical volatility are insignificantly different from zero. For a forecasting horizon of 20 days implied volatilities in fact tend to yield predictions inferior to those using historical volatilities.
In this study, the values of R^2 all are somewhat below those in Bank of Japan (1995). The coefficient of determination exhibits a hump-shaped pattern and is highest for forecasting horizons of 40 or 60 days.

$$
\begin{aligned}
er_t &= \lambda_0 + \lambda_1 h_t + \epsilon_t, \qquad (3.17)\\
\epsilon_t|\epsilon_{t-1}, \epsilon_{t-2}, \ldots &\sim N(0, h_t),\\
h_t^2 &= \alpha_0 + \alpha_1 \epsilon_{t-1}^2 + \beta_1 h_{t-1}^2 + \delta \sigma_{IV,t-1}^2,
\end{aligned}
$$

where $\alpha_0 > 0, \alpha_1 > 0, \beta_1 > 0, \delta > 0$. They also consider an EGARCH(1,1) specification,

$$
\begin{aligned}
\ln(h_t^2) = {} & \alpha_0 + \beta_1 \ln(h_{t-1}^2) + \alpha_1 \left(\theta \psi_{t-1} + \gamma \left(|\psi_{t-1}| - (2/\pi)^{1/2}\right)\right) \qquad (3.18)\\
& + \delta \ln(\sigma_{IV,t-1}^2),
\end{aligned}
$$

where $\alpha_1 = 1$. Implied volatility is estimated using a GLS-version of the approach suggested by Whaley (1982),

$$
\min_{\sigma_{IV,t}} \sum_{i=1}^{n} \left[w_i \left(C_{i,t} - C_{i,t}^{BS}(\sigma_{IV,t}) \right) \right]^2. \qquad (3.19)
$$

n is the number of available strike prices and the weights w_i correspond to each option's share in trading volume. Generally, trading volume is highest for at or close to the money options. Both empirical models are estimated for weekly excess returns from Wednesday to Wednesday and from Friday to Friday. Only for the Wednesday returns can Day and Lewis (1992) reject $\delta = 0$. Hence, implied volatilities seem to contribute to the prediction of the conditional variance of weekly excess returns measured from Wednesday to Wednesday. However, implied variances turn out to be inefficient forecasts because the authors fail to reject $\alpha_1 = \beta_1 = 0$. As far as the Friday excess returns are concerned, implied volatilities do not play any significant role in predicting conditional return variances. Day and Lewis (1992) argue that this disappointing result might be due to the fact that options usually expire on Fridays and, therefore, volatility increases on Thursdays and Fridays (see Day and Lewis (1988)).

Day and Lewis (1992) also perform the regression analyses (3.14) and (3.15) on the Wednesday excess-return series. Apart from implied variance they consider historical variance and GARCH/EGARCH-model-based forecasts of the conditional excess-return variance.[27] In the simple regressions (3.14) both the coefficients on the GARCH and on the EGARCH forecasts are significantly different from zero. Estimation of the multiple regression (3.15) shows neither implied volatilities nor GARCH and EGARCH forecasts to be significant. The authors conclude that weekly return variances seem to be very difficult to forecast.[28]

---

[27] The out of sample forecasts are generated with rolling GARCH/EGARCH models.

[28] Day and Lewis (1992) do not deal adequately with the problem of maturity mismatch. The options' time to expiration which is equal to the forecasting horizon of implied volatilities is different from the one-week forecasting horizon of the GARCH and EGARCH models.

Canina and Figlewski (1993) study the forecasting ability of implied volatilities of S&P 500 index options for the time period from March 1983 to March 1987. They compute implied volatilities from a binomial tree model that explicitly accounts for the early exercise feature of American type options. Then, they combine implied volatilities into groups with respect to time to expiration and moneyness.[29] Generally, implied variances are not significant in predicting actual ex-post S&P 100 return variance with an exemption for some at-the-money options with very short time to expiration.[30] On the other hand, historical volatilities enter the univariate regressions (3.14) with significantly positive coefficients. In addition, in the multiple regressions historical volatilities are often significant but never implied volatilities.[31]

Jorion (1995) investigates the forecasting performance of implied volatilities for foreign-exchange futures He considers foreign exchange rate futures options on US dollar/D-Mark, US dollar/Swiss franc, Japanese yen/US dollar and computes implied volatility as the average of the at-the-money call and put implied volatility. Using data from 1985 to 1992 he finds implied volatilities to be significant in forecasting daily volatilities in the futures prices. Adding historical volatilities and GARCH volatility forecasts as regressors does not change these results. In fact, the coefficients on all the additional variables are not significantly different from zero indicating that these alternative forecasts do not contain additional forecasting information.[32] To avoid maturity mismatch Jorion (1995) repeats the tests using as dependent variable the futures' observed average volatility until the options' expiration. Again,

[29] Canina and Figlewski eliminate options violating a specific arbitrage restriction. However, this biases implied volatilities from options far out of the money. These out-of-the-money options are more sensitive to implied volatility so that measurement errors in option prices lead to relatively large errors in far out-of-the-money implied volatilities. The arbitrage restriction imposed by Canina and Figlewski tends to eliminate options for which the measurement error causes option prices to be much too low. Consequently, since the eliminated options are those with relatively low implied volatilities the remaining sample contains a disproportionate number of out-of-the-money options with implied volatilities being too high due to measurement errors. See Canina and Figlewski (1993, p. 667).

[30] In this study the forecasting horizon is longer than the frequency of observations (daily). Therefore, the time series of return variances is computed from overlapping observations so that the error terms in the regressions follow an MA process (e.g. Lamoureux and Lastrapes (1993, p. 216)). This causes the standard deviations of the OLS estimates to be biased. To counter this problem, Canina and Figlewski (1993) and Lamoureux and Lastrapes (1993) use a corrected estimate of the coefficients' covariances as suggested by Hansen (1982) and Hodrick (1980).

[31] Canina and Figlewski (1993) discuss whether this rather disappointing forecasting performance of implied volatilities might be caused by asynchronous observations. They repeat their tests using transaction data instead of the previously used closing prices but find very similar results.

[32] The GARCH model is estimated on the full data set.

implied volatilities are significant whereas the alternative forecasts are not. However, implied volatilities turn out to be downward-biased predictors of actual volatilities.
In discussing the rather different results compared to those of Canina and Figlewski (1995), Jorion (1995) stresses the effects of measurement errors. First, he argues that it is much more difficult to obtain synchronous observations on the S&P 100 index value and on the corresponding option prices than on foreign exchange options and exchange rates. Stock indices suffer from the 'stale' index problem and, when no concurrent price notations are available, are partially based on stock prices recorded at earlier points in time. Second, transaction costs are lower in option markets than in stock markets. Therefore, new information is more quickly incorporated into option prices than into the stock index value.[33] Further problems are related to measurement errors in option prices (e.g. resulting from bid-ask spreads and discrete price notation) and to the presence of autocorrelation in the time series of actual and implied volatilities. Third, he argues that the sample size available is too small to rely on GMM estimation as in Canina and Figlewski (1993) and Lamoureux and Lastrapes (1993). By means of simulations Jorion (1995) demonstrates that a combination of these problems leads to downward biased regression coefficients on implied volatilities. However, to account for the results presented in Canina and Figlewski (1993) measurement errors would have to be unrealistically large.

Fleming (1998) considers the autocorrelation problem in some detail. His data set consists of observations on S&P 100 index options from October 1985 to April 1992. Using at-the-money options with short time to expiration he computes implied volatilities by means of the binomial option-pricing model by Fleming and Whaley (1994). For each day only data observed within a 10-minute time window at the close of trading is considered in order to reduce the adverse effects of bid-ask spreads, discrete price notations and noncontinuous transactions. Furthermore, observations from the 1987 crash are eliminated from the sample. Fleming argues that the Hansen (1982) and Hodrick (1980) correction fails to remove the bias due to overlapping observations because the forecasting horizon, i.e. the option's time to expiration, is non-constant. The forecasting errors from a specific option contract are highly autocorrelated. In contrast, the correlation of the forecast errors from two different option contracts is much lower. Therefore, the autocorrelation in the time series of forecast errors is affected by switches from one contract to another. Furthermore, for a given contract the correlation of forecast errors rises with declining time to expiration because the relative amount of overlap increases.
Since the time series of both actual and implied volatilities are highly autocorrelated there is a considerable risk that (3.14) estimates a spurious re-

[33] If closing prices are used additional problems arise if the markets for the underlying and the options have different closing times (e.g. Fleming (1998)).

gression.[34] Therefore, Fleming (1998) uses a modified regression to test the unbiasedness hypothesis for implied-volatility-based forecasts,

$$\sigma_{t,T} - \sigma_{IV;t-1,T} = \alpha + \beta\left(\sigma_{IV;t,T} - \sigma_{IV;t-1,T}\right) + \epsilon_{t,T}. \qquad (3.20)$$

The equation is estimated with GMM and a correction for variable overlap in the forecasting horizons is applied. The author rejects the unbiasedness hypothesis ($\alpha = 0, \beta = 1$) and finds implied volatility to overestimate future volatility. Fleming (1995) then continues his study and performs efficiency and orthogonality tests.[35] He considers alternative volatility forecasts based on historical volatility, on the S&P 100 standardized return series, and on a GARCH(1,1) model. Orthogonality of implied volatility's forecast errors cannot be rejected for any alternative volatility forecast. In contrast, orthogonality of historical volatility's prediction errors is strongly rejected. This indicates that implied volatilities contain forecasting information exceeding those in historical volatilities.[36]

In Fleming, Ostdiek, and Whaley (1995) volatility forecasts based on the *Market Volatility Index* (VIX) of the Chicago Board Options Exchange (CBOE) are discussed for the time period from 1986 to 1992.[37] They reject the unbiasedness hypothesis for both VIX- and historical-volatility-based 28-day volatility forecasts. While the VIX is an upward-biased predictor it yields a higher regression R^2 than historical volatility.[38] Orthogonality tests for the residuals from (3.14) do not show any evidence for VIX to contain any forecasting information exceeding those in historical volatilities.

Scott (1992) again looks at implied volatilities from various foreign-exchange options. He tests Black-Scholes implied volatilities computed quarterly from 1983-89 for their predictive power with respect to future ex-post quarterly volatilities. In order to avoid problems resulting from the potential nonstationarity of the volatility time series, Scott (1992) uses the following regression approach[39]

34 For the problem of spurious regression, see e.g. Granger and Newbold (1974) and Phillips (1986).

35 The efficiency and orthogonality tests are based on estimating (3.14) by GMM, using alternative volatility forecasts as instruments, and testing the overidentifying restrictions, see Fleming (1998).

36 Fleming (1985) also considers forecastings horizons of 28 days and 1 day, respectively. This raises a maturity mismatch problem but the results do not change by much.

37 The VIX is constructed from implied volatilities of eight S&P 100 options and is computed for a constant maturity of 30 days. For details, see Fleming, Ostdiek, and Whaley (1995).

38 Fleming, Ostdiek, and Whaley (1995) apply a naive correction to the VIX-forecast bias. They achieve a considerable reduction in the forecast bias without sacrificing much explanatory power.

39 (3.21) is first estimated separately for each currency by OLS. Since the error terms are highly correlated across equations, Scott (1992) also estimates the complete

$$\sigma^2_{i,t+1} = \alpha_i + \beta_i \sigma^2_{i,t} + \gamma_i \left(\sigma^2_{IV,i,t} - \sigma^2_{i,t}\right) + \epsilon_{i,t}. \tag{3.21}$$

The unbiasedness hypothesis ($\alpha_i = 0, \beta_i = 0, \gamma_i = 1$) is rejected for all exchange rates (British pound, D-Mark, Swiss franc and Japanese yen, all against the US dollar). However, the rejection of $\gamma_i = 0$ indicates that implied volatilities have some explanatory power for future actual volatilities.

The general impression from these time-series studies is that implied volatilities seem to contain some information helpful in forecasting future actual volatility. Furthermore, implied-volatility-based forecasts tend to be superior to those derived from historical volatilities or GARCH models but are often strongly biased predictors. Bates (1996a) explains this bias by the existence of risk premia and by option mispricing.[40] Another important conclusion from the studies summarized above is the sensitivity of the results with respect to various aspects of model specification. In particular, overlapping forecast errors and measurement problems might have considerable effects on the results.

Another important strand of the literature examines if actual implied volatilities are forecasts of future implied volatilities. In these studies date-t-implied volatilities are inserted into the option-pricing formulae together with other variables dated $t+1$ in order to compute next period's option price. The difference between the theoretical and observed option prices in $t+1$ can be attributed to two sources: first, the option pricing model might be misspecified. Second, implied volatility in $t+1$ might deviate from implied volatility in t, i.e. implied volatility was not forecast correctly.
Emanuel and MacBeth (1982) compare the Black-Scholes pricing errors to those of a constant-elasticity-of-variance (CEV) model.[41] Their study is based on daily observations on individual stock options in 1976-77. Inserting the at-the-money implied volatility into the Black-Scholes formula along with future values of the other parameters they 'predict' the next day's, next week's, and next month's option prices. They generate competing forecasts based on the CEV model using daily estimates for the model's volatility parameter. Generally, the CEV model's pricing errors turn out to be smaller than those of the Black-Scholes model. Furthermore, the CEV model's relative superiority increases with time to expiration. Emanuel and MacBeth (1982) argue that the CEV model's performance is superior because it provides better forecasts of future implied volatility compared to Black-Scholes implied volatility.
Tucker, Peterson, and Scott (1988) consider data on foreign-exchange options observed in 1983-84 and find the CEV model to be superior for forecasting horizons up to three days. However, for forecasting horizons of more than

system with SURE and GMM. The results summarized in the text are those from the SURE and GMM estimations.

40 For studies on option mispricing see, for example, Fleming (1999) and Engle, Kane, and Noh (1994).

41 The CEV model specifies the stock price process as $dS_t = \mu S_t\, dt + \delta S_t^{\theta/2}\, dB_t$.

ten days the pricing errors of both specifications become statistically indistinguishable. They suggest separating the effect of the implied-volatility forecast from that of the model specification: they also compute the pricing errors that result if the CEV volatility forecast is inserted into the the Black-Scholes formula. It turns out that this specification is only slightly inferior to the CEV model. Hence, the inferior performance of the Black-Scholes model seems to be caused by incorrectly forecasting future implied volatility.

Jackwerth and Rubinstein (1996) study implied volatility forecasts for S&P 500 index options using high-frequency transaction data from 1986-95. They generate implied-volatility forecasts from observed option prices where the option's time to expiration exceeds the forecasting horizon. Various types of implied volatility-forecasts are considered: the Black-Scholes implied volatility (no-change forecast of at-the-money volatility), a relative smile model (implied volatilities depend on moneyness (K/S)), an absolute smile model (implied volatilities depend on strike price), a CEV model, and a binomial model.[42] Before September 1987 the Black-Scholes model has the smallest average pricing error and therefore appears to make the best forecasts of future implied volatility. In the following years, however, the relative and absolute smile models are found to yield superior implied volatility forecasts.[43]

Dumas, Fleming, and Whaley (1998) choose a more general framework. They use *dynamic volatility functions* (DVF), simple functions of exercise price and time expiration, to forecast future implied volatilities. The DVF models are estimated on weekly observations on S&P 500 index options from 1988-93 using a numerical option-pricing model . It turns out that the DVF parameters are unstable and exhibit considerable changes from week to week. The authors report the smallest option-pricing errors for the following very simple DVF model

$$\sigma_{IV,t} = \max[0.01, a_0 + a_1 K + a_2 K^2]. \tag{3.22}$$

Other specifications where implied volatility also depends on time to expiration yield much higher pricing errors. As a benchmark model, the authors insert DVF-based volatility forecasts into the Black-Scholes formula and, surprisingly find the resulting pricing errors to be much lower than those of all consistent DVF specifications. [44] In particular, at-the-money pricing errors

[42] The implied volatilities to estimate the relative and absolute smile are computed from the Black-Scholes formula.

[43] Jackwerth and Rubinstein (1996) also study forecasts that use information in the term structure of implied volatilities. The results obtained with this model do not differ much from the previous ones.

[44] Since theoretically, a DVF is inconsistent with the Black-Scholes formula the pricing performance of the numerical option-pricing model that incorporates the DVF specification should dominate the Black-Scholes formula, see Dumas, Fleming, and Whaley (1998, p. 2086).

decline strongly. Furthermore, the DVF + Black-Scholes specification has a better hedging performance.

Rosenberg (2000) approximates Black-Scholes implied volatilities with deterministic implied volatility functions (DIVF). These functions make possible the separation of the volatility function into two components: first, the "relative implied volatility" that is independent of time to expiration and second, the at-the-money implied volatility which is assumed to be subject to stochastic shocks depending on the rate of return of the underlying asset. Using weekly observations of S&P 500 futures options in 1988-97 the author computes the pricing errors resulting from the DIVF model. In addition, he also presents the DIVF model's forecast errors for implied volatility. With respect to both criteria the DIVF model turns out to be superior to DVF models.

3.2.4 Implied Correlations as Forecasts of Future Correlations

On foreign-exchange markets two options on different currencies can be used to compute the option implied correlation of the two exchange rates against a third country. For example, if $e_{DM/\$;t}$ and $e_{Y/\$;t}$ are the natural logarithms of the D-Mark/US dollar and the Japanese yen/US dollar exchange rate the logarithm of the Japanese yen/D-Mark exchange rate is $e_{Y/DM;t} = e_{Y/\$;t} - e_{DM/\$;t}$. Therefore, the conditional variance of $e_{Y/DM}$ from t to T is

$$\begin{aligned}\sigma^2_{Y/DM;t,T} = {} & \sigma^2_{Y/\$;t,T} + \sigma^2_{DM/\$;t,T} \\ & -2\rho(e_{Y/\$}, e_{DM/\$})_{t,T}\, \sigma_{Y/\$;t,T}\, \sigma_{DM/\$;t,T}.\end{aligned} \tag{3.23}$$

The conditional correlation of the yen/dollar and the D-Mark/dollar exchange rate from t to T results as

$$\rho(e_{Y/\$}, e_{DM/\$})_{t,T} = \frac{\sigma^2_{Y/\$;t,T} + \sigma^2_{DM/\$;t,T} - \sigma^2_{Y/DM;t,T}}{2\sigma_{Y/\$;t,T}\, \sigma_{DM/\$;t,T}}. \tag{3.24}$$

Using the implied variances instead of the actual variances yields the implied correlation ρ^{imp},

$$\rho^{imp}(e_{Y/\$}, e_{DM/\$})_{t,T} = \frac{\sigma^2_{(IV),Y/\$;t,T} + \sigma^2_{(IV),DM/\$;t,T} - \sigma^2_{(IV),Y/DM;t,T}}{2\sigma_{(IV),Y/\$;t,T}\, \sigma_{(IV),DM/\$;t,T}}. \tag{3.25}$$

As with implied volatility, the implied correlation can be interpreted as the expected average correlation of the two exchange rates until the options expire.

Forecasting correlations has important applications. For example, value-at-risk models (see for example Jorion (1997)) are based on historically observed correlations of various asset returns. In contrast, implied correlations refer explicitly to the future. Other applications can be found in the hedging of correlations-based derivatives and in portfolio management.[45] The question whether implied correlations provide useful forecasts for future correlations has been examined in a number of studies.

Bodurtha and Shen (1994) study implied correlations between the exchange rates for D-Mark, US dollar and Japanese yen from 1991 to 1994. They compute implied correlations from foreign-exchange options traded on the Philadelphia stock exchange (PHLX) with time to expiration of up to two months.[46] Using simple regressions like (3.14) they study the predictive ability of implied correlations for forecasting horizons of 30 and 60 days. They compare the forecasting performance of implied correlation between the US dollar/yen and the US dollar/D-Mark exchange rates to that of historical correlation computed with exponentially declining weights and of correlation forecasts derived from a bivariate GARCH(1,1) model as suggested by Engle and Kroner (1995).[47] For both forecasting horizons historical volatilities have the highest explanatory power for actual correlations. In contrast, the regressions on implied correlations yield lower coefficients of determination than any other correlation forecast. Nevertheless, multiple regressions similar to (3.15) show implied correlation to be helpful in predicting future correlations because the coefficient estimate is significantly different from zero.

In contrast to Bodurtha and Shen (1994) Campa and Chang (1998a) use data from the over-the-counter (OTC) market. They argue that prices of OTC options should contain more information than those of exchange traded options because on the OTC market trading volume is much higher. Furthermore, OTC options have a constant time to expiration. This makes it possible to circumvent some problems related to the decline in time to expiration for exchange-traded options. In addition, OTC options are always at-the-money so that Campa and Chang (1998a) effectively avoid problems related to smile effects.[48] Their data set consists of observations on US dollar/Japanese yen, D-Mark/Japanese yen, and US dollar/Japanese yen foreign-exchange rate options from January 1989 to May 1995. They compare the forecasting performance of implied correlations to that of historical correlations, of an exponentially-weighted average of historical correlations and to

[45] Butler and Cooper (1997) discuss how implied correlations can be used to get an insight into the probabilities the market attached to different EU countries entering EMU.

[46] Bodurtha and Shen (1994) estimate implied correlations and implied volatilities jointly whereas in the other studies implied correlations are derived from implied volatilities by (3.25).

[47] The GARCH model is estimated on a rolling sample of 300 observations so that the forecasts are out of sample.

[48] For information on the OTC market for foreign-exchange options, see Campa and Chang (1998a) and Malz (1998a).

that of forecasts generated from a rolling bivariate GARCH(1,1) model. With respect to RMSE implied correlations perform better than any other forecast. The same result can be found by using Diebold-Mariano (1995) tests.[49] In simple regressions of the (3.14) type for forecasting horizons up to one month R^2 generally is higher if implied correlations are used as independent variable. For longer forecasting horizons, forecasts based on implied and on historical correlations are of similar quality and dominate the other candidate variables. Campa and Chang (1998a) show by multiple regressions like (3.15) that only weighted historical correlations (for one month forecasts) and GARCH forecasts (for three months) provide some independent forecasting information relative to implied correlations.

Walter and Lopez (2000) study OTC options on two exchange-rate triples: US dollar, D-Mark and Japanese yen (October 1990 to April 1997) and US dollar, D-Mark and Swiss franc (September 1993 to April 1997). The competing correlation forecasts are similar to those in the previous studies: implied correlation, historical correlation, exponentially-weighted historical correlation, and forecasts from a rolling bivariate GARCH(1,1) similar to that in Bollerslev, Engle, and Wooldridge (1998). Within the first group, implied correlations and GARCH forecasts have the smallest RMSE in predicting exchange-rate corelations over the next month or the next three months. The Diebold-Mariano tests indicate that both forecasts do not differ significantly from the best forecast in RMSE terms. Within the second triple, implied correlations perform well for $\rho(e_{DM/\$}, e_{DM/SFR})$ but not for the other two exchange-rate correlations. The regression analyses also yield mixed results with some coefficients on implied correlations being significant within the first triple. However, for the second triple implied correlations only are significant in the equations for $\rho(e_{DM/\$}, e_{SFR/\$})$.

3.3 The Skewness Premium

In section 3.2.1 we discussed how deviations in the risk-neutral probability density function's skewness relative to the lognormal density were related to asymmetries in the volatility smile. A similar relationship holds for option prices. If the risk-neutral density is symmetric, prices of call and put options equally far out of the money should be identical because the value of these options only depends on the tails of the symmetric risk-neutral probability density. Therefore, differences in out-of-the money call and put prices provide some information about asymmetries in the risk-neutral probability density function.

[49] The Diebold-Mariano test indicates how far a given forecast deviates from the forecast that minimizes RMSE.

Bates (1991, 1996b, 1997, 2000) suggests the skewness premium as a simple measure of the risk-neutral density's asymmetry. He defines the $x\%$ skewness premium as the percentage difference between the prices of a $x\%$ out-of-the-money call and a $x\%$ out-of-the-money put option,

$$SK = \frac{c(F_t, K_c, t)}{p(F_t, K_p, t)} - 1, \tag{3.26}$$

where F is the forward price. Two variants of the skewness premium are considered. For the first, the options' strike prices are symmetric around the forward price. For the second, they are placed geometrically around the forward price,

$$K_p = F(1-x) < F < K_c = F(1+x), \qquad x > 0, \quad \text{or} \tag{3.27}$$

$$K_p = F/(1+x) < F < K_c = F(1+x), \qquad x > 0. \tag{3.28}$$

Bates (1991, 1997) explains that the most commonly used option pricing models assume an almost symmetric slightly positively skewed risk-neutral density. This assumption implies a skewness premium between zero and $x\%$ ($0\% < SK < x\%$). He studies skewness premia for S&P 500 futures option prices from 1983-93 and shows the skewness premium to be significantly negative in 1985-87 and after the October 1987 crash.[50] This implies that out of the money puts are valued much higher than the corresponding out-of-the-money call options because the market attributes a much higher risk-neutral probability to a large decline in the S&P 500 than to a large increase. Significantly positive skewness premia were present in 1985. Only in 1986 does the author find skewness premia consistent with commonly used option-pricing models. Bates shows that skewness premia become significantly negative at the end of 1986. He argues that this can be interpreted as evidence of crash fears among market participants. However, in the weeks before the 1987 crash skewness premia become positive again so that the market does not appear to have anticipated the crash. Generally, the skewness premium is highly correlated with the relative trading volume of call and put options: a higher share for put options in trading volume coincides with negative skewness premia (Bates (2000)).

Bates (1996b) applies this approach to futures options on the D-Mark/US dollar and Japanese yen/US dollar exchange rates traded at the Chicago Mercantile Exchange (CME). For the years 1984-92 he reports the skewness premium changing frequently from positive to negative values. For most of the time it falls outside the interval $(0\%, x\%)$.

The approach suggested by Gemmill (1996) is similar to Bates' method. He computes skewness premia from FTSE 100 index options from July 1985 to December 1990 by focussing on asymmetries in the volatility smile,

[50] Since no pairs of call and put options are usually available for the required strike prices, Bates (1991, 1997, 2000) interpolates option prices using a cubic spline function.

$$SK_\sigma = \left\{ \frac{\sigma(+2\%) - \sigma(-2\%)}{\sigma(+2\%)} \right\} \times 100, \tag{3.29}$$

where $\sigma(+2\%)$ is the implied volatility of a call option with exercise price 2% above the forward price. Accordingly, $\sigma(-2\%)$ is the implied volatility of a put option with exercise price 2% below the forward price. SK_σ is negative if out-of-the-money calls are underpriced relative to out-of-the-money puts.[51] Since at-the-money option prices are approximatly linear in volatility there exists a close relationship between this measure and Bates' skewness premium for small x. Gemmill (1996) reports frequent changes from positive to negative values in SK_σ but does not find evidence for a negative trend after the October 1987 crash as documented in Bates (1991, 1997, 2000) for S&P 500 futures options.[52]

Direct evidence on asymmetries in the risk-neutral density is provided by prices of *risk reversals*. Risk reversals are combinations of options traded on the OTC market and consist of a long call and a short put option that both are equally far out of the money (as measured by their *deltas*). For a symmetric risk-neutral density the prices of both options are equal so that the risk reversal price is zero. If however, risk-reversal prices are positive, market participants assign a higher probability to large positive returns than to extremely negative returns and the risk-neutral density is postively skewed.[53]

3.4 Summary

There already exists a broad literature on the information content of derivative prices. While in early studies, the predictive ability of forward and futures prices for future spot prices is investigated, later studies focus on the forecasting performance of option-implied volatilities. Theoretically, implied volatility can be interpreted as the expected average volatility of the underlying's price until the options' expiration.[54] However, this interpretation refers to the risk-neutral volatility process so that implied volatility might provide

[51] In order to compute SK_σ implied volatilities are interpolated linearly, see Gemmill (1996, p. 885).

[52] Gemmill (1996) argues that this result might be due to the smaller depth of the FTSE index option market where mostly small speculative transactions occur. The S&P index options market however, is much more liquid and makes it possible for institutional investors to pursue portfolio insurance strategies that might raise the prices of out-of-the-money puts.

[53] The information content of risk reversals is discussed in some lenght in Malz (1996b).

[54] This relationship is exploited, for example, by Lyons (1988, 1998) who studies risk premia on foreign-exchange markets. He uses implied volatility as a proxy variable for expected volatility.

biased volatility forecasts in the presence of a risk premium.
Depending on technique, data, and time period, empirical analyses of the forecasting performance of implied volatilities arrive at different results. Studies for individual stock options show implied volatilities to contribute significantly to forecasting future actual volatilities. However, relative efficiency of implied volatility-based forecasts generally is rejected. For stock indices, most studies tend to find implied volatilities to be significant in forecasting future S&P 100 volatilities. However, implied volatilities turn out to be biased predictors of future index volatility. Furthermore, relative efficiency of implied volatility-based forecasts is rejected in most cases. For exchange rates implied volatilities are found to yield superior and relatively efficient volatility forecasts compared to historical volatilities. For bonds futures implied volatilities in most cases are shown to have significant explanatory power for future volatilities. Most often, however, implied volatility-based forecasts are not relatively efficient.
The literature surveyed in this chapter also indicates that, on the methodological side, it is important to deal appropriately with maturity-mismatch problems, autocorrelation in the (implied) volatility time series and measurement errors that can severely affect the empirical results.

Another interesting question is whether or not future implied volatilities are predictable. For stocks and foreign-exchange options it has been shown that until the mid 1980s constant-elasticity-of-variance (CEV) models are quite capable of making useful implied volatility predictions. For more recent periods, simple volatility functions that relate implied volatility to moneyness or to the exercise price have performed well.

A number of studies consider the forecasting ability of implied correlations. Implied correlations are derived from implied volatilities of foreign-exchange-rate options and can be interpreted as being risk-neutral expectations of future exchange-rate correlations. Depending on the selected exchange rates and on the sample periods, these studies have arrived at mixed conclusions about the forecasting ability of implied correlations.

Other approaches use observed option prices to obtain general information about the shape of the risk-neutral probability density function. For example, the shape of the implied volatility smile indicates deviations in the risk-neutral density's skewness and kurtosis relative to the lognormal density. Studies on stock and stock-index options show that the risk-neutral density tends to be more positively skewed than the lognormal density.

The skewness premium and prices of risk reversals depend on the relative risk-neutral probabilities of large positive or negative returns and provide some information about asymmetries in the risk-neutral density function.

The literature reviewed in this chapter clearly shows that derivative prices contain important information about the future. The other chapters in this book review, discuss, and apply approaches that aim at extracting much more information from option prices than only implied volatility.

4

Presenting and Interpreting Risk-Neutral Probabilities

In this chapter we discuss various methods of presenting risk-neutral probabilities extracted from option prices. Most common are graphical displays of the risk-neutral probability density function or of the cumulative distribution function. In many cases the information in the risk-neutral density function is also summarized by computing selected distributional statistics.

However, before turning to the presentation and interpretation of risk-neutral probabilities an important question has to be discussed: Do risk-neutral probabilities convey information about the true subjective probabilities market participants attach to specific events? As emphasized in Chapter 2 the risk-neutral density is not identical to the 'true' density of the underlying's price process because it results from the transformation of the 'true' probability measure. Therefore, in the first section we consider the conditions under which risk-neutral densities can be used to gain insights into the expectations of market participants.

4.1 Interpretation Problems Concerning Risk-Neutral Probabilities

Interpreting risk-neutral proabilities with respect to the subjective expectations of market participants is complicated because of two problems:

First, it is not certain whether the risk-neutral probability density function, i.e. the equivalent martingale measure, can be backed out uniquely from observed option prices. From a theoretical perspective, market imperfections such as transaction costs or liquidity constraints create a situation where the equivalent martingale measure is nonunique. This problem has not yet been studied extensively (see Cont (1999)).[1] From an applied perspective, it turns out that it is not possible to identify the risk-neutral probability density function exactly from a limited number of discretely observed option prices: observed option prices only give information on the conditional expectation and the probability mass between neighbouring exercise prices but not on the exact shape of the density. For example, we can always construct a stepwise density function consistent with observed option prices, where the density is constant between two neighbouring strikes. (Melick and Thomas (1997, 1998)). Since option prices are composed by expressions of the type

$$\mathbf{E}_Q\big[\max[S_T - K, 0]\big] = \big(\mathbf{E}_Q\big[S_T | S_T \geq K\big] - K\big) \cdot (1 - F(K)) \tag{4.1}$$

they only contain information on the probability mass (i) above the highest strike price, (ii) below the lowest strike price and (iii) between two strike prices (Melick and Thomas (1997, p. 98)). For example, it is possible to compute the probability mass between two strike prices using four options with different exercise prices (Neuhaus (1995)). A discrete approximation to (see Ch. 2)

$$\frac{\partial C(S_t, K)}{\partial K} = -e^{-r(T-t)}(1 - \int_{-\infty}^{K} q(S_T|S_t)\, dS_T) \tag{4.2}$$

is

$$\frac{C(S_t, K + \Delta) - C(S_t, K - \Delta)}{2\Delta} = -e^{-r(T-t)}(1 - \int_{-\infty}^{K} q(S_T|S_t)\, dS_T), \tag{4.3}$$

where Δ is the difference between strike prices. Consequently, four options with strike prices spaced by Δ provide enough information to compute the probability mass between K and $K + \Delta$,

$$\begin{aligned} &\frac{[C(S_t, K + \Delta) - C(S_t, K - \Delta)] - [C(S_t, K + 2\Delta) - C(S_t, K)]}{2\Delta} \\ &= e^{-r(T-t)} \left[\int_{-\infty}^{K} q(S_T|S_t)\, dS_T - \int_{-\infty}^{K+\Delta} q(S_T|S_t)\, dS_T \right] \\ &= -e^{r(T-t)} \int_{K}^{K+\Delta} q(S_T|S_t)\, dS_T. \end{aligned} \tag{4.4}$$

How this probability mass is distributed between two strike prices is more or less determined by the technique chosen to extract the risk-neutral density. That means the identification problem resulting from the absence of a continuum of observed option prices is solved by selecting a specific technique with its implicit identifying assumptions.

Second, in interpreting risk-neutral probabilities we have to be aware that they result from the interaction of the 'true' (subjective) conditional probabilities for the underlying's price with market participants' risk preferences.

[1] In addition, in reality we usually deal with incomplete markets that also lead to the equivalent martingale measure not necessarily being unique.

Risk-neutral probabilities are derived from the valuation of state dependent payoffs. For each individual, this value depends both on the probability of the event occurring and on the subjective value of a payoff in this particular state of the world (Chang and Melick (1999, p. 7)).[2] For example, a high risk-neutral probability for a low future value of a stock index might correspond to a low 'true' probability if risk-averse agents highly value payouts in this state of the world, i.e. if their relative marginal utility is high.
In the basic Black/Scholes-Merton model the only difference between the true and the risk-neutral probability density is the drift, i.e. expected values differ by a risk premium. Standard deviation and higher moments coincide under both probability measures.[3]. However, for the Hull and White (1987) model the volatility process is also modified by a risk premium so that neither expected value, nor standard deviation or higher moments can be expected to be the same under both densities (compare Ch. 3).

For an illustration we consider a simple two-period example: an agent can invest in a risky asset with a state-dependent payoff in the next period. Assume the payoff to be negatively correlated with the business cycle. In state 1 (boom) the payoff is 100, in state 2 (recession) it is 120. Let the risk-free rate of interest be equal to 10% and assume that the forward price of the asset is 94.55. Risk-neutral probabilities can be computed as 80% for state 1 and 20% for state 2 $\left((0.8 \times 100 + 0,2 \times 120)/1.1 = 94.55\right)$. Suppose the true subjective probability for state 1 is 95%. If market participants were risk-neutral the forward price should equal $(0.95 \times 100 + 0.05 \times 112)/1,1 = 91.82$. Since risk aversion makes the market participants highly value payoffs in recession when their income from other sources is low they try to insure themselves by investing in the asset negatively correlated with the business cycle, thus driving up its forward price and the risk-neutral probability for state 1.

Without additional identifying assumptions the effects of risk aversion and of the true subjective probabilities on risk-neutral probabilities cannot be separated.[4] The usual assumption is that risk preferences are constant throughout the observation period so that changes in risk-neutral probabilities convey information about changes in the 'true' probabilities, i.e. about changes in market participants' expectations.[5] This assumption is plausible in cases where the observation period is not too long.

[2] See also Galati and Melick (2002, p. 6), Leahy and Thomas (1996, p. 2), and Malz (1998b, p. 112).

[3] This argument is generalized by Nakamura and Shiratsuka (1999)

[4] An additional problem that is not discussed here comes from the fact that the interpretation of risk-neutral probabilities is based on an representative agent concept (Cont (1999)).

[5] Compare Bahra (1997, p. 25), Galati and Melick (1999, p. 6), and Melick and Thomas (1998, p. 296). An alternative identifying assumption is to specify a utility function for all economic agents. Rubinstein (1998) shows that for a logarithmic utility function 'true' and risk-neutral probabilities do not differ significantly.

4.2 Graphical Presentations of the Risk-Neutral Probability Density

If we assume risk-preferences to remain unchanged throughout the observation period we can investigate revisions in market expectations by studying changes in risk-neutral probabilities. Therefore, we require techniques to present and to analyze carefully changes in implied probabilities. The simplest approaches are based on graphical presentations where graphical displays of the risk-neutral density function or of the cumulative distribution function are a starting point. First insights into peculiar properties of the risk-neutral density can be gained by comparing the risk-neutral density to a suitable benchmark, e.g. a lognormal density fitted to option prices (the Black/Scholes-Merton model).[6] However, much more interesting are comparisons of risk-neutral densities or cumulative distribution functions computed from data on the same option contract, i.e. with identical expiration date, for different days (e.g. Leahy and Thomas (1996), Melick and Thomas (1997)). Here, changes in the risk-neutral probabilities over time indicate changes in market participants' expectations.

In addition, the futures or forward prices on the relevant days are often also graphed because they represent the densities' expected values.[7] Marked changes in the risk-neutral distributions indicate significant revisions in market expectations. Most obvious to visual inspection of densities are changes in the futures price, i.e. shifts in the expected value. The same is true for pronounced changes in standard deviations or in the range of the distribution. These observations are evidence of marked changes in the uncertainty in market participants' expectations.

As an illustration of this approach, figure 4.1 compares risk-neutral probability density functions (PDFs) for the Euribor on two days in January 2000. The risk-neutral probabilities have been estimated using the mixture of lognormal approach.[8] On January, 28, the euro reference rate declined below one US dollar for the first time since the euro's introduction. Clearly, this event caused

[6] See, for example, Leahy and Thomas (1996), Levin, McManus, and Watt (1998), McManus (1999), and Melick and Thomas (1997). Some authors, e.g. Levin, McManus, and Watt (1998, p. 234) prefer to present the density or the cumulative distribution function with respect to the logarithm of the exercise price. They argue that this approach makes it easier to compare the risk-neutral probabilities to the benchmark model, which in this case is a normal distribution.

[7] The futures price can deviate significantly from the expected value if futures prices exhibit large changes and hit the limits on maximum price movements imposed by the exchange. In this case trading in the futures contract is suspended while trading in the corresponding option continues.

[8] See Chapter 5. For details on data and estimation method and a detailed discussion of the results, see Mandler (2002).

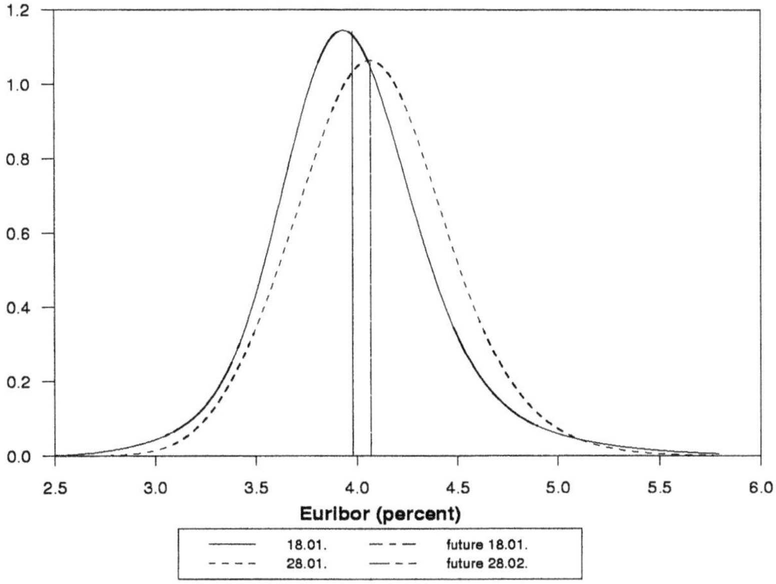

Fig. 4.1. Risk-neutral PDFs for three-month Euribor futures (June contract) on January 18 and January 28, 2000

a shift in the risk-neutral density to the right and an increase in the expected value of future interest rates, i.e. in the futures implied interest rate.

Another approach is to compare graphically two implied density functions computed for the same point in time but from options with different time to maturity. Large discrepancies between these densities indicate differences in expectations with respect to different dates in the future, e.g. varying levels of uncertainty in expectations about alternative points in time. For example, a significant increase in the range of the risk-neutral density computed from three-month options compared to that computed from one-month options indicates a considerable uncertainty about events between one and three months in the future. Obviously, these different types of graphical presentations can be combined with each other, for example, to investigate changes over time in risk-neutral probability densities for different expirations.

Some authors (Levin, McManus, and Watt (1998), McManus (1999)) prefer to graph the cumulative distribution instead of the risk-neutral density function. They argue that the cumulative distribution function can be interpreted more easily: it shows the probability of the underlying's price at expiration being below a given threshold. To supplement the graphical presentation they also present tables containing selected values of the cumulative distribution function and of the inverse cumulative distribution function at different points in time in order to provide some insight into the evolution of market participants' expectations.

Since the risk-neutral probability density function is a point estimate it is desirable to construct confidence intervals to get some measure for the accuracy of the estimation. Furthermore, this might provide researchers with the possibility of deciding whether observed differences between risk-neutral densities are statistically significant. For these reasons, Melick and Thomas (1998) discuss how to construct confidence intervals using the bootstrap method.[9] By drawing repeatedly from the set of observed option prices they generate a large number of pseudo samples. For each of these samples a risk-neutral density function is estimated. Finally, confidence intervals are constructed from the densities' empirical distribution function.
However, this approach suffers from the problem that the loss of observations in constructing the pseudo-samples worsens the identification problem., as discussed option prices only contain information on the probability mass between neighbouring strike prices but not on its exact distribution. With fewer observed option prices used for density estimation, the risk-neutral probabilities will be more dependent on the chosen technique and the estimation results might become quite variable (Melick and Thomas (1998, p. 318)).[10]

4.3 Distributional Statistics and Percentiles

In many applications the information incorporated in risk-neutral probability density functions is summarized by computing various moments. The most commonly used moments are the expected value, standard deviation (reflecting the dispersion of expectations), skewness and kurtosis statistics.[11]
Skewness statistics provide information on the asymmetry in the risk-neutral density, i.e. on the "directional bias" in expectations. A risk-neutral probability density with increasingly positive skewness indicates that market participants put more weight on extremely high realizations of the underlying's price process than on extremely low values.
Kurtosis in the risk-neutral density is usually measured relative to the standard normal distribution. Excess kurtosis, i.e. a more leptokurtic density, assigns higher probabilities to extreme events (fat tails) and leads to a sharper center of the density. These effects offer two different interpretations for an

[9] For the bootstrap see, for example, Horowitz (2001).
[10] Note that this approach yields confidence bands that per se are not probability density functions since the upper confidence band integrates to more than one and the lower band to less than one. See Bliss and Panigirtzoglou (2002). p. 386.
[11] See, for example, Bahra (1997), Campa, Chang, and Reider (1998), Coutant, Jondeau, and Rockinger (2001), Jondeau and Rockinger (2000), Levin, McManus, and Watt (1998), McManus (1999), and Nakamura and Shiratsuka (1999).

increase in excess kurtosis (Nakamura and Shiratsuka (1999)). According to the first interpretation, market participants expect strong deviations from the underlying's current price level to be more likely in the future – uncertainty increases. On the other hand, an increase in excess kurtosis might indicate that agents become more confident in the current price level so that the density becomes sharper at the center. In order to discriminate between these two interpretations Nakamura and Shiratsuka (1999) suggest looking simultaneously at changes in excess kurtosis and standard deviation: increasing excess kurtosis and standard deviation are interpreted as signs of rising uncertainty with respect to extreme future price realizations, i.e. the distribution's fat tails are emphasized. However, if the standard deviation declines while excess kurtosis increases, an interpretation of increasing confidence in the persistence of the underlying's current price is suggested because market participants assign higher probabilities to only very small changes. Accordingly, Nakamura and Shiratsuka (1999) interpret a decline in excess kurtosis coinciding with a rising standard deviation as evidence of a drop in confidence in the current price level. Finally, a decline in excess kurtosis together with a decline in standard deviation is a sign of decreasing uncertainty with respect to extreme future realizations.

The skewness and excess kurtosis statistics predominantly used in applied work, $sp2$ and $wp3$, are defined as

$$sp2 = \frac{\mathbf{E}^Q\left[\left(\ln(S_T) - \mathbf{E}^Q[\ln(S_T)]\right)^3\right]}{\operatorname{var}\left(\ln(S_T)\right)^{3/2}}, \tag{4.5}$$

$$wp3 = \frac{\mathbf{E}^Q\left[\left(\ln(S_T) - \mathbf{E}^Q[\ln(S_T)]\right)^4\right]}{\operatorname{var}\left(\ln(S_T)\right)^2} - 3. \tag{4.6}$$

$\operatorname{var}(\ln(S_T)) = \mathbf{E}^Q\left[\left(\ln(S_T) - \mathbf{E}^Q[\ln(S_T)]\right)^2\right]$ is the variance of $\ln(S_T)$. The notation $\mathbf{E}^Q$ indicates that expectations are taken with respect to the (conditional) risk-neutral density Q. Adjusting the variance for time to expiration yields a measure of the annualized volatility $\sigma_{S,ann} = \sqrt{\operatorname{var}\left(\ln(S_T)\right)/(T-t)}$. Note, that the statistics are computed with respect to the logarithm of the underlying ($\ln(S_T)$) in order to facilitate comparisons with the Black/Scholes-Merton model. In this benchmark model the risk-neutral density is lognormal so that the log of the underlying's price is distributed normally with $sp2 = 0$ and $wp3 = 0$.

Campa, Chang, and Reider (1998) suggest computing relative intensities as alternative skewness statistics. Relative intensities are derived from conditional expected values for the underlying asset's price being above an upper threshold $\bar{S}$ or below a lower threshold $\underline{S}$. $\bar{S}$ and $\underline{S}$ are placed symmetrically around the futures price.

$$int_{\bar{S},+} = \int_{\bar{S}}^{\infty} (S_T - \bar{S})\, q(S_T)\, dS_T, \tag{4.7}$$

$$int_{\underline{S},-} = \int_{0}^{\underline{S}} (\underline{S} - S_T)\, q(S_T)\, dS_T. \tag{4.8}$$

Relative intensity is defined as the difference $int_{\bar{S},+} - int_{\underline{S},-}$.[12] Consequently, relative intensity considers the relative importance of price realizations in both tails of the risk-neutral density.[13] Campa, Chang, and Reider (1998) suggest choosing the distance between the thresholds and the futures price to be a positive function of standard deviation. This makes it possible to separate effects stemming from changes in skewness from those caused by changes in standard deviation. For example, an increase in standard deviation with constant skewness could make relative intensity increase (Campa, Chang, and Reider (1998, p. 141)).
Melick and Thomas (1998, p. 229) compare the probability mass in the density's upper tail to that in its lower tail and derive an alternative skewness statistic

$$rpr = \frac{\int_0^{\underline{S}} q(S_T)dS_T}{\int_{\bar{S}}^{\infty} q(S_T)dS_T}. \tag{4.9}$$

However, Campa, Chang, and Reider (1998, p. 141) point out that *rpr* can give ambigious results. Consider the following example: for a positively skewed distribution *rpr* is greater than one for thresholds very close to the futures price because a positively skewed distribution has more probability mass to the left of the expected value than to the right. When moving the thresholds away from the futures price, *rpr* declines below one because the right tail begins to dominate. This shows that the sign of *rpr* crucially depends on the location of $\bar{S}$ and $\underline{S}$.

Using these statistics, characteristic features of risk-neutral probability density functions can be compared for different points in time, for example, in the context of event studies. Furthermore, in time-series studies, the evolution of the statistics can be tracked over an extended period of time. Time series and event studies of statistics computed from risk-neutral probabilities do not constitute entirely separate approaches because many time-series studies also investigate changes in market expectations related to specific events (e.g. the French snap election in Jondeau and Rockinger (1998)). Nakamura and Shiratsuka (1999), however, prefer not to focus on changes in market expectations related to specific events. They try to identify general trends and characteristic patterns in the relationship between the underlying's price and the distributional statistics for individual option contracts across various underlyings. By this procedure they try to establish typical patterns that should serve as benchmarks for event studies (Shiratsuka (1999)).

[12] This is equal to $e^{r(T-t)}\big(C(S_t, \bar{S}, t) - P(S_t, \underline{S}, t)\big)$.
[13] By definition relative intensity is zero for $\bar{S} = \underline{S} = F$.

Apart from standard deviation, percentiles of the risk-neutral density are used in many empirical studies to capture the uncertainty in market expectations. The evolution of percentiles through time is often displayed together with the futures/forward price.[14] Percentiles can be presented either as absolute or as relative values, i.e. divided by the futures/forward price (Coutant, Jondeau, and Rockinger (2001)). Very high and very low orders of the percentiles (e.g. 5% and 95%) should be avoided since these often fall outside the strike price range spanned by observed option prices (Neuhaus (1995, p. 47)). Working with these percentiles would make the results very dependent on the selected technique, which has a considerable effect on the shape of the risk-neutral density's tails where no observed option prices are available.[15] Therefore, it is preferable to use percentiles within the range covered by observed option prices. Percentile differences, e.g. the interquartile range, can be computed again as absolute values or relative to the forward/futures price. These percentile differences are often used as relatively robust measures for dispersion and uncertainty in expectations.
Generally, the percentiles of the risk-neutral density are not symmetric around the expected value. Some authors therefore compute symmetric bands centered on the expected value and containing a given probability mass (e.g. 90% or 95%). As a statistic for dispersion they use half of the difference between the upper and lower bounds expressed as a percentage value of the forward/futures price.

Most studies focus on changes in percentiles, percentile ranges and in other statistics over time. However, these statistics often turn out to be affected by the decline in the option contract's time to expiration. For example, with decreasing time to expiration the percentiles slowly converge to the futures/forward price. The economic reason for this behaviour is that, assuming the stochastic process of the underlying's price to be sufficiently smooth, for less time to expiration ceteris paribus the probability of deviations from the current price level declines. Such maturity dependence effects are particularly relevant for exchange-traded options because expiration dates are set by the exchange.[16] Maturity dependence might not be limited to percentiles and percentile ranges but might be also present in other distributional statistics such as skewness and kurtosis statistics or in standard deviation.[17]

[14] See, for example Bahra (1997), Coutant, Jondeau, and Rockinger (2001), Neuhaus (1995), and Söderlind (2000). These percentiles are frequently called "confidence bands" (e.g. Coutant, Jondeau, and Rockinger (2001)), a notion that is not exactly accurate.

[15] The same problem applies to other statistics that are strongly influenced by the distribution's tails, such as range, standard deviation, skewness, and kurtosis statistics (Neuhaus (1995)).

[16] On the other hand, OTC option data consist of reported option transactions based on a constant time to expiration.

[17] For example, if the underlying's price process is a random walk we would have $sp2 = 1/\sqrt{T-t}$ and $wp3 = 1/(T-t) - 3$ for the 'true' density function. Therefore,

In the literature two approaches can be found for dealing with maturity dependence. Butler and Davies (1998) estimate risk-neutral density functions for different times to expiration and construct statistics based on a constant maturity by interpolation. Melick and Thomas (1998) suggest a regression approach to eliminate time-to-expiration effects from a time series of relative interquartile ranges (IQR) and demonstrate their approach using foreign-exchange options. They estimate the regression

$$\ln(IQR_t) = \bar{\omega} + \rho \cdot \ln(T_1 - t) + \delta \cdot \ln(T_2 - t) + \eta \cdot d_t + \epsilon_t, \tag{4.10}$$

where d_t is a contract-switch dummy. Option contracts with a very short remaining time to expiration are thought to have only very limited information content. Most of the trading volume has already shifted into another contract with a longer time to expiration. Therefore, in most empirical studies, options coming close to expiration are ignored and a contract with a longer time to expiration is chosen instead. The dummy variable is designed to capture these contract switches that might take place several times.[18]
$T_1 - t$ and $T_2 - t$, respectively, is the time to expiration remaining (1) if no contract switch occurs or (2) if a contract switch occurs. The logarithmic specification was selected by the authors after an inspection of the IQR series and can be altered for other studies.[19] Melick and Thomas (1998) suggest adjusting time series that exhibit maturity dependence by running a regression similar to (4.9) and constructing a constant maturity series from the regession residuals.

4.4 Summary

The interpretation of risk-neutral probabilities is complicated by two problems. First, it is not possible to determine uniquely the risk-neutral probability density function from a limited number of observed option prices. Therefore, risk-neutral probabilities might be sensitive to the choice of technique. The

it is possible that the risk-neutral moments might also depend on the time to expiration. With respect to standard deviation in many cases the ad-hoc correction of dividing by the time to expiration is applied.

[18] Generally, the critical threshold for switching into another contract is selected for each study individually. See, for example Abken, Madan, and Ramamurtie (1996, p. 13), Bates (1991, p. 1019), or Bliss and Panigirtzoglou (2002, p. 396).

[19] In addition, Melick and Thomas (1998, p. 307) also consider alternative specifications for equation (4.9) using information on options for all available expiration dates.
They apply their correction (4.9) to foreign-exchange options and compare the residuals to IRQ from OTC options with constant maturity. It turns out that the adjusted IRQ series no longer exhibit significant dependence on time to expiration.

discussion of how empirical results derived from different techniques to extract risk-neutral probabilities compare to each other in Chapter 6 will shed further light on this issue. Second, since the market participants' expectations and their risk preferences both determine risk-neutral probabilities, market expectations cannot be identified without imposing additional restrictions. Assuming that risk preferences are constant over time, changes in risk-neutral densities convey information about changes in the market participants' expectations.

Changes in risk-neutral probability densities are either examined within event studies or in a broader time-series context. In the first case we compare the density functions and statistics derived thereof before and after the event of interest. On the other hand, time-series studies track the evolution of risk-neutral densities over extended periods of time but often in relation to an important event too.
Various methods can be used to present the information in risk-neutral probabilities. First, graphical displays of risk-neutral probability density functions can be used to compare risk-neutral densities at different points in time or to contrast the estimated density with a benchmark, e.g. a lognormal density. However, the visual inspection can usually only provide some very basic information because only pronounced shifts in the density or large changes in its dispersion can be detected. Therefore, statistics are often computed to capture symmetry/asymmetry, dispersion and uncertainty in the risk-neutral probability density function. These include the expected value, standard deviation, moments-based skewness and excess-kurtosis statistics, relative intensity, percentiles and percentile differences. Many statistics exhibit some dependence on time to expiration and some techniques were suggested that make appropriate adjustments to the statistics' time series.

In Chapters 8 and 9 the methods for the presentation and interpretation of risk-neutral probabilities discussed here will be used to analyze our empirical results with regard to the effects of ECB council meetings on uncertainty in expectations of money-market participants. However, the next step will be a thorough discussion of various techniques to extract risk-neutral probabilities from option prices.

5

Techniques for Extracting Risk-Neutral Probabilities from Option Prices

In this chapter we discuss the recently developed techniques for extracting risk-neutral probabilities from option prices. We present the most important approaches in some detail so that the reader will be able to implement them with appropriate software. Various extensions and modifications are surveyed briefly. Before we consider the three most important types of techniques, section 5.1 shows a direct approach suggested by Neuhaus (1995) where the risk-neutral cumulative distribution function is approximated by a scaled first-order difference quotient of the call option-pricing function.

Section 5.2 considers techniques that rely on identifying assumptions about the shape of the risk-neutral density. A sufficiently flexible parametric density is selected and the free parameters are estimated from observed option prices (5.2.1). Expansion methods model the deviations of the risk-neutral density from a normal or lognormal density (5.2.2). Other related techniques include the minimization of the risk-neutral density's deviation from a prior density and an approach that explicitly considers the risk-neutral density's smoothness as an optimization criterion.

Approaches within the second category (in section 5.3) compute the risk-neutral density function as a scaled second-order difference quotient of the call option-pricing function. The call option pricing function itself is constructed by inter- and extrapolation of the few discretely observed option prices. However, most authors prefer to interpolate the volatility smile instead of option prices. For modelling the volatility smile, global or local polynomials (5.3.1 and 5.3.2) and nonparametric techniques are most widely used.

Finally, we consider techniques that derive the risk-neutral density by assuming a particular stochastic process for the underlying. An implied volatility tree model as an extension of the binomial option-pricing model is discussed together with an approach in which the free parameters of an option-pricing function derived from a specified stochastic process are estimated. Some further issues related to data selection and preparation are described in section 5.5. The last section summarizes and concludes.

5.1 The Direct Approach

Neuhaus (1995) presents a technique to directly compute the risk-neutral cumulative distribution function. His approach does not require any additional identifying assumptions. As shown in Chapter 2 the first derivative of the call option-pricing function is equal to the negative of the discounted risk-neutral probability for the call option being in the money at expiration,

$$-\partial C/\partial K = e^{-r(t-t)}\left(1 - Q(K)\right), \tag{5.1}$$

where $Q(K) = \text{prob}(S_T \leq K|S_t)$. This derivative can be discretely approximated by a first-order difference quotient,

$$(1 - Q(K)) = e^{r(T-t)}\,\frac{C_{i-1} - C_{i+1}}{2\,\Delta K}. \tag{5.2}$$

Here, call prices are ordered for increasing strike prices ($C_i = C(K_i)$) and it is assumed that strike prices are spaced by ΔK.
The risk-neutral probability of the underlying's price in T falling between K_i and K_{i+1} can be written as the difference of (5.2) for two neighbouring strike prices,

$$\begin{aligned}\text{prob}(K_i \leq S_T \leq K_{i+1}) &= Q(K_{i+1}) - Q(K_i) \\ &= e^{r(T-t)}\,\frac{[C_{i-1} - C_{i+1}] - [C_i - C_{i+2}]}{2\,\Delta K}.\end{aligned} \tag{5.3}$$

However, this approach does not provide any information about the cumulative distribution function for strike prices within $[K_i, K_{i+1}]$. Therefore, the number of observed call prices available has an important influence on the amount of information that can be extracted by using this technique.

5.2 Fitting Density Functions to Option Prices

5.2.1 Estimating Parametric Density Functions

A comparatively simple way to extract the risk-neutral probability density function from observed option prices is to assume a specific parametric form for the density and to estimate its free parameters. Assuming a particular parametric density does not imply the assumption of a specific stochastic process for the underlying because a variety of price processes is consistent with a given conditional density for the underlying's price at expiration (e.g. Melick and Thomas (1997)). Since the parametric density should be sufficiently flexible to allow for a wide range of possible shapes for the risk-neutral density, in most applications mixtures of density functions or generalized density functions are selected.

Mixtures of Univariate Lognormal Distributions

Drawing upon a contribution by Ritchey (1990), Bahra (1997), and Melick and Thomas (1997) specify the risk-neutral density as a weighted sum of k univariate lognormal density functions,

$$q(S_T|S_t) = \sum_{i=1}^{k} \theta_i \, \ell(\mu_i, \sigma_i; S_T), \qquad \sum_{i=1}^{k} \theta_i = 1, \qquad \theta_i \geq 0, \tag{5.4}$$

where θ_i are the weights to be estimated in addition to the two parameters (μ_i, σ_i) from each lognormal density,

$$\ell(\mu_i, \sigma_i; S_T) = \frac{1}{\sqrt{2\pi}\,\sigma_i\, S_T} \exp\left[-\frac{1}{2}\left(\frac{\ln(S_T) - \mu_i}{\sigma_i}\right)^2\right]. \tag{5.5}$$

This mixture approach can accomodate risk-neutral density functions of various shapes – even a multimodal density function. For example, a number of theoretical option-pricing models, such as the Hull and White (1987) model or the *jump-diffusion* models by Merton (1973) or Bates (1991), yield risk-neutral density functions that can be represented as a mixture of lognormal densities (Levin, McManus, and Watt (1998, p. 239)).
The number k of lognormal densities is limited by the number of observed option prices because each additional lognormal density increases the number of parameters to be estimated by three $(\mu_i, \sigma_i, \theta_i)$. Since the number of available option prices usually is quite low $k = 2$ oder $k = 3$ is chosen in most applications.[1]

Theoretical option prices can be derived as

$$\hat{C}_t(K) = e^{-r(T-t)} \int_K^{\infty} (S_T - K) \sum_{i=1}^{k} \theta_i \, \ell(\mu_i, \sigma_i; S_T) \, dS_T, \tag{5.6}$$

$$\hat{P}_t(K) = e^{-r(T-t)} \int_0^{K} (K - S_T) \sum_{i=1}^{k} \theta_i \, \ell(\mu_i, \sigma_i; S_T) \, dS_T. \tag{5.7}$$

---

[1] Bahra (1997), Levin, McManus, and Watt (1998), McManus (1999), Söderlind (2000), and Söderlind and Svensson (1998) use a mixture of two lognormals. Leahy and Thomas (1996) and Melick and Thomas (1997) choose $k = 2$.

If a number of observed option prices with different exercise prices and the risk-free interest rate are given, the parameters of the risk-neutral density $\eta' = (\mu_1, ..., \mu_k, \sigma_1, ..., \sigma_k, \theta_1, ..., \theta_k)$ can be estimated by minimizing the sum of squared deviations of theoretical from observed option prices,

$$\min_{\eta} \left[\sum_{i=1}^{n} [C(K_i,t) - \hat{C}(K_i,t)]^2 + \sum_{i=1}^{m} [P(K_i,t) - \hat{P}(K_i,t)]^2 \right. \\ \left. + [F(t,T) - \hat{F}(t,T)]^2 \right], \tag{5.8}$$

where n is the number of observed call prices and m is the number of observed put prices.[2] The last term in (5.8) represents the difference of the forward (futures) price and its theoretical value $\hat{F}(t,T) = \mathbf{E}^Q[S_T|S_t]$ and is often used as an additonal restriction (*martingale restriction*),

$$\hat{F}(t,T) = \mathbf{E}^Q[S_T|S_t] = \sum_{i=1}^{k} \theta_i \, e^{\mu_i + \frac{1}{2}\sigma_i^2}. \tag{5.9}$$

For $k = 2$ Bahra (1997) derives closed form solutions for (5.6) and (5.7),

$$\hat{C}_t(K) = e^{-r(T-t)} \{ \theta \left[e^{\mu_1 + \frac{1}{2}\sigma_1^2} \, \Phi(d_1) - K \, \Phi(d_2) \right] \\ + (1-\theta) \left[e^{\mu_2 + \frac{1}{2}\sigma_2^2} \, \Phi(d_3) - K \, \Phi(d_4) \right] \}, \tag{5.10}$$

$$\hat{P}_t(K) = e^{-r(T-t)} \{ \theta \left[-e^{\mu_1 + \frac{1}{2}\sigma_1^2} \, \Phi(-d_1) + K \, \Phi(-d_2) \right] \\ + (1-\theta) \left[-e^{\mu_2 + \frac{1}{2}\sigma_2^2} \, \Phi(-d_3) + K \, \Phi(-d_4) \right] \}, \tag{5.11}$$

$$d_1 = \frac{-\ln(K) + \mu_1 + \sigma_1^2}{\sigma_1}, \qquad d_2 = d_1 - \sigma_1,$$

$$d_3 = \frac{-\ln(K) + \mu_2 + \sigma_2^2}{\sigma_2}, \qquad d_4 = d_3 - \sigma_2.$$

Call and put prices are weighted sums of two Black-Scholes prices based on the two component lognormal density functions. Minimizing (5.8) with (5.9)-(5.11) yields an estimate for the parameter vector η that can be used in (5.4) and (5.5) to compute the risk-neutral density.

For $k \geq 3$ (5.6) and (5.7) become (Coutant, Jondeau, and Rockinger (2001, p. 1966))

---

[2] Bliss and Panigirtzoglou (2002) discuss various weighting schemes for the loss function. It turns out that the theoretically correct weighting scheme crucially depends on various assumptions about the properties of observed option prices. Empirically, different weighting schemes only have very limited effects on the resulting risk-neutral density.

$$\hat{C}(K,t) = e^{-r(T-t)} \sum_{i=1}^{k} \theta_i \big[e^{\mu_i + \frac{1}{2}\sigma_i^2} \Phi(\frac{-\ln(K) + \mu_i + \sigma_i^2}{\sigma_i}) \\ -K\,\Phi(\frac{-\ln(K) + \mu_i}{\sigma_i})\big], \tag{5.12}$$

$$\hat{P}(K,t) = e^{-r(T-t)} \sum_{i=1}^{k} \theta_i \big[-e^{\mu_i + \frac{1}{2}\sigma_i^2} \Phi(\frac{\ln(K) - \mu_i - \sigma_i^2}{\sigma_i}) \\ +K\,\Phi(\frac{\ln(K) - \mu_i}{\sigma_i})\big]. \tag{5.13}$$

Melick and Thomas (1997) apply the mixture approach to American-type futures options. To account for the early-exercise premium, they specify theoretical option prices as a weighted average of upper and lower bounds for American-type options (see Chaudhury and Wei (1994), Melick und Thomas (1997)),

$$C_t^u(K) = \mathbf{E}^Q[\max[0, F_T - K]|F_t], \tag{5.14}$$
$$C_t^\ell(K) = \max\big[\mathbf{E}^Q[F_T|F_t] - K, e^{-r(T-t)}\,\mathbf{E}^Q[\max[0, F_T - K]|F_t]\big],$$
$$P_t^u(K) = \mathbf{E}^Q[\max[0, K - F_T]|F_t], \tag{5.15}$$
$$P_t^\ell(K) = \max\big[K - \mathbf{E}^Q[F_T|F_t], e^{-r(T-t)}\,\mathbf{E}^Q[\max[0, K - F_T]|F_t]\big].$$

The upper bounds (C_t^u, P_t^u) are the undiscounted values of the corresponding European-type options and the minimum lower bounds (C_t^l, P_t^l) are equal to the European option prices. Therefore, the maximum difference between the upper and lower bounds is the factor $e^{r(T-t)}$, so that this approximation turns out to be quite accurate.
Introducing an error term because of the approximation involved, Melick and Thomas (1997) write theoretical option prices as

$$\hat{C}_t^{am}(K) = w_C\, C_t^u(K) + (1 - w_C)\, C_t^\ell(K) + \epsilon_C(K) \tag{5.16}$$
$$\hat{P}_t^{am}(K) = w_P\, P_t^u(K) + (1 - w_P)\, P_t^\ell(K) + \epsilon_P(K), \tag{5.17}$$

with weights $w_C = \omega_1, w_P = \omega_2$, if $K < F_t$, and $w_C = \omega_2, w_P = \omega_1$, if $K \geq F$. (ω_1, ω_2) also have to be estimated so that $\eta' = (\mu_1, \mu_2, \mu_3, \sigma_1 \sigma_2, \sigma_3, \theta_1, \theta_2, \omega_1, \omega_2)$.

Using (5.14)-(5.17), the option prices can be expressed in terms of conditional expectations and cumulative distribution functions,[3]

[3] Since Melick and Thomas (1997) consider futures options the discount factor in front of the expressions can be dropped.

$$\hat{C}_t^{am}(K) = \\ w_C\left[\left(\mathbf{E}^Q[F_T|F_T \geq K, F_t] - K\right)(1 - F(K|F_t))\right] + (1 - w_C) \\ \cdot \max\left[\mathbf{E}^Q[F_T|F_t] - K, e^{-r(T-t)}\left(\mathbf{E}^Q[F_T|F_T \geq K, F_t] - K\right)(1 - F(K|F_t))\right], \tag{5.18}$$

$$\hat{P}_t^{am}(K) = \\ w_P\left[\left(K - \mathbf{E}^Q[F_T|F_T \leq K, F_t]\right) F(K|F_t)\right] + (1 - w_P) \\ \cdot \max\left[K - \mathbf{E}^Q[F_T|F_t], e^{-r(T-t)}\left(K - \mathbf{E}^Q[F_T|F_T \leq K, F_t]\right) F(K|F_t)\right]. \tag{5.19}$$

The individual expressions are (Melick and Thomas (1997, p. 112)),

$$\mathbf{E}^Q[F_T|F_t] = \sum_{i=1}^{3} \theta_i\, e^{\mu_i + \frac{\sigma_i^2}{2}}, \tag{5.20}$$

$$1 - F(K|F_t) = \sum_{i=1}^{3} \theta_i \left(1 - \Phi\left[\frac{\ln(K) - \mu_i}{\sigma_i}\right]\right), \tag{5.21}$$

$$F(K|F_t) = \sum_{i=1}^{3} \theta_i\, \Phi\left[\frac{\ln(K) - \mu_i}{\sigma_i}\right], \tag{5.22}$$

$$\mathbf{E}^Q[F_T|F_T \geq K, F_t] = \sum_{i=1}^{3} \theta_i\, e^{\mu_i + \frac{1}{2}\sigma_i^2} \frac{1 - \Phi\left[\frac{\ln(K) - \mu_i - \sigma_i^2}{\sigma_i}\right]}{1 - \Phi\left[\frac{\ln(K) - \mu_i}{\sigma_i}\right]}, \tag{5.23}$$

$$\mathbf{E}^Q[F_T|F_t \leq K, F_t] = \mathbf{E}_Q[F_T|F_t] - \mathbf{E}_Q[F_T|F_T \geq K, F_t]. \tag{5.24}$$

Substituting these expressions into (5.18) and (5.19) and maximizing the loss function (5.8) with respect to η' yields estimates of the free parameters.

Melick and Thomas (1998) show how the mixture approach can be used to construct confidence bands around the risk-neutral density by Monte Carlo simulations. Instead of using the nonlinear least-squares (NLS) approach in (5.8) they estimate η' by constraint-maximum likelihood where the covariance matrix of the estimator $\hat{\eta}'$ results from the Hessian matrix. Under some assumptions $(\eta' - \hat{\eta}') \sim N(0, \Sigma)$. They generate a pseudo distribution of the true parameter vector by drawing 500 times from this distribution. From pseudo distribution they compute risk-neutral density functions and derive the confidence bands (Melick and Thomas (1998, p. 315)).[4] However, they note that some important assumptions for the validity of the Monte Carlo approach are not satisfied. First, the residuals from fitted option prices are not independently distributed and, second, the estimation is carried out under parameter restrictions (Melick and Thomas (1998, p. 317)).

Mizrach (1996) constructs the risk-neutral density as a mixture of three log-normal distributions. He reduces the number of free parameters by assuming

[4] Again, the confidence bands themselves are not probability density functions (see Chapter 4).

the μ-parameters of two distributions to be spaced symmetrically around the third one

$$q(S_T|S_t) = \theta_1\,\ell(\mu-b,\sigma_1;S_T) + \theta_2\,\ell(\mu+b,\sigma_2;S_T) \\ +(1-\theta_1-\theta_2)\,\ell(\mu,\sigma_3;S_T), \qquad \theta_1,\theta_2 \geq 0, \tag{5.25}$$

where μ is specified exogenously. In a study of foreign-exchange options Mizrach (1996) sets μ equal to the interest-rate differential between the home and the foreign country. He then estimates the remaining six parameters $(\theta_1,\theta_2,b,\sigma_1,\sigma_2,\sigma_3)$ with the simulated method of moments by Duffie and Singleton (1993).

Mixtures of Bivariate Lognormal Distributions

Söderlind and Svensson (1998) assume that the underlying's price and the stochastic discount factor $(D_{t,T})$ are jointly distributed as a mixture of two bivariate lognormal distributions,[5]

$$\left(\begin{bmatrix} d \\ s \end{bmatrix}\right) = \sum_{i=1}^{k} \theta_i\,\phi\left(\begin{bmatrix} d \\ s \end{bmatrix};\begin{bmatrix} \bar{d}^i \\ \bar{s}^i \end{bmatrix},\begin{bmatrix} \sigma^i_{dd} & \sigma^i_{ds} \\ \sigma^i_{ds} & \sigma^i_{ss} \end{bmatrix}\right), \tag{5.26}$$

$d = \ln(D_{t,T}), s = \ln(S_T), \sum_{i=1}^{k} \theta_i = 1, \theta_i \geq 0$. In addition, they assume $\bar{d}^i = \bar{d}$ and $\sigma^i_{dd} = \sigma_{dd}$ so that the price of a European-type call is

$$\hat{C}_t(K) = e^{-r(T-t)} \sum_{i=1}^{k} \theta_i \\ \cdot\left[e^{\bar{s}^i+\frac{1}{2}\sigma^i_{ss}+\sigma^i_{ds}}\,\Phi\left(\frac{\bar{s}^i+\sigma^i_{ss}+\sigma^i_{ds}-\ln(K)}{\sqrt{\sigma^i_{ss}}}\right)\right. \\ \left.-K\,\Phi\left(\frac{\bar{s}^i+\sigma^i_{ds}-\ln(K)}{\sqrt{\sigma^i_{ss}}}\right)\right], \tag{5.27}$$

and the forward price is

$$F_t = \sum_{i=1}^{k} \theta_i\, e^{\bar{s}^i+\sigma^i_{ds}+\frac{1}{2}\sigma^i_{ss}}. \tag{5.28}$$

[5] This assumption is much more restrictive than simply approximating the risk-neutral density by a mixture of parametric distributions because it assumes knowledge of the 'true' probability density.
Note, that a stochastic discount factor (*pricing kernel*) allows the price of an asset with stochastic payoff x_T to be written as $V(t,T) = \mathbf{E}[D_{t,T}x_T]$, see e.g. Duffie (1996).

The model's $3k-1$ free parameters $\{\bar{s}^i+\sigma^i_{ds}\}_{i=1}^k$ and $\{\theta_i\}_{i=1}^{k-1}$ can be estimated, for example, by minimizing the sum of squared deviations of theoretical from observed option prices.
In this model the risk-neutral density for S_T is a mixture of two lognormal densities and differs from the 'true' marginal density because the expectations parameter is shifted by σ^i_{ds} (see Söderlind and Svensson (1998, p. 395)),

$$q(s) = \frac{1}{\sqrt{2\pi\sigma^i_{ss}}} e^{-\frac{1}{2}\frac{(s-\bar{s}^i-\sigma^i_{ds})^2}{\sigma^i_{ss}}} . \tag{5.29}$$

However, since in (5.27) $\bar{s}^i$ and σ^i_{ds} only appear as a sum it is not possible to identify them separately. The covariance σ^i_{ds} acts as a risk premium that drives a wedge between the expected values under the 'true' and under the risk-neutral density.[6] If we define the risk-neutral expectation of $\log(S_T)$ as $\mu_i = \bar{s}^i + \sigma^i_{ds}$, (5.27) is identical to (5.12), i.e. the call option-pricing function from the univariate mixture model. Obviously, Söderlind and Svensson (1998) extend the basic univariate mixture model by explicitly modelling the relationship between the risk-neutral and the 'true' density.
Another interesting feature of this approach is that confidence bands can easily be constructed. With the assumptions already made, minimization of the sum of squared deviations of theoretical from observed option prices is equivalent to NLS-estimation, so that the parameter estimates are approximately normally distributed. Hence, confidence bands for the risk-neutral probability density function can be constructed if an estimate of the parameter's covariance matrix is available (see Söderlind and Svensson (1998, p. 397)).

The approach of Söderlind and Svensson (1998) is modified by Fornari und Violi (1998). They extend the technique to be applicable to panels of option prices, i.e. options with different strike prices and different times to expiration. The authors specify the variance of the risk-neutral density in (5.26) as a function of time to expiration given by

$$\sigma^1_{ss} = \sigma_1[(1-e^{-2a_1(T-t)})(1-e^{-a_1(T-t)})^2]/(2a_1^3), \tag{5.30}$$
$$\sigma^2_{ss} = \sigma_2[(1-e^{-2a_2(T-t)})(1-e^{-a_2(T-t)})^2]/(2a_2^3). \tag{5.31}$$

Generalized Parametric Distributions

In other studies the risk-neutral density is approximated by flexible individual parametric densities. Compared to the lognormal or normal distribution these distributions generally have a number of additional free parameters.

[6] The fact that in Söderlind and Svensson (1998) the only difference between the risk-neutral and the 'true' density lies in their expected values stems from the specific assumption made about the 'true' density. Without this restrictive assumption no such clear result can be derived.

Generalized distributions often contain simple distributions as special cases for specific parameter constellations.
For example, Aparicio and Hodges (1998) represent the risk-neutral density function as a generalized beta distribution (GB2) with four parameters,

$$GB2(a,b,p,q;S_T) = \frac{|a|\, S_T^{ap-1}}{b^{ap}\, B(p,q) \left[1 + \left(\frac{S_T}{b}\right)^a\right]^{p+q}}, \qquad S_T > 0. \tag{5.32}$$

B is the beta function

$$B(p,q) = \int_0^1 t^{p-1}(1-t)^{q-1}\, dt. \tag{5.33}$$

They estimate the four parameters (a, b, p, q) by minimizing the sum of squared deviations of observed from theoretical option prices,

$$\hat{C}_t(K) = e^{-r(T-t)} \int_K^{\infty} (S_T - K)\, GB2(a,b,p,q;S_T)\, dS_T, \tag{5.34}$$

$$\hat{P}_t(K) = e^{-r(T-t)} \int_0^{K} (K - S_T)\, GB2(a,b,p,q;S_T)\, dS_T. \tag{5.35}$$

Other examples can be found in Posner und Milevsky (1998) using a density function from the Johnson (1949)-family, in Sherrick, Garcia, and Tirupattur (1996), who use a Burr-III distribution, and in Sherrick, Irwin, and Forster (1992) who recommend an approximation with a Burr XII distribution. Finally, Abadir and Rockinger (1997) construct the risk-neutral density from a mixture of Kummer functions and argue that this allows for maximum flexibility with respect to the resulting risk-neutral density function.

For options with more than one underlying asset, e.g. *spread options*, a multivariate risk-neutral density has to be considered. Rosenberg (1998) assumes the multivariate risk-neutral density to be bivariate lognormal where the variances are polynomials in the underlyings' returns. He specifies

$$q(s_{1,T}, s_{2,T}) = \lambda \phi \left(\begin{bmatrix} s_{1,T} \\ s_{2,T} \end{bmatrix} ; \begin{bmatrix} \bar{s}^1 \\ \bar{s}^2 \end{bmatrix}, \begin{bmatrix} \sigma_{11} & \sigma_{12} \\ \sigma_{12} & \sigma_{22} \end{bmatrix} \right), \tag{5.36}$$

$$\sqrt{\sigma_{11}(s_{1,T}, s_{1,t}, \alpha, a)} = \exp[\alpha_1 + \alpha_2 (s_{1,T} - s_{1,t}) + \alpha_3 (s_{1,T} - s_{1,t})^2 + \cdots + \alpha_a (s_{1,T} - s_{1,t})^{a-1}], \tag{5.37}$$

$$\sqrt{\sigma_{22}(s_{2,T}, s_{2,t}, \beta, b)} = \exp[\beta_1 + \beta_2 (s_{2,T} - s_{2,t}) + \beta_3 (s_{2,T} - s_{2,t})^2 + \cdots + \beta_b (s_{2,T} - s_{2,t})^{b-1}], \tag{5.38}$$

with λ representing a scaling factor that sets the complete probability mass equal to one, $s_{1,T} = \ln(S_{1,T}), s_{2,t} = \ln(S_{2,T})$. Rosenberg (1998) estimates his model by the method of moments.

5.2.2 Expansion Methods

Expansion methods model the deviations of the risk-neutral from a reference density – in most cases a normal or lognormal density. The reference density is adjusted by various correction terms that generally depend on high-order moments of the risk-neutral probability density. Truncating the expansion at a finite order allows us to derive a parametric representation for the option price and to estimate the free parameters. The risk-neutral density can then be computed by substituting the parameter estimates in the expansion equation (Cont (1999), Jackwerth (1999)). By using expansion methods it is possible to have a flexible parametric representation for the risk-neutral density which is based on a very simple reference density. However, a problem of this approach is that truncating the expansion at a finite order entails an approximation error that can lead to negative values for the risk-neutral density in some intervals (Aparicio und Hodges (1998, p. 11) and Cont (1999)).

Hermite-Polynomial Approximation

This expansion method is based on a theoretical model by Madan and Milne (1994). They define the risk-neutral and the 'true' density functions as the product of a *change-of-measure density* and the standard normal reference density,

$$p(z) = \nu(z)\,\phi(z), \qquad \text{(true density)} \qquad (5.39)$$

$$q(z) = \lambda(z)\,\phi(z). \qquad \text{(risk-neutral density)} \qquad (5.40)$$

They specify the underlying's price process under the reference measure to be a geometric Brownian motion,

$$S_T = S_t\, e^{\mu(T-t)+\sigma\sqrt{(T-t)}z_t - \frac{\sigma^2(T-t)}{2}} = S_t\, e^{\eta(T-t)}, \qquad (5.41)$$

where $z_t \sim N(0,1)$ and $\eta \sim N\left(\mu - \frac{\sigma^2}{2}, \frac{\sigma^2}{T-t}\right)$. Furthermore, they assume the densities $p(z)$ and $q(z)$ to be square integrable with respect to the standard normal distribution so that the density $q(z)$ can be written as (see Abken, Madan, and Ramamurtie (1995, p. 31))

$$q(z) = \sum_{k=0}^{\infty} b_k\, h_k(z)\, \phi(z), \qquad \text{i.e. } \lambda(z) = \sum_{k=0}^{\infty} b_k\, h_k(z). \qquad (5.42)$$

Next, Madan and Milne (1994) assume that the set of all conditional payoff functions is a separable Hilbert space for which an orthonormal basis exists. This basis is constructed from standardized Hermite polynomials $\{h_k\}_{k=1}^{\infty}$,

$$h_k(z) = \frac{H_k(z)}{\sqrt{k!}}, \qquad H_k(z) = (-1)^k \frac{\partial^k \phi(z)}{\partial z^k} \frac{1}{\phi(z)}. \tag{5.43}$$

The Hermite polynomials of order zero to four are $h_0 = 1, h_1 = z, h_2 = (z^2-1)/\sqrt{2}, h_3 = (z^3 - 3z)/\sqrt{6}, h_4 = (z^4 - 6z^2 + 3)/\sqrt{24}$ (e.g. Kendall und Stuart (1977, p. 69)).
They rewrite the option's payoff function $g(z)$ using the Hermite polynomials,

$$g(z) = \sum_{k=0}^{\infty} a_k\, h_k(z), \tag{5.44}$$

where,

$$a_k = \int_{-\infty}^{+\infty} g(z)\, h_k(z)\, \phi(z) dz. \tag{5.45}$$

Because of the orthonormality of the basis, the option price can be written as

$$\begin{aligned} V[g(z)] &= e^{-r(T-t)} \int_{-\infty}^{+\infty} g(z)\, q(z) dz \\ &= \sum_{k=0}^{+\infty} a_k\, \pi_k, \qquad \pi_k = e^{-r(T-t)} b_k. \end{aligned} \tag{5.46}$$

As shown in Madan and Milne (1994), the coefficients for a European-type call option are

$$a_k^{call}(S_t, K, \mu, \sigma, T-t) = \left.\frac{\partial^k \Psi(u, S_t, K, \mu, \sigma, T-t)}{\partial u^k}\right|_{u=0} \frac{1}{\sqrt{k!}}, \tag{5.47}$$

$$\begin{aligned} \Psi(u, S_t, K, \mu, \sigma, T-t) &= S_t\, e^{\mu(T-t)+\sigma\sqrt{(T-t)}u}\, \Phi\big(d_1(u)\big) \\ &\quad - K\, \Phi\big(d_2(u)\big), \end{aligned} \tag{5.48}$$

$$\begin{aligned} d_1(u) &= \frac{\ln \frac{S_t}{K} + \left(\mu + \frac{\sigma^2}{2}\right)(T-t)}{\sigma\sqrt{T-t}} + u \\ d_2(u) &= d_1(u) - \sigma\sqrt{T-t}. \end{aligned} \tag{5.49}$$

The coefficients of the corresponding European-type put option can be derived from the call coefficients using European put-call parity,

$$a_k^{put}(S_t, K, \mu, \sigma, T-t) = \frac{\partial^k \Xi(u, S_t, K, \mu, \sigma, T-t)}{\partial u^k}\bigg|_{u=0} \frac{1}{\sqrt{k!}}, \tag{5.50}$$

where (Abken, Madan, and Ramamurtie (1995, p. 39)),

$$\begin{aligned} \Psi(u, S_t, K, \mu, \sigma, T_t) - \Xi(u, S_t, K, \mu, \sigma, T_t) + K \\ = S_t\, e^{\mu(T-t)+\sigma\sqrt{(T-t)}u}, \end{aligned} \tag{5.51}$$

i.e.,

$$\begin{aligned} a_0^{put}(S_t, K, \mu, \sigma, T-t) &= a_0^{call}(S_t, K, \mu, \sigma, T-t) - S_t\, e^{\mu(T-t)}, \\ a_k^{put}(S_t, K, \mu, \sigma, T-t) &= a_k^{call}(S_t, K, \mu, \sigma, T-t) - S_t\, e^{\mu(T-t)} \frac{(\sigma\sqrt{T-t})^k}{\sqrt{k!}}, \\ & k \geq 1. \end{aligned} \tag{5.52}$$

Abken, Madan, and Ramamurtie (1995) truncate the approximation (5.46) after $k = 4$, so that the call price is approximated as

$$C(K_i) = \sum_{k=0}^{4} \pi_k\, a_k^{call} + \epsilon_i^{call}, \qquad \text{where} \tag{5.53}$$

$$\begin{aligned} a_0^{call} &= S_t\, e^{\mu(T-t)}\, \Phi(d_1) - K\, \Phi(d_2), \\ a_1^{call} &= \sigma\sqrt{T-t}\, S_t\, e^{\mu(T-t)}\, \Phi(d_1) + S_t\, e^{\mu(T-t)}\, \phi(d_1) - K\, \Phi(d_2), \\ a_2^{call} &= \frac{1}{\sqrt{2}}\big[(\sigma\sqrt{T-t})^2 S_t\, e^{\mu(T-t)}\, \Phi(d_1) + 2\sigma\sqrt{T-t}\, S_t\, e^{\mu(T-t)}\, \phi(d_1) \\ &\quad + S_t\, e^{\mu(T-t)}\, \phi'(d_1) - K\, \phi'(d_2)\big], \\ a_3^{call} &= \frac{1}{\sqrt{6}}\big[(\sigma\sqrt{T-t})^3 S_t\, e^{\mu(T-t)}\, \Phi(d_1) + 3(\sigma\sqrt{T-t})^2 S_t\, e^{\mu(T-t)}\, \phi(d_1) \\ &\quad + 3\sigma\sqrt{T-t}\, S_t\, e^{\mu(T-t)}\, \phi'(d_1) + S_t\, e^{\mu(T-t)}\, \phi''(d_1) - K\, \phi''(d_2)\big], \\ a_4^{call} &= \frac{1}{\sqrt{24}}\big[(\sigma\sqrt{T-t})^4 S_t\, e^{\mu(T-t)}\, \Phi(d_1) + 4(\sigma\sqrt{T-t})^3 S_t\, e^{\mu(T-t)}\, \phi(d_1) \\ &\quad + 6(\sigma\sqrt{T-t})^2 S_t\, e^{\mu(T-t)}\, \phi'(d_1) + 4\sigma\sqrt{T-t}\, S_t\, e^{\mu(T-t)}\, \phi''(d_1) \\ &\quad + S_t\, e^{\mu(T-t)}\, \phi^{(3)}(d_1) - K\, \phi^{(3)}(d_2)\big], \end{aligned} \tag{5.54}$$

for d_1 and d_2 with $u = 0$. ϵ^{call} is a pricing error resulting from the finite order of the approximation and from measurement errors in the data.

Accordingly, the put option price is approximated as,

$$P(K_i) = \sum_{k=0}^{4} \pi_k\, a_k^{put} + \epsilon_i^{put}, \tag{5.55}$$

where the coefficients a_k^{put} are given by (5.50).

From equations (5.53) and (5.55), which are the empirical counterparts of (5.46), the parameters μ, σ and the Hermite polynomial coefficients $\{\pi_k\}_{k=0}^4$ can be estimated. Abken, Madan, and Ramamurtie (1995) impose the restrictions $\pi_0 = e^{-r(T-t)}, \pi_1 = 0, \pi_2 = 0$. The first restriction results from $q(z)$ being a density function that must integrate to one. The second and the third restrictions imply that the first two moments of the return process η (see (5.41)) coincide under the reference and the risk-neutral measure.[7]
The coefficients π_k can be interpreted as the prices of the basis risks $h_k(z)$. Since the Hermite polynomial of order k depends on a k-th order moment, π_3 and π_4 are denoted the prices of skewness and kurtosis (Jondeau and Rockinger (1999, p. 13)). It is also possible to impose the martingale restriction, i.e. to restrict the drift of S_t to be equal to the risk-free rate of interest under both probability measures ($\mu = r$) (Jondeau and Rockinger (2000, p. 889)).

Truncating the expansion of the risk-neutral density (5.42) after $k = 4$ yields for $q(z)$

$$
\begin{aligned}
q(z) &= \sum_{k=0}^{4} b_k\, h_k(z)\, \phi(z), && (5.56)\\
&= \left[\left(b_0 - \frac{b_2}{\sqrt{2}} + \frac{3b_4}{\sqrt{24}}\right) + \left(b_1 - \frac{3b_3}{\sqrt{6}}\right)z + \left(\frac{b_2}{\sqrt{2}} - \frac{6b_4}{\sqrt{24}}\right)z^2\right.\\
&\quad \left. + \frac{b_3}{\sqrt{6}}z^3 + \frac{b_4}{\sqrt{24}}z^4\right]\phi(z), && (5.57)
\end{aligned}
$$

or imposing the restrictions,

$$
\begin{aligned}
q(z) = &\left[\left(1 + \frac{3b_4}{\sqrt{24}}\right) - \frac{3b_3}{\sqrt{6}}z - \frac{6b_4}{\sqrt{24}}z^2\right.\\
&\left. + \frac{b_3}{\sqrt{6}}z^3 + \frac{b_4}{\sqrt{24}}z^4\right]\phi(z). \qquad (5.58)
\end{aligned}
$$

(5.58) is a *Gram-Charlier* expansion of type A of the risk-neutral density truncated after the fifth term (e.g. Kendall and Stuart (1977, p. 169)). $q(z)$ can be easily computed using the parameter estimates for $\pi_k = e^{-r(T-t)}b_k, k = 3, 4$. The coefficients b_3 and b_4 in (5.58) are the values of the third central moment and of the fourth central moment minus three of z under the risk-neutral density. In order to transform these moments into the corresponding

[7] $\pi_k = e^{-r(T-t)}b_k$. As shown in Abken, Madan, and Ramamurtie (1995, p. 26), b_1 determines the shift in the expected value of η with respect to $q(z)$ relative to the reference measure and b_1 and b_2 jointly determine the shift in the variance. Since μ and σ, the parameters of η under the reference measure, are estimated from option prices, i.e. under the risk-neutral density, assuming the first two moments to be the same under both probability measures is not restricitve.

moments of S_T, the following change of variables must be performed: $z = \frac{\ln(S_T)-\ln(S_t)-(\mu-\frac{\sigma^2}{2})(T-t)}{\sigma\sqrt{T-t}}$.

Abken, Madan, and Ramamurtie (1995) estimate the system (5.53) and (5.55) with GMM and use a kernel estimator for the cross-moment matrix of the error terms $\epsilon\epsilon'$. However, estimation by minimizinig the sum of squared deviations of theoretical from observed option prices is also possible. The authors favor the GMM method in order to test for the validity of another theoretically derived restriction on the b-coefficients for options with different times to expiration,

$$b_{k,T-s} = b_{k,T-t}\left(\frac{T-s}{T-t}\right)^{\frac{k}{2}}. \tag{5.59}$$

The hypothesis is rejected. Nevertheless, Coutant, Jondeau, and Rockinger (2001) suggest using this restriction to construct a risk-neutral density with constant time to expiration from exchange-traded options.

Approximation (5.58) does not guarantee the risk-neutral density to be positive everywhere for all possible combinations of b_3 and b_4. In order to prevent negative probabilities, Jondeau and Rockinger (2001) present an algorithm which appropriately restricts the b-coefficients (see Appendix 5A).

Gram-Charlier Expansion

Corrado and Su (1996b) and Longstaff (1995) use the Gram-Charlier expansion of the risk-neutral density as the starting point for their empirical studies. They assume drift and variance to be the same under the risk-neutral and the reference measure but, in addition, they set the drift equal to the risk-free rate of interest. As in the model described above, $q(z)$ represents the risk-neutral density for the standardized variable $z = \frac{\ln(S_T)-\ln(S_t)-(r-\frac{\sigma^2}{2})(T-t)}{\sigma\sqrt{T-t}}$, from which the risk-neutral density for S_T can be derived. Corrado and Su (1996b) use (5.58) to write the call option-pricing function as

$$\begin{aligned} C(K) &= C^{BS} + b_3\,A_3 + (b_4-3)A_4, && (5.60)\\ C^{BS} &= S_t\,\Phi(d_1) - K\,e^{-r(T-t)}\Phi(d_2),\\ A_3 &= \frac{1}{6}S_t\,\sigma\sqrt{T-t}\left((2\sigma\sqrt{T-t}-d_1)\,\phi(d_1) - \sigma^2(T-t)\,\Phi(d_1)\right),\\ A_4 &= \frac{1}{24}S_t\,\sigma\sqrt{T-t}\left((d_1^2-1-3\sigma\sqrt{(T-t)}\,d_2)\,\phi(d_1), +\sigma^3\sqrt{T-t}^{3/2}\Phi(d_1)\right),\\ d_1 &= \frac{\ln(\frac{S_t}{K})+\left(r+\frac{\sigma^2}{2}\right)(T-t)}{\sigma\sqrt{T-t}}, \qquad d_2 = d_1 - \sigma\sqrt{T-t}. && (5.61)\end{aligned}$$

This shows that the option price can be written as the sum of the Black-Scholes price (C^{BS}) and two correction terms with coefficients that are equal to the skewness (b_3) and the excess kurtosis ($b_4 - 3$)of the risk-neutral density.

$$\min_{\sigma,b_3,b_4} \sum_{j=1}^{n} \Big[C(K_j) - \big(C^{BS}(K_j,\sigma) + b_3\, A_3(\sigma,K_j) + (b_4-3)\, A_4(\sigma,K_j)\big)\Big]^2 \tag{5.62}$$

produces estimates for the parameters σ (implied volatility), b_3 and b_4. Using these estimates in (5.58) and applying the transformation from z into S_T the risk-neutral density can be computed.

Edgeworth Expansion

Jarrow and Rudd (1982) use an Edgeworth expansion to approximate the risk-neutral probability density function around a lognormal density,

$$\begin{aligned} q(S_T) = \ell(S_T) &+ \frac{\big(\kappa_2(Q)-\kappa_2(L)\big)}{2!}\frac{\partial^2 \ell(S_T)}{\partial S_T^2} - \frac{\big(\kappa_3(Q)-\kappa_3(L)\big)}{3!}\frac{\partial^3 \ell(S_T)}{\partial S_T^3} \\ &+ \frac{\big[\big(\kappa_4(Q)-\kappa_4(L)\big) + 3\big(\kappa_2(Q)-\kappa_2(L)\big)\big]^2}{4!}\frac{\partial^4 \ell(S_T)}{\partial S_T^4} \\ &+ \epsilon(S_T), \end{aligned} \tag{5.63}$$

where,

$$\ell(S_T) = \frac{1}{S_T\sigma\sqrt{(T-t)2\pi}} \exp\left[-\frac{1}{2}\frac{\big(\ln(S_T)-\ln(S_t)-(\mu-\frac{\sigma^2}{2})(T-t)\big)^2}{\sigma^2(T-t)}\right]. \tag{5.64}$$

$\kappa_i(Q)$ and $\kappa_i(L)$ are the cumulants of the risk-neutral and the lognormal density, respectively. If under a given probability measure moments of a random variable exist up to order n, the cumulants are implicitly defined by (Kendall and Stuart (1977, p. 69))

$$\ln\big(\xi(L)\big) = \sum_{j=1}^{n-1} \kappa_j(L)\frac{(it)^j}{j!} + o(t^{n-1}). \tag{5.65}$$

The cumulants for Q can be computed analogously.[8] Cumulants and moments up to order four are related by

$$\begin{aligned} \kappa_1 &= \mathbf{E}[S_T],\ \ \kappa_2 = \mathbf{E}\big[\big(S_T - \mathbf{E}[S_T]\big)^2\big], \\ \kappa_3 &= \mathbf{E}\big[\big(S_T - \mathbf{E}[S_T]\big)^3\big],\ \ \kappa_4 = \mathbf{E}\big[\big(S_T - \mathbf{E}[S_T]\big)^4\big] - 3\kappa_2. \end{aligned} \tag{5.66}$$

[8] $\xi(L)$ is the characteristic function of L.

With the above assumptions $\kappa_1(Q) = \kappa_1(L) = S_t\, e^{r(T-t)}$, i.e. $\mu = r$. ϵ is an approximation error resulting from truncating the expansion after the cumulant of order four. Thus, equation (5.63) describes the deviations of the risk-neutral from the lognormal density by correction terms that depend on the deviations of the risk-neutral density's second, third and fourth moments from the lognormal benchmark.

From the Edgeworth expansion Jarrow and Rudd (1982) derive an approximation formula for the call option price,

$$\begin{aligned} C(K) = C^{BS} &+ e^{-r(T-t)} \frac{\big(\kappa_2(Q) - \kappa_2(L)\big)}{2!} \ell(S_T)|_{S_T=K} \\ &- e^{-r(T-t)} \frac{\big(\kappa_3(Q) - \kappa_3(L)\big)}{3!} \frac{\partial \ell(S_T)}{\partial S_T}\bigg|_{S_T=K} \\ &+ e^{-r(T-t)} \frac{\Big[\big(\kappa_4(Q) - \kappa_4(L)\big) + 3\big(\kappa_2(Q) - \kappa_2(L)\big)^2\Big]}{4!} \frac{\partial^2 \ell(S_T)}{\partial S_T^2}\bigg|_{S_T=K} \\ &+ \epsilon(K). \end{aligned} \tag{5.67}$$

C^{BS} is the call price assuming a lognormal risk-neutral density, i.e. the Black-Scholes price. The cumulants of the lognormal distribution in (5.67) are

$$\begin{aligned} \kappa_1(L) &= S_t\, e^{r(T-t)}, \\ \kappa_2(L) &= [\kappa_1(L)\, \delta]^2, \\ \kappa_3(L) &= [\kappa_1(L)\, \gamma]^3 (3\delta + \delta^3), \\ \kappa_4(L) &= [\kappa_1(L)\, \delta]^4 (16\delta^2 + 15\delta^4 + 6\delta^6 + \delta^8), \end{aligned} \tag{5.68}$$

$\delta = (e^{\sigma^2(T-t)} - 1)^{1/2}$ and assuming $\mu = r$.
Setting equal the variances of the risk-neutral and the true density leads to

$$\begin{aligned} C(K) = C^{BS} &+ - e^{-r(T-t)} \frac{\big(\kappa_3(Q) - \kappa_3(L)\big)}{3!} \frac{\partial \ell(S_T)}{\partial S_T}\bigg|_{S_T=K} \\ &+ e^{-r(T-t)} \frac{\big(\kappa_4(Q) - \kappa_4(L)\big)}{4!} \frac{\partial^2 \ell(S_T)}{\partial S_T^2}\bigg|_{S_T=K} + \epsilon(K). \end{aligned} \tag{5.69}$$

However, Corrado and Su (1996a, 1997) decide not to estimate the cumulants but the skewness and excess kurtosis statistics

$$\gamma_1(Q) = \frac{\kappa_3(Q)}{[\kappa_2(Q)]^{3/2}}, \qquad \gamma_2(Q) = \frac{\kappa_4(Q)}{[\kappa_2(Q)]^2}, \tag{5.70}$$

so that theoretical call prices can be rewritten in terms of γ_1 and γ_2,

$$\begin{aligned} C(K) = C^{BS} &- e^{-r(T-t)} (\gamma_1(Q) - \gamma_1(L)) \frac{\kappa_2(L)^{3/2}}{3!} \frac{\partial \ell(S_T)}{\partial S_T}\bigg|_{S_T=K} \\ &+ e^{-r(T-t)} (\gamma_2(Q) - \gamma_2(L)) \frac{\kappa_2(L)^2}{4!} \frac{\partial^2 \ell(S_T)}{\partial S_T^2}\bigg|_{S_T=K} + \epsilon(K). \end{aligned} \tag{5.71}$$

They estimate the following system by NLS,

$$\begin{aligned}
\min_{\sigma,\gamma_1,\gamma_2} \sum_{j=1}^{n} \quad & \left[C(K_j) - \left(C^{BS}(K_j,\sigma) + \nu_1\, A_3(\sigma, K_j)\right.\right. \\
& \left.\left. +\nu_2\, A_4(\sigma, K_j)\right)\right]^2, \qquad (5.72) \\
\gamma_1(Q) &= \nu_1 + \gamma_1[L(\sigma)], \\
\gamma_2(Q) &= \nu_2 + \gamma_2[L(\sigma)], \\
A_3 &= -(S_t\, e^{r(T-t)})^3 (e^{\sigma^2(T-t)} - 1)^{3/2} \frac{e^{-r(T-t)}}{3!} \frac{\partial \ell(S_T)}{\partial d S_T}\bigg|_{S_T=K}, \\
A_4 &= (S_t\, e^{r(T-t)})^4 (e^{\sigma^2(T-t)} - 1)^{2} \frac{e^{-r(T-t)}}{4!} \frac{\partial^2 \ell(S_T)}{\partial d S_T^2}\bigg|_{S_T=K}, \\
\frac{\partial \ell(S_T)}{\partial S_T}\bigg|_{S_T=K} &= \frac{\ell(K)(d_2 - \sigma\sqrt{T-t})}{K\,\sigma\sqrt{T-t}}, \\
\frac{\partial^2 \ell(S_T)}{\partial S_T^2}\bigg|_{S_T=K} &= \frac{\ell(K)}{K^2\sigma^2(T-t)}\left[(d_2 - \sigma\sqrt{T-t})^2\right. \\
& \left. -\sigma\sqrt{T-t}\,(d_2 - \sigma\sqrt{T-t}) - 1\right].
\end{aligned}$$

Corrado and Su (1996a, p. 625) argue that the assumption $\kappa_2(Q) = \kappa_2(L)$ is very important for the identification of the parameters. Since in (5.67) the second term on the right-hand side (including the cumulants of second-order) is highly correlated with A_4, estimation results including the second order cumulants are very unstable. In addition, without this assumption the model is overidentified since the implied variance σ^2, i.e. the log price variance, is estimated simultaneously with the variance of the underlying's price κ_2.

The risk-neutral density can be easily obtained by substituting the parameter estimates into (5.69) and differentiating twice with respect to K (Jondeau and Rockinger (2000)) or, alternatively, by using (5.63) with $\kappa_2(L) = \kappa_2(Q)$ from (5.68) together with the following iteration formulae (Jondeau and Rockinger (2000, p. 894)). Note that the expression for the risk-neutral density resulting from the Edgeworth expansion is not exactly identical to the result derived by Hermite polynomial approximation. However, in empirical applications both approaches are likely to yield very similar results (Jondeau and Rockinger (2000)).

$$
\begin{aligned}
\frac{\partial \ell(S_T)}{\partial S_T} &= -\left(1 + \frac{\ln(S_T) - m}{\sigma^2(T-t)}\right)\frac{\ell(S_T)}{S_T}, \\
\frac{\partial^2 \ell(S_T)}{\partial S_T^2} &= -\left(2 + \frac{\ln(S_T) - m}{\sigma^2(T-t)}\right)\frac{1}{S_T}\frac{\partial \ell(S_T)}{\partial S_T} - \frac{1}{S_T^2\sigma^2(T-t)}\ell(S_T), \\
\frac{\partial^3 \ell(S_T)}{\partial S_T^3} &= -\left(3 + \frac{\ln(S_T) - m}{\sigma^2(T-t)}\right)\frac{1}{S_T}\frac{\partial^2 \ell(S_T)}{\partial S_T^2} - \\
&\quad \frac{2}{S_T^2\sigma^2(T-t)}\frac{\partial \ell(S_T)}{\partial S_T} + \frac{1}{S_T^3\sigma^2(T-t)}\ell(S_T), \\
\frac{\partial^4 \ell(S_T)}{\partial S_T^4} &= -\left(4 + \frac{\ln(S_T) - m}{\sigma^2(T-t)}\right)\frac{1}{S_T}\frac{\partial^3 \ell(S_T)}{\partial S_T^3} - \\
&\quad \frac{3}{S_T^2\sigma^2(T-t)}\frac{\partial^2 \ell(S_T)}{\partial S_T^2} + \frac{3}{S_T^3\sigma^2(T-t)}\frac{\partial \ell(S_T)}{\partial S_T} - \\
&\quad \frac{1}{S_T^4\sigma^2(T-t)}\ell(S_T),
\end{aligned}
\tag{5.73}
$$

$m = \ln(S_t) + (r - \frac{\sigma^2}{2})(T-t)$.

Another expansion method that should be mentioned is presented in Potters, Cont, and Bouchaud (1998). They expand the risk-neutral around the normal density and derive an option-pricing function that is then truncated after the n-th term. Instead of fitting their theoretical to observed option prices and estimating the cumulants they invert the valuation function in order to get an expression for the volatility smile as an n-order polynomial. Fitting the theoretical to the observed volatility smile they obtain implicit solutions for the cumulants from which the risk-neutral density can be computed (see Cont (1999)).

5.2.3 Minimization of Deviations from a Prior Density

Entropy Maximization

Buchen and Kelly (1996) apply the principle of entropy maximization to the estimation risk-neutral probability density functions. This is a a Bayesian approach that determines the distribution of a random variable under limited information from a finite number of expectations (Jaynes (1979, 1982)). The maximum entropy criterion selects the risk-neutral density that is least prejudiced with respect to unknown or missing information – in other words the density that maximizes the amount of missing information (Jackwerth (1999, p. 70)).

For the risk-neutral density $q(S_T)$ entropy is defined as[9]

[9] This is a special case of the Kullback-Leibler information criterion distance between the risk-neutral density and the prior density $\pi(S_T)$, $H(q, \pi) =$

$$H(q) = - \int_0^{+\infty} q(S_T) \ln(q(S_T)), dS_T. \tag{5.74}$$

As a density function $q(S_T)$ must integrate to one and correctly price the observed options,

$$\int_0^{+\infty} q(S_T)\, dS_T = 1, \tag{5.75}$$

$$\int_0^{+\infty} c(K_i, S_T)\, q(S_T)\, dS_T = e^{r(T-t)} C(K_i), \qquad i = 1, ..m, \tag{5.76}$$

where $c(K_i, S_T)$ is the call option payoff.[10] Coutant, Jondeau, and Rockinger (2001) also impose the *martingale restriction*[11]

$$\int_0^{+\infty} S_T q(S_T)\, dS_T = F_t. \tag{5.77}$$

For entropy maximization, the Hamiltonian is constructed,

$$\mathcal{H}(q) = - \int_0^{+\infty} q(S_T) \ln(q(S_T))\, dS_T + (1+\gamma)\Big(\int_0^{+\infty} q(S_T)\, dS_T - 1\Big)$$
$$+ \sum_{i=0}^{m} \lambda_i \Big(\int_0^{+\infty} c(K_i, S_T)\, q(S_T)\, dS_T - e^{r(T-t)} C(K_i)\Big). \tag{5.78}$$

$\mathcal{H}(q)$ is maximized if the Frêchet derivative is equal to zero,

$$\delta\mathcal{H} = \int_0^{+\infty} \Big[- \ln(q(S_T)) + \gamma + \sum_{i=0}^{m} \lambda_i\, c(K_i, S_T) \Big] \delta q(S_T)\, dS_T = 0. \tag{5.79}$$

Therefore,

$\int_0^{+\infty} q(S_T) \ln\left[\frac{q(S_T)}{\pi(S_T)}\right] dS_T$. (5.74) follows for a uniform prior (Buchen and Kelly (1996, p. 148)).

[10] The approach can be applied to put options analogously. However, McManus (1999) suggests simplifying the estimation by converting put prices into call prices via the European put-call parity.

[11] This restriction can be written in the form of (5.76): $\int_0^{+\infty} c(K_0, S_T)\, q(S_T)\, dS_T = e^{r(T-t)} C(K_0)$, with $K_0 = 0, C_0 = e^{-r(T-t)} F_t$.

$$q(S_T) = \frac{1}{\xi} \exp\left[\sum_{i=0}^{m} \lambda_i \, c(K_i, S_T)\right], \qquad \text{with}$$

$$\xi \equiv \frac{1}{e^{\gamma}} = \int_{0}^{+\infty} \exp\left[\sum_{i=0}^{m} \lambda_i \, c(K_i, S_T)\right] dS_T, \tag{5.80}$$

so that,

$$H(\lambda_0, \lambda_1, \cdots, \lambda_m) = \int_{0}^{+\infty} q(S_T)\left[-\ln(\xi) + \sum_{i=0}^{m} \lambda_i \, c(K_i, S_T)\right] dS_T \tag{5.81}$$

$$= -\ln(\xi) + \sum_{i=0}^{m} \lambda_i e^{r(T-t)} C(K_i).$$

Since the payoff functions $c(K_i, S_T)$ are piecewise linear functions and consist of a constant and of a linear segment with slope equal to $+1$, the risk-neutral density consists of $m+1$ segments of exponential curves (see (5.80)).

Coutant, Jondeau, and Rockinger (2001) consider how to estimate the density via entropy maximization. First, the strike prices are placed in increasing order $K_1 < K_2 < \cdots < K_m$. Then, they define the following variables $a_i \equiv \lambda_0 + \lambda_1 + \cdots + \lambda_i$, $b_i \equiv -(\lambda_1 K_1 + \lambda_2 K_2 + \cdots + \lambda_i K_i)$, i.e. $b_i = b_{i-1} - (a_i - a_{i-1})K_i$, and $b_0 = 0, K_0 = 0, K_{m+1} = +\infty$ so that the risk-neutral density can be written as

$$q(S_T) = \begin{cases} \frac{1}{\xi} e^{a_i S_T + b_i}, & \text{for } K_i < S_T < K_{i+1}, i = 0, ..., m-1, \\ \frac{1}{\xi} e^{a_m S_T + b_m}, & \text{for } K_m < S_T. \end{cases} \tag{5.82}$$

They show that the normalizing constant can be expressed as

$$\xi = \frac{1}{a_0}\left(e^{a_0 K_1 + b_0} - e^{a_0 K_0 + b_0}\right) + \frac{1}{a_1}\left(e^{a_1 K_2 + b_1} - e^{a_1 K_1 + b_1}\right)$$
$$\ldots + \frac{1}{a_m}\left(e^{a_m K_{m+1} + b_m} - e^{a_m K_m + b_m}\right), \tag{5.83}$$

and that the option prices obey

$$\xi e^{r(T-t)} C(K_i) = \sum_{k=i}^{m} \left[\left(\frac{K_{k+1} - K_i}{a_k} - \frac{1}{a_k^2}\right) e^{a_k K_{k+1} + b_k} - \left(\frac{K_k - K_i}{a_k} - \frac{1}{a_k^2}\right) e^{a_k K_k + b_k}\right]. \tag{5.84}$$

Coutant, Jondeau, and Rockinger (2001) estimate the $\{a_i\}_{i=0}^{m}$ parameters by minimizing the sum of squared deviations of theoretical from observed option prices. In order to improve the convergence of the optimization algorithm they recommend the following procedure: first, $\hat{q}(S_T)$ is parameterized as a lognormal density that is evaluated on a number of discrete values for S_T; second, the parameters $\{\lambda_i\}_{i=0}^m$ are estimated by OLS from

$$\hat{q}(S_T) = \frac{1}{\xi} \exp\left[\sum_{i=0}^{m} \lambda_i \, c(K_i, S_T)\right]$$
$$\Rightarrow \ln\big(\hat{q}(S_T)\big) = -\ln(\xi) + \sum_{i=0}^{m} \lambda_i \, c(K_i, S_T) + \epsilon. \tag{5.85}$$

These results provide suitable starting values for the $\{a_i\}_{i=0}^m$ coefficients.

Due to the lack of restrictions on the smoothness of the resulting density, the method of maximum entropy often leads to multimodal risk-neutral probability density functions exhibiting sharp 'spikes'. It is possible to modify this approach by using a loss function that also considers the smoothness of the density (as in Jackwerth and Rubinstein (1996)), but this makes the results strongly dependent on the relative weights for entropy and smoothness (Cont (1999, p. 19)).

The maximum-entropy method is also applied by Stutzer (1996). However, he considers discretely spaced exercise prices computed from the historical return series. Furthermore, he does not restrict the estimated risk-neutral density function to be consistent with observed option prices but only imposes the restriction that the underlying is correctly priced under the risk-neutral density.

Rubinstein's Approach

Rubinstein (1994) estimates risk-neutral probabilities $\{q_i\}_{i=0}^n$ for discretely spaced strike prices $S_0 < S_1 < \cdots < S_n$, with $n \gg m$ (the number of options) by minimizing the sum of squared deviations of risk-neutral probabilities from prior probabilities $\{\pi\}_{i=0}^n$. The constraints imposed on the risk-neutral probabilities are that underlying and options are valued correctly between observed bid and ask prices,

$$\min_{q_i} \sum_{j=0}^{n} (q_j - \pi_j)^2, \qquad \text{subject to:} \tag{5.86}$$

$$\sum_{j=0}^{n} q_j = 1, \quad q_j \geq 0, \quad j = 0, ..., n,$$
$$S^b \leq S \leq S^a, \quad \text{and } C_i^b \leq C_i \leq C_i^a, \quad i = 0, ..., m,$$

where,

$$S = \frac{\sum_{j=0}^{n} q_j \, S_j}{(1+r)^{T-t}},$$

$$C_i = \frac{\sum_{j=0}^{n} q_j \max[0, S_j - K_i]}{(1+r)^{T-t}}. \tag{5.87}$$

Rubinstein explains that, as the number of observed option prices increases, the prior probabilities' influence on the results is diminished and in the limit the risk-neutral probabilities are completely determined by the constraints (Rubinstein (1994), Jackwerth and Rubinstein (1996)). In his application he selects a prior distribution derived from the binomial option pricing model of Cox, Ross, and Rubinstein (1979), $\pi_j = \binom{n}{j} \tilde{p}^j \, (1-\tilde{p})^{n-j}$, where $\tilde{p}$ denotes the probability of the underlying's price increasing over the next time interval.

In Jackwerth and Rubinstein (1996) and Rubinstein and Jackwerth (1999) alternative loss functions are discussed, like the "goodness-of-fit" function $\sum_j (q_j - \pi_j)^2/\pi_j$, the sum of absolute deviations, $\sum_j |q_j - \pi_j|$ or the maximum entropy principle. It turns out that risk-neutral probabilities at the center of the distribution are very similar and almost independent from the selected loss function. However, the probabilities of options with very low exercise prices are more heavily affected by the type of loss function because only very few far-in-the-money option prices are available and, as a consequence, the restrictions imposed on the risk-neutral density are very weak.
An important problem of Rubinstein's approach is that it tends to create implausibly ragged density functions that exhibit little smoothness. This leads Jackwerth and Rubinstein (1996) to consider an alternative optimization criterion that emphasizes the smoothness of the risk-neutral density.

5.2.4 The Maximum-Smoothness Criterion

Jackwerth and Rubinstein (1996) suggest minimizing the curvature of the risk-neutral density using the following discrete approximation

$$\min_{q_i} \sum_j (q_{j-1} - 2q_j + q_{j+1})^2, \qquad \text{with } q_{-1} = q_{n+1} = 0. \tag{5.88}$$

They simplify the optimization problem so that it finally can be written as a system of linear equations. Since the risk-neutral probability density function is related to option prices by $q_j = (1+r)^{T-t} \frac{\partial^2 C_j}{\partial K_j^2}$, the loss function can be restated as a fourth-order difference of the call option-pricing function,

$$\min_{C_j} \Omega = \sum_j (C_{j-2} - 4C_{j-1} + 6C_j - 4C_{j+1} + C_{j+2})^2, \quad \text{s.t.} \tag{5.89}$$

$$C_j = C_i^m, \qquad \text{if } K_j = K_i, \qquad i = 1, ..., m.$$

The C_j are call option prices for exercise prices K_j on an equally spaced grid. The restriction requires theoretical call prices to be equal to the average of observed bid and ask prices C^m wherever an observed call option is available. n is the number of strike prices on the grid and m the number of observed option prices.[12] By stating the optimization in terms of call prices instead of risk-neutral densities they avoid the probabilistic restrictions from (5.87).

Discrete approximation of the first-order conditions leads to

$$\frac{\partial \Omega}{\partial C_j} = 2C_{j-4} - 16C_{j-3} + 56C_{j-2} - 112C_{j-1} + 140C_j - 112C_{j+1} \\ +56C_{j+2} - 16C_{j+3} + 2C_{j+4} = 0, \quad j = 0, ..., n. \tag{5.90}$$

The constraints from (5.89) are introduced by modifying the objective function by a penalty term, so that $\Omega' = \Omega + \alpha \sum_i^m (C_i - C_i^m)^2$. The first-order conditions become

$$\frac{\partial \Omega'}{\partial C_j} = 2C_{j-4} - 16C_{j-3} + 56C_{j-2} - 112C_{j-1} + (140 + 2\alpha)C_j \\ -112C_{j+1} + 56C_{j+2} - 16C_{j+3} + 2C_{j+4} = 2\alpha C_j^m, \tag{5.91} \\ j = 1, \cdots, n.$$

The boundary conditions set the prices for options with very high strike prices $C_{n+1}, C_{n+2}, C_{n+3}, C_{n+4}$ equal to zero and those for options with very low strike prices $C_{-4}, C_{-3}, C_{-2}, C_{-1}$ equal to $S_t - K_i(1+r)^{T-t}, \quad i = -1, .., -4$. Hence, the probabilities of extremely high and extremely low realizations for the underlyings' price are assumed to be zero. After these simplifications, the call option prices can be simply computed by inverting a banddiagonal matrix of rank n. After having solved (5.91) the risk-neutral probabilities result from the butterfly spread

$$P_j = (1+r)^{T-t}(C_{j-1} - 2C_j + C_{j+1}). \tag{5.92}$$

The approach does not ensure that the risk-neutral probabilities will always be positive. Therefore, the authors propose an iterative technique to prevent risk-neutral probabilities from becoming negative: if negative probabilities occur they replace the observed option price for the highest strike price by zero and that for the lowest strike price by $S_t - K_i(1+r)^{T-t}$. Then call prices and risk-neutral probabilities are computed again and the procedure is applied repeatedly until only positive probabilities result.

Mayhew (1995) also relies on the maximum-smoothness criterion but considers continuous strike prices. He shows that the resulting risk-neutral density can

[12] The authors construct the grid from the ending nodes of a binomial option-pricing model. However, they deviate from the conventionally used logarithmic spacing by using equally spaced strike prices (Jackwerth and Rubinstein (1996, p. 1624)).

also be derived from fitting a polynomial spline function to observed option prices.[13]

5.3 Estimating Option-Pricing Functions

As shown in equation (2.19) the risk-neutral density can be computed from the second derivative of the call option-pricing function. Since in applied work only a small number of discretely spaced observations on options with alternative strike prices is available, using the relationship (2.19) requires the creation of a set of more densely spaced option prices that can be differentiated numerically.

5.3.1 Fitting Polynomials to the Volatility Smile

Global Polynomials

Shimko (1993) fits a quadratic function in the exercise price to Black-Scholes implied volatilities. From the estimated polynomial he computes a large number of strike/volatility combinations and converts the implied volatilities back into call option prices via the Black-Scholes formula. The risk-neutral density function then results from a second order difference quotient of the option prices. Dumas, Fleming, and Whaley (1998) extend this approach by fitting a quadratic polynomial in exercise price and time to expiration to the implied volatility smile, thus including information from options with different time to expiration (Dumas, Fleming, and Whaley (1998, p. 2080)).

Most authors prefer to interpolate the volatility smile and not option prices directly because this technique is more simple and reliable.[14] It is particularly difficult to adequately model the curvature of the option-pricing function because it consists of both strictly linear and extremely convex segments. Even small errors in the approximation can lead to large deviations in the curvature and can cause large errors in the risk-neutral probabilities. In contrast, the volatility smile can generally be better approximated by conventional techniques and small estimation errors have only a very limited impact on the call option-pricing function's curvature (Cooper und Talbot (1999), p. 75).

These approaches use the Black-Scholes formula twice: first implied volatilities are computed from option prices and then the estimated volatilities are

[13] In addition, Mayhew (1995) presents a cubic-spline approach where the risk-neutral probabilities are constructed from piecewise cubic polynomials under the restrictions that the density integrates to one and that all observed options are correctly priced.

[14] Exceptions are the papers by Bates (1991, 2000) where the call option-pricing function is approximated by cubic-spline functions.

converted back into option prices. Note that this does not presume that the Black-Scholes formula is an accurate representation for the formation of option prices. The Black-Scholes formula is only used as a convenient tool for mapping from price into volatility space and vice versa (e.g. Cooper and Talbot (1999, p. 75), and Malz (1998b, p. 125)).

While Shimko (1993) and Dumas, Fleming, and Whaley (1998) use data on exchange-traded options, Malz (1997, 1998b) considers data for foreign-exchange options from the OTC market. His data set consists of prices of *strangles*, *straddles* and *risk reversals*, i.e. of combinations of put and call options. As is general practice on the OTC market, option prices are quoted in terms of Black-Scholes implied volatilities while strike prices are quoted in terms of *delta*, the derivative of the Black-Scholes price with respect to S_t.[15] Three points on the volatility smile can be computed from prices of *risk reversals* and *strangles*: $\sigma_{25\delta}$ $(\delta = 0.25)$, the implied volatility at the money σ_{atm}, and $\sigma_{75\delta}$ $(\delta = 0.75)$. The *risk reversal* and the *strangle* prices (rr and str) are defined as

$$\begin{aligned} str &= 0.5(\sigma_{75\delta} + \sigma_{25\delta}) - \sigma_{atm}, \\ rr &= \sigma_{25\delta} - \sigma_{75\delta}. \end{aligned} \tag{5.93}$$

Therefore,

$$\begin{aligned} \sigma_{25\delta} &= \sigma_{atm} + str + 0.5rr, \\ \sigma_{75\delta} &= \sigma_{atm} + str - 0.5rr. \end{aligned} \tag{5.94}$$

The implied volatility at the money σ_{atm} can be computed from the *straddle* price in terms of implied volatilities (see Malz (1998a, p. 43)).

Malz fits a quadratic polynomial to these three volatilities,[16]

$$\sigma(\delta; \sigma_{atm}, rr, str) = b_0\, \sigma_{atm} + b_1\, rr(\delta - 0.5) + b_2\, str(\delta - 0.5)^2. \tag{5.95}$$

The requirement that the polynomial fits exactly the three observed volatility/*delta* pairs leads to $b_0 = 1, b_1 = 2$, and $b_2 = 16$ because[17]

[15] On the OTC market for foreign-exchange options, buying a *straddle* implies entering a long position in an at-the-money call and an at-the-money put option. Buying a *risk reversal* means buying an out-of-the money call with $\delta = 0.25$ and selling an out-of-the money put with $\delta = 0.25$. Finally, a *strangle* consists of long positions in both an out-of-the money call $(\delta = 0.25)$ and an out-of-the money put $(\delta = 0.25)$ (see Malz (1998a, p. 43)). The *delta* values of call and put options are related by $\delta(K)^p = \delta(K)^c - 1$. Unless otherwise indicated *delta* values given in the text always refer to call options.

[16] This specification is based on the interpretation of rr as an indicator of skewness and of str as an indicator of kurtosis of the risk-neutral density (Malz (1998b, p. 126)). Compare also section 3.2.1.

[17] For at-the-money options $\delta \approx 0.5$.

$$\begin{aligned}\sigma_{atm} &= \sigma(0.5;\sigma_{atm},rr,str) = b_0\,\sigma_{atm},\\ rr &= \sigma(0.25;\sigma_{atm},rr,str) - \sigma(0.75;\sigma_{atm},rr,str) = \frac{b_1}{2}rr,\\ str &= \frac{\sigma(0.25;\sigma_{atm},rr,str)+\sigma(0.75;\sigma_{atm},rr,str)}{2} - \sigma_{atm} = \frac{b_2}{16}str,\end{aligned} \tag{5.96}$$

so that,

$$\sigma(\delta;\sigma_{atm},rr,str) = \sigma_{atm} + 2rr(\delta-0.5) + 16str(\delta-0.5)^2. \tag{5.97}$$

Now, the *delta*/volatility pairs have to be transformed into strike price/option price space. However, a complication arises since *delta* itself depends on implied volatility,

$$\delta(\sigma,r,K,T-t) = \Phi(d_1), \tag{5.98}$$

$$d_1 = \frac{\ln\left(\frac{S_t}{K}\right) + \left(r+\frac{\sigma^2}{2}\right)(T-t)}{\sigma\sqrt{T-t}}.$$

Consequently σ must be computed from the implicit function

$$\sigma = \sigma_{atm} + 2rr\big(\Phi(d_1(\sigma)) - 0.5\big) + 16str\big(\Phi(d_1(\sigma)) - 0.5\big)^2. \tag{5.99}$$

Solving for σ for given values of K and substituting the results into the Black-Scholes formula yields the call prices that can be differentiated numerically twice in order to arrive at the risk-neutral density function.[18]

For this type of approach there is a problem related to modelling the extreme tails of the risk-neutral density outside the range of observed option prices. Shimko (1993) suggests grafting lognormal tails to the computed risk-neutral density function so that the density integrates to one while Malz (1997, 1998b) extrapolates the estimated quadratic function for the volatility smile.

Local Polynomials

A number of papers use spline functions to model the volatility smile. Campa, Chang, and Reider (1997, 1998) and Rosenberg and Engle (1999) work in strike price/volatility space whereas Bliss and Panigirtzoglou (2002) measure moneyness in terms of *delta*. This causes implied volatilities far out of the

[18] Malz (1997) investigates the accuracy of his approximation of the volatility smile with a data set containing options with *delta* values in addition to $\delta = \{0.25, 0.5, 0.75\}$. He finds large deviations only for very high and very low *delta* values. Since in these regions *vega* $= \frac{\partial C^{BS}}{\partial\sigma}$ is very small, these deviations affect call prices only slightly and therefore have almost negligible effects on the risk-neutral density (see Malz (1997, p. 29)).

money to be grouped more densely than at the money and therefore allows for a more flexible shape at the center of the volatility smile where options are traded more actively (Bliss and Panigirtzoglou (2002)).
Like Campa, Chang, and Reider (1997, 1998) they choose a natural cubic spline function, i.e. they construct the volatilitiy smile from piecewise cubic polynomials,

$$\sigma(\delta) = f_i(\delta) = a_i + b_i\,(\delta - \delta_i) + c_i\,(\delta - \delta_i)^2 + d_i\,(\delta - \delta_i)^3,$$
$$\text{for } \delta_i \le \delta \le \delta_{i+1}, \qquad i = 1, ..., m-1. \tag{5.100}$$

For simplicity define,

$$\sigma(\delta) = f_m(\delta) = a_m + b_m\,(\delta - \delta_m) + c_m\,(\delta - \delta_m)^2 + d_m\,(\delta - \delta_m)^3,$$
$$\text{for } \delta_m \le \delta. \tag{5.101}$$

At the knot points, i.e. at the observed *delta*/volatility pairs, the spline function is required to be continuous with continuous first and second derivatives,

$$f_i(\delta_i) = f_{i-1}(\delta_i), \quad i = 2, ..., m, \tag{5.102}$$
$$f_i'(\delta_i) = f_{i-1}'(\delta_i), \quad i = 2, ..., m, \tag{5.103}$$
$$f_i''(\delta_i) = f_{i-1}''(\delta_i), \quad i = 2, ..., m. \tag{5.104}$$

Bliss and Panigirtzoglou (2002) do not require the spline function to match the (σ_i, δ_i) pairs exactly, i.e. they do not estimate an interpolation smile.[19]

(5.102)-(5.104) provide 3(m-1) linear constraints,

$$\begin{pmatrix} 1\,0\,0\,0 \\ 0\,1\,0\,0 \\ 0\,0\,1\,0 \end{pmatrix} \begin{pmatrix} a_i \\ b_i \\ c_i \\ d_i \end{pmatrix} \tag{5.105}$$
$$= \begin{pmatrix} 1 & (\delta_i - \delta_{i-1}) & (\delta_i - \delta_{i-1})^2 & (\delta_i - \delta_{i-1})^3 \\ 0 & 1 & 2(\delta_i - \delta_{i-1}) & 3(\delta_i - \delta_{i-1})^2 \\ 0 & 0 & 1 & 3(\delta_i - \delta_{i-1}) \end{pmatrix} \begin{pmatrix} a_{i-1} \\ b_{i-1} \\ c_{i-1} \\ d_{i-1} \end{pmatrix},$$

for $i = 2, ..., m$. Together the m polynomials contain $4m$ parameters so that $4m - 3(m-1) = m + 3$ free parameters have to be estimated. If we select these as $\Theta = (a_1, b_1, c_1, d_1, d_2, ..., d_m)'$, the other parameters $\{a_i, b_i, c_i\}_{i=2}^{m}$ can be computed from (5.105). For a natural spline function we also require $f(\delta_1)'' = f(\delta_m)'' = 0$, i.e. $c_1 = c_m = 0$ providing two additional restrictions. Furthermore, Bliss und Panigirtzoglou (2002) extend the spline function linearly outside the range covered by observed *delta*/volatility pairs so that $f(\delta)'' = 0$, for $\delta \le \delta_1$ and $\delta \ge \delta_m$ requiring $c_1 = c_m = d_m = 0$.[20]

[19] For more details on spline functions, see e.g. Härtter (1978).

[20] Campa, Chang, and Reider (1998) extrapolate the first and the last spline segment to a further strike price segment in the tails of the volatility smile and thereafter restrict the functions to be linear.

For estimation they suggest the following objective function:

$$\min_{\Theta} \sum_{i=1}^{m} w_i \left(\sigma_i - f_i(\delta_i, \Theta)\right)^2 + \lambda \int_{-\infty}^{+\infty} f''(\delta; \Theta)^2 d\delta, \tag{5.106}$$

where the w_i are the weights of the individual knot points. Bliss and Panigirtzoglou (2002) choose a weighting scheme based on each option's *vega*, i.e. the value of the derivative of the Black-Scholes price with respect to volatility. This scheme puts the highest weights on at the money options and is theoretically consistent if the errors in option prices are homoskedastic.[21] λ is the relative weight on the penalty term that is based on the smoothness of the estimated volatility smile.

As an alternative, Aparicio und Hodges (1998) choose a cubic B-spline to model the volatility smile. For the tails of the risk-neutral density they follow Shimko (1993) but use the more flexible Ramberg (1979) distribution instead of the lognormal.

5.3.2 A Nonparametric Technique

Aït-Sahalia and Lo (1998) extract the risk-neutral density with a nonparametric or semiparametric technique and estimate the option-valuation function with respect to d parameters $\mathbf{Z}$ using a kernel estimator.[22] Application of such a technique requires only very few assumptions. On the other hand, kernel estimation is a very data-intensive technique.[23] The kernel estimation approach corresponds to constructing the option-valuation function $H(\mathbf{Z})$ as a weighted moving average of the n observed combinations of H and $\mathbf{Z}$. The estimator for the conditional expectation of H at some $\mathbf{Z}$ is given by

$$\hat{H}(\mathbf{Z}) = \mathbf{E}[H|\mathbf{Z}] = \frac{\sum_{i=1}^{n} \mathcal{K}((\mathbf{Z} - \mathbf{Z}_i)/h)\, H_i}{\sum_{i=1}^{n} \mathcal{K}((\mathbf{Z} - \mathbf{Z}_i)/h)}. \tag{5.107}$$

[21] Since $dC = \frac{\partial C}{\partial \sigma} d\sigma$ the assumption of homoscedastic pricing errors requires a direct vega weighting. In contrast, assuming homoscedastic errors in implied volatilities would require an inverse vega weighting, see Bliss und Panigirtzoglou (2002, p. 392).

[22] An extensive discussion of kernel estimation is provided by Härdle (1990), Härdle and Linton (1994), and Silverman (1986). Yatchew (1998) is a good introduction. For nonparametric techniques in the context of option valuation, see Ghysels et. al. (1997).

[23] The data set used by Aït-Sahalia and Lo (1998) consists of more than 14,000 observations.

(5.107) is a *Nadaraya-Watson* kernel estimator. The d dimensional kernel function $\mathcal{K}$ is usually specified to be a probability density function. Hence, option prices with characteristics $\mathbf{Z}_i$ very close to $\mathbf{Z}$ are weighted more heavily than options whose characteristics deviate more strongly from the option to be priced. The bandwidth parameter h increases with sample size n. The closer h is to zero, the more peaked is the kernel density around $\mathbf{Z}$ and the more weight is placed on options with $\mathbf{Z}_i$ very close to $\mathbf{Z}$.

Aït-Sahalia and Lo (1998) assume the option price to depend on five variables, $\mathbf{Z} = [S_t, K, r_{t,\tau}, \delta_{t,\tau}, \tau]'$, where $r_{t,\tau}$ is the risk-free rate of interest in t for the time interval $\tau = T - t$ and $\delta_{t,\tau}$ is the dividend yield in t over the remaining time to expiration τ. The multivariate kernel function $\mathcal{K}$ is the product of five univariate kernel functions k, so that (5.107) becomes

$$\hat{H}(S_t, K, r_{t,\tau}, \delta_{t,\tau}, \tau) \tag{5.108}$$
$$= \frac{\sum_{i=1}^{n} k_S\left(\frac{S_t - S_{t_i}}{h_S}\right) k_K\left(\frac{K-K_i}{h_K}\right) k_r\left(\frac{r_{t,\tau} - r_{t_i,\tau_i}}{h_r}\right) k_\delta\left(\frac{\delta_{t,\tau} - \delta_{t_i,\tau_i}}{h_\delta}\right) k_\tau\left(\frac{\tau - \tau_i}{h_\tau}\right) H_i}{\sum_{i=1}^{n} k_S\left(\frac{S_t - S_{t_i}}{h_S}\right) k_K\left(\frac{K-K_i}{h_K}\right) k_r\left(\frac{r_{t,\tau} - r_{t_i,\tau_i}}{h_r}\right) k_\delta\left(\frac{\delta_{t,\tau} - \delta_{t_i,\tau_i}}{h_\delta}\right) k_\tau\left(\frac{\tau - \tau_i}{h_\tau}\right)}.$$

Obviously, the authors estimate a single option-valuation function from pooled option data, i.e. data observed on different points in time. This implies the assumption that the risk-neutral density function is stable over time, i.e. that all changes in the risk-neutral density are related to changes in the underlying option parameters (including time to expiration) in a predictable way.
Aït-Sahalia and Lo (1998) show that an increase in number of regressors in conjunction with the fact that $\hat{H}$ has to be differenced twice to arrive at the risk-neutral density considerably slows down convergence. Therefore, they decide to reduce the dimension of the kernel estimation from $d = 5$ to $d = 3$ by estimating the implied volatility smile instead of the option-valuation function. Implied volatilities are assumed to depend only on the futures price, the exercise price, and time to expiration, i.e. $\sigma(F_{t,\tau}, K, \tau)$ with $\tilde{\mathbf{Z}} = [F_{t,\tau}, K, \tau]'$. The Nadaraya-Watson kernel estimator for this model is

$$\hat{\sigma}(F_{t,\tau}, K, \tau) = \frac{\sum_{i=1}^{n} k_F\left(\frac{F_{t,\tau} - F_{t_i,\tau_i}}{h_F}\right) k_K\left(\frac{K-K_i}{h_K}\right) k_\tau\left(\frac{\tau-\tau_i}{h_\tau}\right) \sigma_i}{\sum_{i=1}^{n} k_F\left(\frac{F_{t,\tau} - F_{t_i,\tau_i}}{h_F}\right) k_K\left(\frac{K-K_i}{h_K}\right) k_\tau\left(\frac{\tau-\tau_i}{h_\tau}\right)}. \tag{5.109}$$

Using the estimated volatility function call option prices can be computed via the Black-Scholes formula. Finally, the risk-neutral probabilities are derived by differentiation,

$$\hat{H}(S_t, K, r_t, \delta_t, \tau) = C^{BS}(S_t, K, r_{t,\tau}, \delta_{t,\tau}, \tau; \hat{\sigma}(F_{t,\tau}, K, \tau)), \tag{5.110}$$

$$\hat{q}(S_T) = e^{r_{t,\tau}\tau} \left(\frac{\partial^2 \hat{H}(S_t, K, r_{t,\tau}, \delta_{t,\tau}, \tau)}{\partial K^2} \right) \Bigg|_{K=S_T}. \tag{5.111}$$

For estimation Aït-Sahalia and Lo (1998) select kernel functions of order four and two, $k_S = k_\tau = k_\delta = k_\tau = k_{(4)}, k_K = k_{(2)}$ and $k_F = k_\tau = k_{(4)}, k_K = k_{(2)}$, respectively.[24] Generally, the choice of the kernel function has only a limited impact on the results of nonparametric regressions. Much more important is an appropriate bandwidth selection. If the bandwidth is too small, observations far away from point $\mathbf{Z}$, where the function is to be estimated, are given too small weights so that the estimated function is undersmoothed. On the other hand, too large a bandwidth causes oversmoothing, i.e. the variance of the estimate is low and the bias is high. Aït-Sahalia and Lo (1998) argue that the optimum trade-off between bias and variance is found with the following choice for the bandwidth parameter

$$h_j = c_j\, s(\mathbf{Z_j})\, n^{-1/(d+2p)}. \tag{5.112}$$

where $j = 1, ..., d$. d is the number of regressors, $p = p_1 = p_2 = ... = p_d$ is the number of continuous derivatives existing for the option-pricing function $H(\bullet)$ with respect to the j-th regressor. $s(\mathbf{Z_j})$ is the j-th regressor's unconditional standard deviation. The coefficients c_j depend on the type of kernel function used (Aït-Sahalia and Lo (1998, p. 537)). The authors set $c_j = c_{j0}/\ln(n)$, where c_j0 is a constant.

Rookley (1997) also uses a nonparametric technique but avoids the pooling of option prices observed on different trading days. From each day's data he estimates the volatility smile using a bivariate locally polynomial kernel regression with moneyness and the time of observation as regressors.

5.3.3 The Maximum-Smoothness Criterion for the Volatility Smile

The approach in Jackwerth und Rubinstein (1996) is modified by Jackwerth (2000) who focusses on the second derivative of the volatility smile instead of minimizing the curvature of the call option-pricing function. He imposes the restriction that estimated implied volatilities should not deviate too much from observed implied volatilities,

$$\min_{\sigma_j} (1-\alpha) \sum_{j=1}^{n} (\sigma_j'')^2 + \alpha \sum_i \left(\frac{\sigma_i - \bar{\sigma}_i}{std_i} \right)^2. \tag{5.113}$$

σ_j is the implied volatility for strike price $K_j = S_j$. As before, the strike prices are fixed on a grid with constantly spaced intervals Δ. σ_i is the estimated implied volatility of a traded option with strike price K_i for which an implied

[24] The order s of a kernel function is defined as the even integer that satisfies $\int_{-\infty}^{+\infty} z^j k(z)dz = 0$ for $j = 1, ..., s-1$, and $\int_{-\infty}^{+\infty} |z|^s k(z)dz < +\infty$. For the order selection and the determination of the bandwidth, see Aït-Sahalia and Lo (1998, p. 535).

volatility $\bar{\sigma}_i$ is observed. $\boldsymbol{std_i}$ is the standard deviation of $\bar{\sigma}_i$ on the trading day. Dividing by $\boldsymbol{std_i}$ places a greater weight on implied volatilities from at-the-money options for which $\boldsymbol{std_i}$ is typically the smallest (Jackwerth (2000)). σ'' is approximated by

$$\sigma'' = \frac{\sigma_{j-1} - 2\sigma_j + \sigma_{j+1}}{\Delta^2}. \tag{5.114}$$

Estimating the volatility smile with the techniques discussed so far does not necessarily lead to arbitrage-free option prices. Therefore, the option prices computed from the estimated volatility smile should be checked for the absence of arbitrage possibilities. A violation of the no-arbitrage condition can lead to negative risk-neutral probabilities. Hodges (1993), for example, provides some theoretical restrictions on the slope of the volatility smile that ensure arbitrage-free option prices.

5.3.4 Further Extensions

Since implied volatilities depend on the exercise price and time to expiration it makes sense to incorporate the maturity dependence into modelling the implied volatility structure. However, maturity dependence of implied volatilities is inconsistent with the Black-Scholes formula. Using the Black-Scholes formula to compute implied volatilities from observed option prices and to convert estimated volatilities back into call prices can be justified on the grounds that the exercise price is a constant characteristic of the option that does not change over time. In contrast, it is not possible to use the Black-Scholes formula to compute option prices from estimated implied volatilities that depend on time to expiration since volatility would change deterministically through time.
Deterministic volatility functions that model the (nonstochastic) dependence of implied volatilities on the exercise prices and on time to expiration are investigated by Dumas, Fleming, and Whaley (1998). They estimate implied volatility as polynomials in the exercise price and in time to expiration. In computing theoretical option prices they rely on a finite-difference method where volatilities are discretely spaced on a grid.[25]

Finite-difference methods and deterministic volatility functions are also considered in Levin, McManus, and Watt (1998), Bodurtha and Jermakyan (1999), Coleman, Li, and Verma (1998), and Lagnado and Osher (1997). The latter three studies also use the smoothness of the fitted volatility surface in determining a solution. Other related work is by Avellaneda et. al. (1997), Carr and Madan (1998), and Laurent and Leisen (1998). The main focus of all these papers is on pricing exotic or illiquid options by using information from

[25] For finite-difference techniques see, e.g. Duffie (1996), Ch. 11.

observed prices of standard options. However, in principle, these approaches can be used to extract risk-neutral probabilities by differencing the estimated option-pricing function.

5.4 Process-Based Techniques

5.4.1 Implied-Volatility Trees

Implied tree models are extensions to the binomial option-pricing model by Cox, Ross, and Rubinstein (1979).[26] The standard binomial option-pricing model is a discrete approximation to the Black/Scholes-Merton model and, hence, it is based on the assumption of constant (local) volatility. Implied volatility trees, however, accomodate the empirically observed strike and maturity dependence of implied volatilities. These models were developed in order to improve the hedging and valuation of exotic options relative to the standard binomial tree model (Chriss (1997, p. 362)). Implied-volatility trees were first presented independently by Derman and Kani (1994) and Dupire (1994). The following discussion is based on Chriss (1997) who suggests a slightly different approach that can be more easily extended to American-type options.

Implied-volatility trees are constructed by iteration. The information for each time step is computed from the information of the preceding one. The following notation will be used: $i = 0, 1, ..., n$ denotes the time steps on the tree with equal intervals of $\Delta t = t_i - t_{i-1}$. The possible stock-price nodes on step i are denoted $S_{i,j}$ in ascending order, $j = 0, ..., i$, and $p_{i,j}$ is the risk-neutral probability of the stock price moving upward from node $S_{i,j}$ to $S_{i+1,j+1}$. From these probabilities the Arrow-Debreu prices, i.e. the prices of securities with a payoff of one if the stock price is at node $S_{i,j}$ in t_i and of none elsewhere, can be computed: the Arrow-Debreu prices for each node are equal to the discounted risk-neutral probability for the stock price being at that node in t_i.

Let us assume that all relevant information for step $(i-1)$ has been computed. The next step of the tree will be constructed from the known values of $S_{i-1,\bullet}$, from the Arrow-Debreu prices $\lambda_{i-1,\bullet}$, and from some observed European-type option prices. The option prices are used to inter- and extrapolate option prices for various strike prices and times to expiration.[27]
As a starting point, a first stock-price node at time step i must be determined.

[26] This section requires some familiarity with the binomial option-pricing model. For introductions see, e.g. Chriss (1997) and Hull (1997).

[27] The following algorithm can also be applied to the first step on the tree since the necessary values for the preceding step, i.e. the vertex, are known to be the current price of the underlying S_0 and $\lambda_0 = 1$.

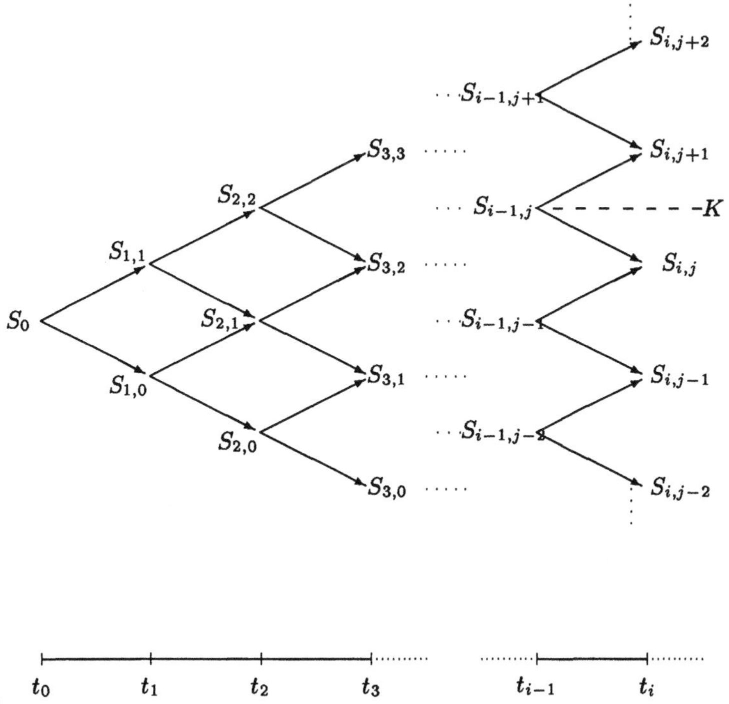

Fig. 5.1. Implied volatility tree

Assigning the first stock price to a node on step i is completely arbitrary because $i+1$ stock price nodes and i transition probabilities from step $i-1$ to i must be determined from i forward prices and i interpolated option prices (one for each node on step $i-1$) leaving one free parameter. Derman and Kani (1994) and Chriss (1996) suggest fixing the middle node first. How this is done depends on whether i is odd or even.

If i is **even** the number of nodes on this time step is odd. The stock-price value on the middle node can be set either equal to the current price of the underlying asset $S_{i,i/2} = S_0$ or equal to the forward price $S_{i,i/2} = S_0 e^{ri\Delta t}$, depending on whether the tree is centered on the spot or on the forward price (r is the risk-free rate of interest from t_0 to t_i).

If i is **odd** the number of nodes on time step i is even so that the stock-price values of the two middle nodes $S_{i,(i+1)/2}$ and $S_{i,(i-1)/2}$ are determined first. In order to compute these values the price of a European-type at-the-money put option with expiration t_i and strike price $K = S_{i-1,i/2}$, *at the node* $S_{i-1,i/2}$ is required ($\nu^{put}_{i-1,i/2}$). This option price can be computed from an interpolated put option price with expiration t_i and strike price $S_{i-1,i/2}$, $P(t_i, S_{i-1,i/2})$

(see Appendix B),

$$\nu^{put}_{i-1,i/2} = \frac{P(t_i, S_{i-1,i/2}) - \Sigma}{\lambda_{i-1,i/2}}, \tag{5.115}$$

$$\Sigma = \sum_{k=0}^{i/2-1} \lambda_{i-1,k} \left(e^{-r_i \Delta t} S_{i-1,i/2} - S_{i-1,k} + e^{-r_i \Delta t} D_i\right),$$

where r_i is the forward rate from t_{i-1} to t_i and D_i is the dividend payment in t_i. Now, define

$$u = \frac{\nu^{put}_{i-1,i/2} + S_{i-1,i/2}}{e^{-r_i \Delta t} S_{i-1,i/2} - \nu^{put}_{i-1,i/2}}. \tag{5.116}$$

If the tree is centered on spot prices set

$$S_{i,(i+1)/2} = S_{i-1,i/2}\, u \qquad \text{and} \quad S_{i,(i-1)/2} = S_{i-1,i/2}/u, \tag{5.117}$$

or for centering on forward prices[28]

$$S_{i,(i+1)/2} = S_{i-1,i/2} u, \qquad \text{and} \quad S_{i,(i-1)/2} = \left(S_{i-1,i/2} e^{r_i \Delta t}\right)/u. \tag{5.118}$$

The transition probability from node $(i-1, i/2)$ to $(i, (i+1)/2)$ is

$$p_{i-1,i/2} = \frac{e^{r_i \Delta t} S_{i-1,i/2} - D_i - S_{i,(i-1)/2}}{S_{i,(i+1)/2} - S_{i,(i-1)/2}}. \tag{5.119}$$

After the first node or the first pair of nodes has been computed, the rest of the i-th step can be completed easily. The nodes in the **lower half** are filled iteratively going downward: for a known node $S_{i,j+1}$, the node $S_{i,j}$, $j < (i-1)/2$ can be computed from the interpolated price of a European-type put option with expiration t_i and strike price $S_{i-1,j}$ $(P(t_i, S_{i-1,j})$. First, the price of the put option at node $S_{i-1,j}$ is

$$\nu^{put}_{i-1,j} = \frac{P(t_i, S_{i-1,j}) - \Sigma}{\lambda_{i-1,j}}, \tag{5.120}$$

$$\Sigma = \sum_{k=0}^{j-1} \lambda_{i-1,k} \left(e^{-r_i \Delta t} S_{i-1,j} - S_{i-1,k} + e^{-r_i \Delta t} D_i\right),$$

and from this,

$$S_{i,j} = \frac{\nu^{put}_{i-1,j}\, S_{i,j+1} + \left(S_{i-1,j} - e^{-r_i \Delta t} S_{i,j+1}\right) S_{i-1,j}}{\nu^{put}_{i-1,j} + S_{i-1,j} - e^{-r_i \Delta t} S_{i,j+1}}. \tag{5.121}$$

[28] Derman and Kani (1994) center the tree on the spot price while Barle and Cakici (1995, 1998) suggest centering on forward prices.

Going down the tree in this way all nodes down to $S_{i,0}$ can be completed. The transition probabilities to each node are

$$p_{i-1,j} = \frac{e^{r_i \Delta t} S_{i-1,j} - D_i - S_{i,j}}{S_{i,j+1} - S_{i,j}}. \tag{5.122}$$

In the **upper half** the nodes are filled going upward. The node $S_{i,j+1}, j+1 > (i+1)/2$ is computed from the node $S_{i,j}$ and the interpolated price of a European-type call option $C(t_i, S_{i-1,j})$. First, the call option price at node $S_{i-1,j}$ is

$$\nu_{i-1,j}^{call} = \frac{C(t_i, S_{i-1,j}) - \Sigma}{\lambda_{i-1,j}}, \tag{5.123}$$

$$\Sigma = \sum_{k=j+1}^{i-1} \lambda_{i-1,k} \big(S_{i-1,k} - e^{-r_i \Delta t} D_i - e^{-r_i \Delta t} S_{i-1,j} \big).$$

From this follows

$$S_{i,j+1} = \frac{\nu_{i-1,j}^{call} S_{i,j} + \big(-e^{-r_i \Delta t} S_{i,j} - S_{i-1,j}\big) S_{i-1,j}}{\nu_{i-1,j}^{call} + e^{-r_i \Delta t} S_{i,j} - S_{i-1,j}}, \tag{5.124}$$

and the transition probabilities in (5.122). With this procedure all nodes in the upper half of the tree up to $S_{i,i}$ can be computed.[29]

In order to complete the time step i, the nodes' Arrow-Debreu prices are derived iteratively from the preceding time step,

$$\begin{aligned} \lambda_{i,i} &= e^{-r_i \Delta t}\, p_{i-1,i-1}\, \lambda_{i-1,i-1}, \\ \lambda_{i,0} &= e^{-r_i \Delta t}\, (1 - p_{i-1,0})\, \lambda_{i-1,0}, \\ \lambda_{i,j} &= e^{-r_i \Delta t}\, (p_{i-1,j-1}\, \lambda_{i-1,j-1} + (1 - p_{i-1,j})\, \lambda_{i-1,j}), \quad j = 2, \cdots, i-1. \end{aligned} \tag{5.125}$$

Finally, the risk-neutral probabilities that are equal to the Arrow-Debreu prices can simply be read from the completed tree (Chriss (1996)).

However, the alogorithm sometimes yields transition probabilities in (5.122) that are not between zero and one. To discuss this problem, equation (5.122) must be considered in some more detail. It is derived from the forward condition that sets the forward price at node $(i-1, j)$ equal to the expected value of the stock price in t_i,

$$p_{i-1,j}\, S_{i,j+1} + (1 - p_{i-1,j})\, S_{i,j} = S_{i-1,j}\, e^{r_i \Delta t} - D_i = F \tag{5.126}$$

[29] It is not required to construct the upper half of the tree from call and the lower part from put option prices. European put-call parity shows that the opposite is possible as well. However, one advantage of the algorithm described above is that the interpolated option prices are always out of the money and therefore more sensitive to volatility than in-the-money options (Chriss (1997, p. 390)).

Inadmissible transition probabilities indicate that the forward price is not within the interval $[S_{i,j}, S_{i,j+1}]$ (see fig. 5.2), i.e. that the forward condition is violated. Two alternative situations are possible: either we are in the process of going down the i-th step of the tree and the node to be computed $S_{i,j+1}$ is above the forward price of $S_{i-1,j+1}$ (case a), or we are going up the upper half of the tree and the forward price $S_{i-1,j}e^{r_i \Delta t} - D_i$ turns out to be above $S_{i,j+1}$ (case b).
If negative transition probabilities occur, Derman and Kani (1994) and Chriss

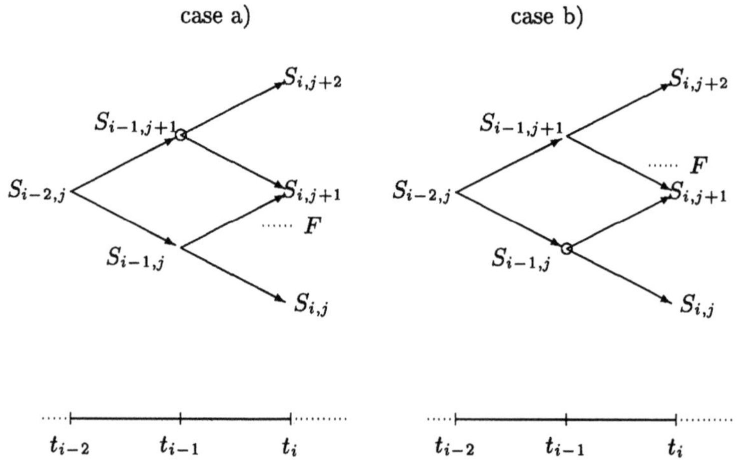

Fig. 5.2. Violation of the forward condition (based on Chriss (1997, p. 380)).

(1996) suggest changing the value of $S_{i,j+1}$ so that the forward condition is valid again. For case (a) the authors recommend replacing $S_{i,j+1}$ by

$$S'_{i,j+1} = \frac{S_{i,j+2}\, S_{i-1,j}}{S_{i-1,j+1}}, \qquad (5.127)$$

and for case (b) by

$$S'_{i,j+1} = \frac{S_{i,j}\, S_{i-1,j+1}}{S_{i-1,j}}. \qquad (5.128)$$

These values set the stock-price ratio of the two neighbouring nodes on the current step equal to that of the two corresponding nodes on the preceding step.[30]

If the forward condition is still not satisfied after this adjustment the authors recommend setting $S_{i,j+1}$ in such a way that the forward condition can no longer be violated,

[30] This relation is of great importance since it determines local volatility (see Chriss (1997, p. 381)): $\sigma_{i,j} = \frac{1}{\sqrt{\Delta t}} \sqrt{p_{i,j}\,(1 - p_{i,j})} \ln(S_{i+1,j+1}/S_{i+1,j})$.

$$S'_{i,j+1} = S^{r_i \Delta t} S_{i-1,j} - D_i \pm \epsilon, \tag{5.129}$$

for small positive ϵ implying that the stock price at the node is put just above/below the forward price. In applied work, 'bad' probabilities occur more often the greater the number of steps in the tree. Hence, implied-volatility trees with a large number of steps tend to become numerically unstable (Jackwerth (1999, p. 75)).

An implied-volatility tree can also be constructed from prices of American-type options if an iteration method that accounts for early exercise is used for the solution of (5.115), (5.120), and (5.123) (see Chriss (1997), Ch. 9).

Eliminating 'bad' probabilities as shown above implies a loss of information because the relevant nodes are set arbitrarily without reference to the data. Barle and Cakici (1998) discuss how the occurence of 'bad' probabilities can be reduced by modifying the approach of Derman and Kani (1994). They set the interpolated options' strike prices equal to the forward price on the preceding node [$(K = S_{i-1,j}\, e^{r\Delta t} - D_i)$ instead of $(K = S_{i-1,j})$]. Derman, Kani, and Chriss (1996) extend the binomial model to a trinomial implied-volatility tree and use the additional free parameters to set the stock-price values at the nodes more or less independently from the data. Then, observed option prices are used to determine the transition probabilities. They argue that an appropriately designed state space avoids most cases of 'bad' probabilities. However, none of these modifications can definitely rule out this problem so that in most applications arbitrary interventions remain necessary. In the modified models 'bad' probabilities almost exclusively occur near the boundaries of the tree, i.e. in regions where the risk-neutral probabilities are usually very low (Barle and Cakici (1998, p. 146)).

While the implied tree models by Rubinstein (1994) and Jackwerth (1997) are both based on a set of options with a common time to expiration, the implied-volatility tree models by Derman and Kani (1994), Dupire (1994), and Chriss (1996) use information contained in prices of options for various expiration dates. However, the most important difference is that Rubinstein (1994) requires risk-neutral probabilities as an input to the construction of the tree that is calibrated to reproduce these risk-neutral probabilities whereas implied volatility trees produce risk-neutral probabilities as a result.[31]

More recent extensions incorporate stochastic volatility into implied-volatility trees, see e.g Derman and Kani (1998), Britten-Jones and Neuburger (2000), and Ledoit and Santa-Clara (1999).

[31] The basic model in Rubinstein (1994) also cannot be applied to American-type options but that limitiation is relaxed by Jackwerth (1996). Brown and Toft (1999) extend the model further so that it can be based on risk-neutral probabilities for different times to expiration.

5.4.2 Estimation of Stochastic Process Parameters

Malz (1996, 1998c) computes risk-neutral probabilities with explicit reference to a specific option-pricing model. For foreign-exchange options he assumes the underlying exchange rate to follow a jump-diffusion process and derives its risk-neutral representation

$$dS_t = (r - r^\star - \lambda \mathrm{E}[k])\, S_t\, dt + \sigma_B\, S_t\, dB_t + S_t\, k\, dq_{t,T}. \tag{5.130}$$

r and $r^\star$ are the constant domestic and foreign interest rates. $q_{t,T}$ is a Poisson distributed jump variable on the interval (t,T) and denotes the number of jumps in the exchange rates. The average number of jumps is equal to λ and the stochastic jump size is k.[32] Malz (1996, 1998c) simplifies the model by assuming k to be nonstochastic and focusses on the so called *"Bernoulli version"* of the jump-diffusion model where there is either one jump or no jump at all (Ball and Torous (1983, 1985)). For this model the option-valuation formulae are

$$\begin{aligned} &C\;(S_t, T-t; K, \sigma_B, r, r^\star, \lambda, k) \qquad\qquad (5.131)\\ &= (1-\lambda(T-t))\left[\frac{S_t\, e^{-r^\star(T-t)}}{1+\lambda\, k\,(T-t)}\,\Phi(d_0+\sigma_B\sqrt{T-t}) - K\, e^{-r(T-t)}\,\Phi(d_0)\right]\\ &\quad +\lambda(T-t)\left[\frac{S_t\, e^{-r^\star(T-t)}}{1+\lambda\, k\,(T-t)}(1+k)\,\Phi(d_1+\sigma_B\sqrt{T-t}) - K\, e^{-r(T-t)}\,\Phi(d_1)\right],\\ &P\;(S_t, T-t; K, \sigma_B, r, r^\star, \lambda, k) \qquad\qquad (5.132)\\ &= (1-\lambda(T-t))\left[K\, e^{-r(T-t)}\,\Phi(-d_0) - \frac{S_t\, e^{-r^\star(T-t)}}{1+\lambda\, k\,(T-t)}\,\Phi(-d_0-\sigma_B\sqrt{T-t})\right]\\ &\quad +\lambda(T-t)\left[K\, e^{-r(T-t)}\,\Phi(-d_1) - \frac{S_t\, e^{-r^\star(T-t)}}{1+\lambda\, k\,(T-t)}\,\Phi(-d_1-\sigma_B\sqrt{T-t})\right], \end{aligned}$$

where

$$d_0 = \frac{\ln\left(\frac{S_t}{K}\right) - \ln\left(1+\lambda\, k\,(T-t)\right) + \left(r - r^\star - \frac{\sigma_B^2}{2}\right)(T-t)}{\sigma_B\sqrt{T-t}}, \tag{5.133}$$

$$d_1 = \frac{\ln\left(\frac{S_t}{K}\right) - \ln\left(1+\lambda\, k\,(T-t)\right) + \ln(1+k) + \left(r - r^\star - \frac{\sigma_B^2}{2}\right)(T-t)}{\sigma_B\sqrt{T-t}}.$$

This implies that option prices are a weighted average of the Black-Scholes price if no jump occurs and of the Black-Scholes price if a jump occurs where the weights are the probabilities for no jump or one jump (see Malz (1996a, p. 728)).

---

[32] Merton (1976) and Bates (1991) derive the relevant option-valuation formulae.

Provided there are at least three observed option prices available, the free parameters λ, k, and σ_B can be estimated.[33] A problem arising in estimation is that for σ_B close to the Black-Scholes implied volatility the estimates for λ and k become very small. Therefore, Malz (1996a, 1998c) decides to apply a two-stage estimation procedure that fixes σ_B on a grid.
Since λ and k mostly appear as a product in (5.131)-(5.133), they are difficult to estimate seperately (Malz (1996a, 1998c)). The author therefore first estimates the model with all parameters unrestricted and then repeats the estimation for $k = -0.05$ so that only λ and σ_B remain to be estimated.[34]

From (5.130) in the Bernoulli version the risk-neutral cumulative distribution function can be derived as a mixture of two lognormal distributions,

$$Q(K) = \text{prob}(S_T \leq K) = (1-\lambda)\Phi\left[\frac{\ln\frac{K}{F} + \ln(1+\lambda\, k) + \frac{\sigma_B^2}{2}}{\sigma_B}\right] \tag{5.134}$$
$$+\lambda\Phi\left[\frac{\ln\frac{K}{F} + \ln(1+\lambda\, k) - \ln(1+k) + \frac{\sigma_B^2}{2}}{\sigma_B}\right].$$

Finally, the risk-neutral probabilities result from substituting the parameter estimates into (5.134).[35]

5.5 Data Selection and Preparation

Depending on the technique to be applied, often some effort must be made to prepare the option data. For example, while some approaches can deal with both call and put options simultaneously, other techniques require a specific type of option so that option prices of one type must be converted into option prices of the other, e.g. by the European put-call parity (for European-type options) or the binomial option pricing model (for American-type options). Since some specific requirements of the various techniques have already been discussed, this section will focus on some general information about issues related to data selection and preparation that are particularly relevant for exchange-traded options.

[33] An inconsistency implicit in this approach is that the model assumes the parameters to be constant through time at least for a given option contract, while estimating the parameters repeatedly for each day allows them to vary.

[34] Other studies that estimate implicit parameters of stochastic processes from option prices are Bates (1991, 1996b, 1996c, 2000) and in a regime-switching context Bollen, Gray, and Whaley (2000). However, these studies do not derive risk-neutral probabilities. In contrast, Jondeau and Rockinger (2000) consider an underlying price process with stochastic volatility and estimate the risk-neutral density.

[35] $F = S_t\, e^{(r-r^*)(T-t)}$ is the forward rate.

A first important step is to check the observed option prices for arbitrage violations because the existence of arbitrage possibilities can lead to negative risk-neutral probabilities. Nonmonotonicity and nonconvexity or violations of put-call parity for European-type options are the most easily checked indicators for arbitrage violations. Other useful criteria are suggested, for example, by Longstaff (1995), who checks for violations of the arbitrage bounds from Merton (1973), and Jackwerth and Rubinstein (1996), who search for arbitrage possibilities in form of profitable spreads.

Computing risk-neutral probabilities requires simultaneous observations on option prices and of the the underlying's price.[36] However, simultaneous observations on options and underlying are usually quite difficult to obtain. Particularly in the case of index options, it is well known that the index lags the index future and that traders use the index future to hedge the options (see, e.g.Jackwerth and Rubinstein (1996, p. 1616) for the S&P 500). In such cases an adequate alternative is to obtain an *implicit* index value from the futures price (e.g. Jackwerth and Rubinstein (1996), p. 1616.). Other researchers prefer to use settlement prices instead of closing prices or trading prices.[37] Settlement prices are determined by the exchange each day at the close of trading und provide the basis for the daily marking to the market. Söderlind (2000) argues that we can expect settlement prices to be close to equilibrium prices because the members of the clearing house deciding on the settlement prices usually also act as brokers or themselves hold open positions in options. Therefore, they have an interest in establishing prices close to equilibrium. However, depending on the institutional features of the exchange in question nonsynchronicity problems can still arise (Bliss and Panigirtzoglou (2002, p. 388)).

For some types of underlying (stocks, stock indices) the dividend yield must be obtained. In many studies ex-post dividend yields are used (e.g. Jackwerth (2000), Jackwerth and Rubinstein (1996), and Longstaff (1995)). Other authors compute the *implied* dividend yield from futures and spot prices using the relationship $F_t = S_t\, e^{(r_{t,T}-\delta_{t,T})(T-t)}$ (Aït-Sahalia and Lo (1998, p. 520)). Risk-free interest rates for a time of maturity exactly matching the options' time to expiration generally cannot be observed. Frequently found approximations use weighted averages of risk-free rates that bracket the options' expiration date or consider only the yield to maturity of an appropriate government security maturing close to the options' expiration date. Jackwerth

[36] Generally, exactly simultaneously observed prices are not available so that prices observed within a relatively short time window are used. See Dumas, Fleming, and Whaley (1998), p. 2071, and Longstaff (1995)).

[37] Nakamura and Shiratsuka (1999, p. 6), and Neuhaus (1995, p. 45) explain that the problems in obtaining simultaneous observations might also apply to closing prices.

und Rubinstein (1996) compute implicit risk-free interest rates from European put-call parity.[38]

Furthermore, the researcher must choose between various option contracts with different times to expiration and decide on the range of strike prices that will be used to extract risk-neutral probabilities. On the one hand, it makes sense to include as many options as possible, i.e. to work with the complete range of strike prices available. On the other hand, options far out of the money or far in the money are traded less frequently and are less liquid. Therefore, these option prices might contain information of inferior quality compared to the actively traded at-the-money or slightly out-of-the-money options. In addition, often prices for options far away from the money are not supported by trades. For these reasons, many researchers decide to exclude options below and above prespecified upper and lower bounds for moneyness (e.g. Dumas, Fleming, and Whaley (1998, p. 2070) and Jackwerth (2000)).[39] Options significantly out of the money have prices close to zero and might suffer from large relative pricing errors due to the fact that prices of exchange-traded options are quoted in discrete steps (*minimum tick size*) (Bliss and Panigirtzoglou (2002, p. 388) and pp. 418).[40] Therefore, it is recommended to eliminate options with very low prices from the sample.
Similar considerations apply to the problem of deciding on time to expiration. Options with very short time to expiration are not usually traded very actively because trading volume has already shifted into another contract. In addition, while time to expiration decreases, the number of actively traded strike prices declines and the trading volume remaining for this option contract concentrates in an increasingly limited number of strikes at or near the money. Consequently, only a few options contain reliable information. The number of eligible strike prices in some cases becomes too low, so that a number of techniques cannot be applied anymore. Depending on the individual properties of the option contract and the underlying asset, the minimum time to expiration required is often found to be between one month and one week (e.g. Dumas, Fleming, and Whaley (1998, p. 2070) and Nakamura and Shiratsuka (1999, p. 6).).

The appropriate decisions on these issues obviously depend on the nature of the economic problem to be investigated and on the properties of the available data, etc. In some cases additional more specific issues might arise.[41]

[38] As an alternative, Bliss and Panigirtzoglou (2002) suggest computing implied risk-free rates of interest and the implicit price of the underlying simultaneously by minimizing deviations from put-call parity.

[39] Compare also Chang und Melick (1999, p. 6).

[40] The maximum absolute pricing error due to the discrete price notation is half the minimum tick size.

[41] An example is how to deal with bid and ask prices or transaction-based prices (see e.g. Longstaff (1995)).

5.6 Summary

A variety of techniques to extract risk-neutral probabilities from option prices have been discussed and explained in some detail. First, there are techniques that rely on identifying assumptions about the shape of the risk-neutral density function. Most widely used is a mixture approach where the risk-neutral probability density function is assumed to be a mixture of lognormal densities the parameters of which can be estimated from observed option data. Expansion methods model the deviations of the risk-neutral density function from a normal or lognormal reference density. The difference between the risk-neutral probability density function and the reference density is related to the risk-neutral density's skewness and kurtosis that can be estimated from observed option prices. Other approaches are based on maximizing the risk-neutral density's entropy, on minimizing deviations from given prior probabilities, or on estimating a risk-neutral density as smooth as possible, all subject to correctly pricing observed options.
Second, an option-pricing function can be constructed from observed data and the risk-neutral density can be derived by numerical differentiation. It is usually more convenient to construct the option-pricing function from the estimated or interpolated volatility smile than to directly interpolate option prices. Global or local polynomials can be fitted to the volatility smile or non-parametric estimation techniques can be applied.
Third, there are approaches that focus on the stochastic process of the underlying's price. Implied volatility trees as an extension of the binomial option-pricing model are calibrated to observed option prices and yield risk-neutral probabilities from the nodes' Arrow-Debreu prices. Assuming a jump-diffusion model for the underlying's price process, a theoretical option-pricing function and its corresponding risk-neutral density can be derived to estimate the free parameters from observed option prices.

Obviously, the various techniques are very different with respect to the depth of the theoretical foundations and the degree of complexity. On the one hand, there are relatively simple ad-hoc approaches and on the other hand, there are methods based on elaborated theoretical modelling like the Hermite polynomial approximation or the estimation of jump-diffusion parameters.
In applied work (see Chapter 7) the more simple approaches dominate. In particular, the spline estimation of the volatility smile and the mixture approach with lognormal densities are encountered most often with the Hermite polynomial approximation a distant third.

At the end of this chapter some issues relevant to the data-selection and preparation process have been discussed. For example, the data should be checked for arbitrage possibilities that might cause negative risk-neutral probabilities. Another important issue relates to nonsynchronous observations and some ways to alleviate this problem have been discussed. In deciding upon the range of strike prices and the appropriate time to expiration of the options used to estimate risk-neutral probabilities one should be careful to avoid putting too much weight on options containing little reliable information.

Which one of these techniques should be used in our empirical investigation? In order to answer this question we must compare the various techniques with respect to implementation, robustness, and consistency of results.

Appendix 5A: Restrictions to Ensure a Positive Density in the Gram-Charlier Expansion

In order to prevent the coefficients b_3 and b_4 from attaining values that yield negative risk-neutral probabilities, Jondeau and Rockinger (2001) first compute numerically the set of combinations $\{b_3, b_4\}$ for which $q(z)$ is positive. Technically, they let b_4 take on values from 0 to 4 in steps of 10^{-4} and set b_3 equal either to 0 or to 1.3. For each combination they compute the value $q(z)$ for various z in $[-5, 5]$. At the lower boundary of b_3, $q(z)$ is always positive; at the upper boundary it is negative for some z. They then adjust b_3, so that $q(z)$ still has opposite signs for at least one z. Since $q(z)$ is symmetric the algorithm can be limited to positive values of b_3. From this procedure a boundary $D = \{b_3, b_4 | q(z) = 0\}$ is obtained that bounds the combinations of b_3 and b_4 for which $q(z)$ is always positive.

Next, they force the estimates for b_3 and b_4 within the set of admissible values by using the NLS method to estimate the transformed parameter $\tilde{b}_4 = v(\tilde{b}_4; 0, 4)$ instead of b_4 $(0 \leq b_4 \leq 4)$, where

$$v(x, \alpha, \beta) = \alpha + (\beta - \alpha)\frac{e^x}{1 + e^x}.$$

The function $v(x, \alpha, \beta)$ maps the argument x into the interval (α, β), so that b_4 is restricted on $(0, 4)$. Now the corresponding boundary values for b_3 are linearly interpolated where the lower boundary values result from the symmetry of $q(z)$,

$$b_3^u = \frac{b_{3,i}\, b_{4,i+1} - b_{3,i+1}\, b_{4,i}}{b_{4,i+1} - b_{4,i}} + \frac{b_{3,i+1} - b_{3,i}}{b_{4,i+1} - b_{4,i}} k,$$
$$b_3^\ell = -b_3^u,$$

where i, such that $b_{4,i} \leq b_4 < b_{4,i+1}$, $b_{3,i}, b_{3,i+1}$ corresponding to $b_{4,i}, b_{4,i+1}$ and all in the boundary D. Finally, b_3 can be forced into the admissible set by the transformation $b_3 = v(\tilde{b}_3; b_3^\ell, b_3^u)$.

Appendix 5B: Deriving (5.120) and (5.123)[42]

Computing $\nu^{put}_{i-1,j}$ from $P(t_i, K), K = S_{i-1,j}$. At each node above $(i-1, j)$ the put option is worthless because it can never finish in the money, $\nu^{put}_{i-1,k} = 0, k > j$. For nodes below $(i-1, j)$ the put value is

$$\nu^{put}_{i-1,k} = e^{-r_i \Delta t}(p_{i-1,k}\,(K - S_{i,k+1}) + (1 - p_{i-1,k})\,(K - S_{i,k})), \quad k < j.$$

Using the forward price at node $(i-1, k)$,

$$p_{i-1,k}\, S_{i,k+1} + (1 - p_{i-1,k})\, S_{i,k} = e^{r_i \Delta t} S_{i-1,k} - D_i,$$

yields

$$\nu^{put}_{i-1,k} = e^{-r_i \Delta t} K - S_{i-1,k} + e^{-r_i \Delta t} D_i, \quad k < j.$$

The put value $P(t_i, K)$ is the sum of all $\nu^{put}_{i-1,k}$ weighted with the each node's Arrow-Debreu price,

$$\begin{aligned} P(t_i, K) &= \sum_{k=0}^{j} \lambda_{i-1,k}\, \nu^{put}_{i-1,k} \\ &= \sum_{k=0}^{j-1} \lambda_{i-1,k}(e^{-r_i \Delta t} K - S_{i-1,k} + e^{-r_i \Delta t} D_i) + \lambda_{i-1,j}\, \nu^{put}_{i-1,j}. \end{aligned}$$

Solving for $\nu^{put}_{i-1,j}$ yields (5.116)

$$\begin{aligned} \nu^{put}_{i-1,j} &= \frac{P(t_i, K) - \Sigma}{\lambda_{i-1,j}}, \\ \Sigma &= \sum_{k=0}^{j-1} \lambda_{i-1,k}\big(e^{-r_i \Delta t} K - S_{i-1,k} + e^{-r_i \Delta t} D_i\big), \end{aligned}$$

(note: $K = S_{i-1,k}$).

Applying a similar argument to the call option yields

$$\begin{aligned} C(t_i, K) &= \sum_{k=j}^{i} \lambda_{i-1,k}\, \nu^{call}_{i-1,k} \\ &= \sum_{k=j+1}^{i} \lambda_{i-1,k}(S_{i-1,k} - e^{r_i \Delta t} D_i - e^{-r \Delta t} K) + \lambda_{i-1,j}\, \nu^{call}_{i-1,j} \end{aligned}$$

[42] This section follows Chriss (1997, pp. 371-73).

and therefore

$$\nu_{i-1,j}^{call} = \frac{C(t_i, S_{i-1,j}) - \Sigma}{\lambda_{i-1,j}},$$

$$\Sigma = \sum_{k=j+1}^{i} \lambda_{i-1,k}\big(S_{i-1,k} - e^{-r_i \Delta t} D_i - e^{-r_i \Delta t} S_{i-1,j}\big).$$

6

The Advantages and Disadvantages of Selected Techniques

For empirical applications one of the techniques reviewed in Chapter 5 must be selected. In taking this decision an important criterion is whether or not different techniques produce similar results for the risk-neutral density. If this is the case, the choice of technique will not be a major problem but otherwise the results of the application will depend heavily on the approach used. Another relevant issue when choosing between the various approaches relates to implementation problems. Depending on the data set for some techniques, problems are often encountered in the convergence of the optimization algorithm.

Implementation problems described in the literature are discussed in the first section. The second and the third sections compare the techniques with respect to the similarity of their results. First, studies are reviewed that apply different approaches to the same data set and compare the results. Second, robustness studies are discussed that compare the relative performance of the different techniques by means of simulation studies. However, to date the very few existing robustness studies only consider the two most widely used approaches, the mixture of lognormals and the spline-based estimation of the volatility smile.

6.1 Implementation

Very few papers explicitly discuss issues related to implementation in the context of the mixture-of-lognormals approach.

In some applications of this technique convergence problems occur and the global minimum is not attained. This problem is particularly relevant for interest-rate option data (Coutant, Jondeau, and Rockinger (2001), McManus (1999)). In contrast, expansion methods generally converge relatively fast. If

convergence problems are encountered, Jondeau and Rockinger (1999) recommend using parameter restrictions, e.g. a logistic transformation, to prevent the estimation algorithm from entering regions where it diverges. In addition, they suggest fixing a subset of parameters on a grid for a preliminary estimation. After that, all parameters can be estimated unrestricted using the preliminary estimates as starting values. This method is particularly useful for the mixture-of-lognormals approach because there a weight close to one is often assigned to only one lognormal component in the estimation. If this occurs, the other lognormal components often degenerate and are estimated with a variance approaching zero because their parameters retain only a negligible influence on the objective function. Fixing the weights on a grid avoids this problem in most cases (see Jondeau and Rockinger (2000)).
The objective function for the mixture-of-lognormals approach sometimes turns out to have multiple minima. In this situation Jondeau and Rockinger (2000) recommend fixing additional parameters on a grid and experimenting with different starting values. Furthermore, they restrict the admissible range for the μ_i parameters by a logistic transformation. Melick and Thomas (1998) point out that it is often necessary to place constraints upon the standard deviations of the individual lognormal components. If the standard deviation of one of the lognormal densities becomes too small relative to the space between adjacent strike prices, all probability mass falls between just two neighbouring strikes. Since the technique cannot discriminate between alternative density functions that feature the same probability mass and the same expected value between two neighbouring exercise prices, the mixture parameters are not identified if the standard deviation is too small.
Estimations with the maximum-entropy approach also converge very slowly in some applications, e.g. for interest-rate options (see McManus (1999, p. 19)). For the Rubinstein (1994) method Campa, Chang, and Reider (1998) note implausibly high probabilities resulting for the extreme tails of the risk-neutral density and recommend ignoring these in computing distributional statistics. Jackwerth and Rubinstein (1996) show that the choice of the prior density strongly affects the convergence of the estimated probabilities. Specifying a uniform prior instead of a lognormal one considerably slows down the estimation. However, the resulting risk-neutral probabilities turn out to be very similar for both priors.

Techniques that derive the risk-neutral density from numerically differentiating call-option prices also are burdened by some problems. First, numerically computed second-order derivatives are known to be unstable (e.g. Jondeau and Rockinger (2001)). Second, the option prices to be differenced are derived from an estimated volatility smile the shape of which is partially dependent on the selected model. From the estimated volatility smile the effects of the chosen technique carry over to option prices and from there to the risk-neutral density. Any effect of the technique used to model the volatility smile that affects the option-pricing function's curvature might be magnified by the computational instability of numerical second-order derivatives. Among the process-based approaches, experience with estimating the parameters of jump-diffusion models indicates problems in identifying the jump parameters if the jumps are only infrequently observed and therefore the risk-neutral density is close to a lognormal (McManus (1999, p. 19)).

Even if the same technique is applied to the same data set, the results might differ across applications because most approaches rely on constrained nonlinear optimization techniques and small differences in the optimization algorithms lead to significantly altered results, particularly when complex functions are estimated as in many of the approaches discussed (see McCollough and Vinod (1999)).

6.2 Comparing the Results

Many studies compare the estimated risk-neutral density to a risk-neutral density based on the Black-Scholes formula or on one of its modifications, i.e. a lognormal density. This is done to demonstrate that the technique used to construct the risk-neutral density is able to produce results that could not have been derived in the benchmark case of the Black-Scholes formula.

Melick and Thomas (1997) compare a risk-neutral density for crude-oil futures estimated as a mixture of three lognormal densities to a single lognormal. Despite almost identical expected values they find substantial differences in various conditional expected values and in the probability of extreme price increases. The simple lognormal density leads to an underpricing of out-of-the-money calls and in-the-money puts relative to the mixture density. They show that the risk-neutral density is multimodal on some days, a property that cannot be replicated by a single lognormal probability density.[1]
Levin, McManus, and Watt (1998) in an application for Canadian-dollar futures options compare the mixture-of-lognormals model to a single lognormal density and find important differences. The mixture approach yields a higher standard deviation for the risk-neutral density and very different results for skewness and kurtosis statistics. Leahy and Thomas (1996) using Canadian-dollar futures options find much lower mean-squared pricing errors for a mixture of three lognormal densities than for only one lognormal.
McManus (1999) estimates risk-neutral probabilities for Eurodollar futures using a mixture of two lognormal densities, a jump-diffusion model, a Hermite polynomial approximation and the method of maximum entropy. He compares

[1] Multimodal risk-neutral densities often occur if there is considerable uncertainty among market participants and if their expectations can be described by two or more very different scenarios or regimes, see Cont (1999) and Campa, Chang, and Reider (1998).

the results to the single lognormal density from Black's (1976) futures-options-pricing model. All techniques lead to lower deviations of theoretical from observed option prices and exhibit standard deviations, skewness and kurtosis strongly different from the single lognormal.[2] Similar results are documented by Jondeau and Rockinger (2000) for French franc/D-Mark options. They consider, among others, the mixture-of-lognormals approach, Hermite polynomial approximation, the Edgeworth approximation and two process-based techniques. Jackwerth and Rubinstein (1996) find important differences between the results from the single lognormal model and those from various approaches that are based on prior probabilities using alternative types of objective functions. A Burr III distribution is considered by Sherrick, Garcia, and Tirupattur (1996) for soybean futures. Their estimated pricing errors are always smaller than those for a single lognormal distribution. Bates (2000) compares the pricing errors resulting from a stochastic volatility model with jumps to those from the Black-Scholes formula and from a deterministic volatility specification and finds the stochastic volatility model superior.
In applications of expansion methods to S&P 500 index options Corrado and Su (1996a, 1997) present smaller estimated pricing errors for the Edgeworth expansion and the Gram-Charlier expansion relative to the Black-Scholes formula. Coutant (1999) investigates the Hermite polynomial approximation for CAC40 options where the resulting risk-neutral density has a larger standard deviation than the lognormal benchmark.
Aït-Sahalia and Lo (1998) explicitly test the risk-neutral density against the benchmark lognormal within their nonparametric approach and find the lognormal to be rejected.

Also of interest are comparisons of the results derived from different techniques using the same set of option prices. Levin, McManus, and Watt (1998) estimate risk-neutral probabilities from Canadian-dollar futures options using the mixture of two lognormals and a deterministic volatility model (see 5.3.5). They show the resulting risk-neutral densities to have only slightly different appearances. Jackwerth and Rubinstein (1996) arrive at similar conclusions considering different types of objective functions in an approach based on prior probabilities. The density functions are very similar at the money but strong differences are found in the tails. McManus (1999) presents both similarities and strong differences in risk-neutral densities estimated from Eurodollar futures options. Particularly, the method of maximum entropy does not lead to a smooth density and often produces negative probabilities in the extreme tails. The smallest mean-squared pricing error is found for the mixture of two lognormal densities followed by the Hermite polynomial approximation and

[2] Generally, it is not possible to test for significant differences between the distributional statistics from various approaches because performing statistical tests in most cases contradicts some basic assumptions made by the option-pricing models. For details see Bates (1996a, p. 587) and Clement, Gourieroux, and Montfort (2000).

a jump-diffusion model. Generally, the mixture density and the density from the jump-diffusion model exhibit higher standard deviations than those derived from the Hermite polynomial approximation and from the method of maximum entropy. No clear ranking emerges for higher moments where considerable changes from day to day are encountered.

Jondeau and Rockinger (2000) study French franc/D-Mark options with similar results. The standard deviations from the Hermite polynomial approximation, the Edgeworth expansion, the mixture of lognormals, a jump diffusion model and a stochastic volatility model are close to each other. However, moments of higher order differ strongly. Looking at the graphs of the risk-neutral densities shows very close results for both expansion methods. In contrast to the other approaches, the stochastic volatility model produces only a slightly asymmetrical and strongly leptokurtic risk-neutral density. Jondeau and Rockinger (2000) argue that the stochastic volatility model is unable to capture the asymmetry present in the option prices and transforms it into a higher kurtosis.[3] The authors compute bands containing 95% probability mass from the risk-neutral densities and show them to be roughly equal for most models with the exception of the stochastic volatility model. Coutant, Jondeau, and Rockinger (2001) using PIBOR options study the results from different techniques and find the estimated standard deviations to be very similar while moments of higher order exhibit large differences. As previously, the maximum-entropy approach produces a risk-neutral density with many spikes.

Campa, Chang, and Reider (1998) compare risk-neutral densities computed as a mixture of lognormals, by estimating the volatility smile with a cubic spline and by the approach of Rubinstein (1994) for various exchange rates (US dollar/D-Mark, US dollar/Japanese yen, British pound/D-Mark, D-Mark/French franc, D-Mark/Italian lira). The standard deviation from the spline approach is lower than that from the other techniques and large differences are present in moments of higher order.

Melick (1999) asks a number of researchers to estimate risk-neutral densities from Eurodollar futures options using their favorite technique. Among the methods applied are the estimation of the volatility smile, the mixture of lognormals, jump-diffusion models and the approach suggested by Neuhaus (1995). Each participant was asked to compute the expected value, the median and eleven percentiles of the risk-neutral density. Melick (1999) compares these results and finds considerable divergence in percentiles of very low and very high order while percentiles of medium order turn out to be very close to each other across all methods. This results from the lack of information on the tails of the risk-neutral density due to the limited range of observed strike prices, so that the extreme tails depend strongly on assumptions implicit in the chosen technique (see Melick (1999, p. 3)).

---

[3] However, some problems in correctly estimating the skewness in the risk-neutral density are found for the expansion methods, too.

This survey makes clear that the different methods pick up deviations in the risk-neutral probability density function from the lognormal benchmark, i.e. from the Black/Scholes-Merton model. However, moments of higher order differ strongly across the methods. These differences often go unnoticed by visual inspection because even very small deviations in the tail probabilities can translate into large discrepancies between high-order moments. Since the choice of technique has relatively strong effects on the shape of the risk-neutral density's tails, one should not rely exclusively on statistics based on the extreme tail probabilities. Furthermore, the maximum-entropy method emerges as a technique that tends to produce 'spiked' density functions.

6.3 Robustness

Bliss and Panigirtzoglou (2002), Cooper (1999), and Söderlind (2000) examine how robust selected techniques are for extracting risk-neutral probabilities from option prices. Since the interpretation of risk-neutral probabilities is focussed on changes, particularly on changes in statistics computed from the density, it is important that these changes are caused by market participants revising their expectations. If the risk-neutral density function were very sensitive to measurement errors in observed option prices, the information content in changes in risk-neutral probabilities would be diminished. Most robustness studies rely on Monte Carlo methods. Resampling approaches like the bootstrap are much less suitable because in most cases only a very limited number of observed option prices is available.

Söderlind (2000) estimates the risk-neutral density as a mixture of lognormal densities using interest-rate options. He simulates 100 data sets with theoretical option and forward prices using the estimated parameters. Theoretical prices then are modified either by a normally distributed random variable with expectation zero and variance equal to the variance of the pricing errors in the first estimation (Monte Carlo approach) or they are directly drawn from the option-price residuals (bootstrap). From the simulated data sets risk-neutral probability density functions are estimated and for each the 95% and 5% percentiles computed. Söderlind (2000) constructs confidence bands for the 95% and 5% percentiles of the risk-neutral density and finds them to differ only by a few basis points so that some confidence can be had in his estimated percentiles.

Cooper (1999) performs a Monte Carlo analysis in order to compare the mixture approach with two lognormal densities to the cubic-spline estimation of the volatility smile. His focus is on the effects of measurement errors in option prices.[4] He constructs artificial option prices using the stochastic volatility

[4] The objective function for the mixture model does not contain the martingale restriction.

model of Heston (1993). Six data sets are created with alternative volatility (high/low) and skewness characteristics (strongly negative, weakly positive, strongly positive). For each scenario the artificial data set consists of theoretical option prices with time to expiration of one month, three months, and six months and strike prices in steps of one unit of currency. Finally, theoretical prices are distorted by a univariate random variable on the interval $[-0.025; 0.025]$ that captures the effects of a minimum tick size equal to 0.5. 100 artificial data sets of each type are constructed and from each a risk-neutral density is extracted using both techniques. The relative performance of the alternative methods is evaluated by comparing the mean values of various statistics to their theoretical values in the option-pricing model. In addition, for each statistic percentiles are computed using the empirical distribution function.
For all scenarios and times to expiration, the mean deviations of the expected value and of the standard deviation are marginally smaller for the smile-based approach. No clear ranking is possible for the moment-based skewness and kurtosis statistics. With respect to the standard deviations of the statistics relative to their true values the mixture approach is inferior to the spline-based method for almost all scenarios and times to expiration. Therefore, Cooper (1999) concludes that the mixture of lognormals yields more unstable results compared to the spline estimation of the volatility smile. In particular if volatility is low and skewness is either strongly positive or strongly negative mean-squared deviations from the true values are much larger for the lognormal mixture. In order to investigate this issue in some detail Cooper (1999) focusses on the scenario with low volatility and strongly positive skewness and compares the shape of the risk-neutral densities as estimated by the two techniques to the theoretical one. It turns out that particularly for short time to expiration the mixture of lognormal densities exhibits considerable variability and in many cases 'spikes' appear, i.e. the variance of one of the lognormal components collapses towards zero. Furthermore, some density functions estimated with the mixture technique deviate considerably in skewness from the theoretical density. For longer times to expiration 'spiked' densities are encountered less often, but the performance of this model is still inferior to the spline based technique. Cooper (1999) concludes that the mixture approach is more sensitive to measurement errors in option prices that lead to considerable deviations of the estimated from the theoretical risk-neutral density.

Neuhaus (1999) points out that the artificial data sets constructed by Cooper (1999) are "too complete". He argues that strike prices are spaced too densely so that the artificial data sets contain cross sections with a much larger number of options than are actually available. Particularly if time to expiration is very short only a very small number of actively traded strike prices for a given option contract can be obtained. In his opinion, the much more densely populated data sets used by Cooper (1999) tend to favor the smile-based approach because interpolation there is much easier while, on the other hand, one of the advantages of the mixture approach is found in applications where only a very small number of option prices is observed. The superior performance of the smile approach then could be attributed to the fact that only small errors in implied volatility are caused by the pricing errors that are easily smoothed away in the estimation of the volatility smile from the dense set of observations. In addition, Bliss and Panigirtzoglou (2002) point out that within the smile-based approach the effect of a specific measurement error is confined to a small section on the estimated volatility smile. For the lognormal mixture, however, any measurement error affects the whole estimated density (see Bliss and Panigirtzoglou (2002), p. 407).[5]

Bliss and Panigirtzoglou (2002) criticize robustness studies based on artificial option prices generated by assuming a particular risk-neutral density because the properties of the theoretical density might favor one of the techniques to be compared. The important objective is not to extract risk-neutral densities of a specific type but to select a technique that is applicable to a wide range of density functions that might be encountered in applied work. Since in reality the correct risk-neutral density is not known, simulation results derived from a particular assumption for the risk-neutral probability density function are not useful. In addition, they argue that artificial data sets generated from a specific option-pricing model exhibit an unrealistic degree of smoothness. Even if some random pricing errors are introduced, this feature might lead to a convergence pattern in estimation that is different from the one encountered in applied work. They admit that adding estimated pricing errors to theoretical option prices as in Söderlind (2000) alleviates this problem but in reality pricing errors are not necessarily independently distributed and homoskedastic. They therfore suggest relying on observed instead of model based data and generating artificial option prices by adding small pricing errors to *observed* option prices.

They select two data sets consisting of settlement prices observed on the London International Financial Futures Exchange (LIFFE) in 1997 for FTSE 100 index options and options on a short sterling interest rate. Like Cooper (1999), they compare the mixture approach with two lognormal densities to the spline estimation of the volatility smile. From both samples they construct 100 artificial data sets by adding or subtracting a uniformly distributed error term with a maximum absolute value equal to half of the minimum tick size. Risk-neutral densities are then estimated for all days and various times to expiration using both approaches. Statistics are computed from the estimated densities and their changes from day to day are investigated.

Inspection of the estimation results for the original data shows that day-to-day changes in the statistics are greater for the mixture approach, while the means

[5] Furthermore, Neuhaus (1999) criticizes that the artificial data sets are not checked for arbitrage violations that might be caused by the added error terms.

and the standard deviations of the statistics differ only slightly.[6] Therefore, small changes in option prices appear to have more pronounced effects within the mixture-of-lognormals approach. In addition, the changes in the statistics computed by the two alternative techniques are only weakly correlated so that the two approaches might yield different results in empirical applications.
The authors also compare the results for the simulated data by computing standard deviations and percentiles for the various statistics considered. It turns out that percentile ranges from risk-neutral densities are robust with respect to small errors in option prices as long as the percentiles involved are not of too high or too low order, i.e. do not fall into the extreme tails of the density. Percentiles from the smile-based approach are more robust than those computed with the lognormal mixture. The standard deviations of the statistics are up to 100 times larger for the mixture than for the smile-based approach.[7] These results are strengthened by the generally much wider confidence intervals for the statistics computed from the mixture of lognormals. Particularly, for skewness and kurtosis the confidence intervals for the mixture approach are often much larger than the average daily changes in these statistics. The results for the FTSE 100 options are not as strong as those for the interest-rate options but only for very few statistics is the confidence interval small relative to daily observed changes.[8]

6.4 Summary

For some of the techniques discussed in Chapter 5 considerable convergence problems have been noted in the literature. Particularly, the mixture approach with lognormal densities often has difficulties in attaining the global optimum. Imposing appropriate parameter restrictions and fixing some parameters on a grid alleviates these problems. Furthermore, parameter restrictions are often necessary to prevent the standard deviation of one of the lognormal components from collapsing towards zero.
The method of maximum entropy also often converges very slowly while the speed of convergence in the method of Rubinstein (1994) depends on the selection of the prior density. Techniques that derive the risk-neutral density by numerical differentiation might suffer from the well-known instability of numerical derivatives.

All the different techniques yield risk-neutral densities that differ strongly from a lognormal density. While graphically risk-neutral densities appear to

[6] The day-to-day changes for the smile approach relate to the instability of deterministic volatility functions discussed in Dumas, Fleming, and Whaley (1998).

[7] This result still holds if the statistics are adjusted for outliers.

[8] Bliss and Panigirtzoglou (2002) experiment with different weighting schemes in the objective function for the smile-based approach but conclude that these do not significantly influence the results.

be very close to each other, statistics based on moments of order three or higher exhibit vast differences across the various approaches. Similar results are obtained for percentiles. While percentiles of medium order do not differ much, the various approaches estimate very heterogeneous percentiles of very high and very low order because the tails of the risk-neutral density depend more strongly on the choice of technique than the center region.

There are only very few simulation studies on the robustness of techniques to extract risk-neutral probabilities from option prices. In these, the mixture-of-lognormals approach is compared to the spline-based estimation of the volatility smile. Overall, the results indicate that the lognormal mixture is less robust with respect to small measurement errors in option prices than the smile-based technique. This inferiority in particular applies to moments of higher order and percentiles located in the density's tails where small changes in option prices can induce comparatively large changes in the statistics computed from the risk-neutral density. Observed changes in these types of statistics must therefore be interpreted carefully.

These results suggest selecting the spline-interpolation technique for our own empirical studies. In addition, we should be careful in interpreting higher-order moments and other statistics that depend on the risk-neutral densities' extreme tails. Finally, the presence of large fluctuations in the statistics that might be caused purely by measurement errors in option prices requires the development of a methodology to separate changes that are economically significant from this 'noise' component. These issues will play an important role in the empirical studies presented in Chapters 8 and 9.

Part II

Empirical Applications

7

Important Empirical Applications - A Review

In this chapter we review the most important applications of techniques to extract market expectations from option prices. First, some studies on market expectations with regard to exchange rates will be discussed. Specifically, we shall concentrate on a number of studies focussing on the credibility of fixed-exchange-rate regimes. We shall then review empirical applications with regard to market expectations about future interest rates and stock indices. Finally, we shall discuss the results of applications that provide some insight into market participant's risk preferences by exploiting the relationship between the risk-neutral and the true conditional density.

7.1 Exchange Rates

Campa and Chang (1996) investigate the credibility of exchange-rate bands in the European Monetary System (EMS) by computing risk-neutral realignment intensities from the risk-neutral probability density function. They define the risk-neutral realignment intensity as the conditional expectation for the exchange rate being above the upper band ($\bar{S}$) at the options' expiration,[1]

$$R_t = \int_{\bar{S}}^{\infty} (S_t - \bar{S}) q(S_t) dS_t. \tag{7.1}$$

Obviously, the risk-neutral realignment intensity is proportional to the value of a European-type call option with strike price $\bar{S}$,

$$R_t = e^{r(T-t)} C(S_t, K = \bar{S}). \tag{7.2}$$

[1] They make the implicit assumption that a realignment only takes place if the exchange rate exceeds the upper band.

Since in most cases a call option with an exercise price exactly equal to $\bar{S}$ is not available, the authors use an interpolation technique to compute the risk-neutral realignment intensity. Campa and Chang (1995) assume the lower exchange rate band $\underline{S}$ to be completely credible. From a given option price with $\underline{S} \leq K \leq \bar{S}$ they derive a lower bound on the risk-neutral realignment intensity.

The value of a European-type call option with exercise price K can be written as

$$
\begin{aligned}
C(S_t, K) &= e^{-r(T-t)} \int_0^\infty \max[S_T - K, 0]\, q(S_T)\, dS_T \\
&= e^{-r(T-t)} \int_{\underline{K}}^\infty (S_T - K)\, q(S_T)\, dS_T \qquad (7.3) \\
&= e^{-r(T-t)} \left[\int_{\bar{S}}^\infty (S_T - \bar{S}) q(S_T)\, dS_T + \int_{\bar{S}}^\infty (\bar{S} - K)\, q(S_T)\, dS_T \right. \\
&\quad \left. + \int_K^{\bar{S}} (S_T - K)\, q(S_T)\, dS_T \right].
\end{aligned}
$$

The first term in brackets is the risk-neutral realignment intensity. Since

$$
\begin{aligned}
&\int_K^{\bar{S}} (S_T - K)\, q(S_T)\, dS_T + \int_{\bar{S}}^\infty (\bar{S} - K)\, q(S_T)\, dS_T \qquad (7.4) \\
&\leq (\bar{S} - K) \int_K^{\bar{S}} q(S_T)\, dS_T \int_{\bar{S}}^\infty (\bar{S} - K)\, q(S_T)\, dS_T = (\bar{S} - K)(1 - Q(K)),
\end{aligned}
$$

(7.3) can be solved for R_t,

$$
R_t \geq C(S_t, K)\, e^{r(T-t)} - (\bar{S} - K)(1 - Q(K)). \qquad (7.5)
$$

If the lower band is fully credible the value of a European-type put option with exercise price K is

$$
\begin{aligned}
P(S_t, K) &= e^{-r(T-t)} \int_{\underline{S}}^K (K - S_T)\, q(S_T)\, dS_T \qquad (7.6) \\
&\leq e^{-r(T-t)} (K - \underline{S}) \int_{\underline{S}}^K q(S_T)\, dS_T = e^{-r(T-t)}\, (K - \underline{S})\, Q(K),
\end{aligned}
$$

i.e.

$$1 - Q(K) \leq 1 - e^{r(T-t)} \frac{P(S_t, K)}{K - \underline{S}}, \tag{7.7}$$

so that the minimum risk-neutral realignment intensity can be derived from (7.5)using the European put-call parity.

$$R_t \geq C(S_t, K)\, e^{r(T-t)} - \left[\frac{\bar{S} - K}{K - \underline{S}}\right] + [F_t - \underline{S} - C(S_t, K)], \tag{7.8}$$

where F_t is the forward price with time to expiration equal to $T - t$.[2]

Campa und Chang (1996) compute minimum risk-neutral realignment intensities for the Italian lira, British pound, and French franc against the D-Mark from September 1991 to August 1994 from daily data on OTC options with times to expiration of three and four months. They focus on the period before the EMS crisis in September 1992. At the beginning of this period minimum risk-neutral realignment intensities for the lira are at about one percent of the central EMS-parity (a result of zero would indicate full credibility of the upper band). Over the four months leading up to the lira's exit from the EMS minimum risk-neutral realignment intensities rise strongly to about 4.5 percent. For the British pound the final weeks before leaving the EMS also show large minimum risk-neutral realignment intensities of 6 to 8 percent. For the French franc, however, the values always are below 2 percent.[3]

For various periods from 1991 to 1995 Campa und Chang (1998c) obtain minimum risk-neutral realignment intensities for the Italian lira, British pound, French franc and Spanish peseta against the D-Mark. They regress the realignment intensities on selected macroeconomic variables and conclude that these 'fundamentals' can only explain a very moderate amount of variability in realignment intensities. A real appreciation against the D-Mark tends to increase the minimum risk-neutral realignment intensity as does an increase in the monetary base relative to Germany. Inflation, output growth, and trade deficit relative to Germany have no significant effects. Campa, Chang, and Refalo (2002) perform a similar analysis for the Brazil *real* plan using

[2] If only call-option prices for strike prices above $\bar{S}$ are observed, (7.6) yields a maximum risk-neutral realignment intensity. The minimum risk-neutral realignment intensity for $K \geq \bar{S}$ is $C(S_t, K)e^{r(T-t)}$. See Campa and Chang (1996, p. 735).

[3] The authors also compute maximum risk-neutral realignment intensities as $C(S_t, K)e^{r(T-t)}, K < \bar{S}$. These turn out to be considerably above the minimum risk-neutral realignment intensities for the lira/D-Mark exchange rate. For the pound/D-Mark and the franc/D-Mark exchange rate, however, the maximum and minimum risk-neutral realignment intensities are close to each other. See Campa und Chang (1996, p. 736). In the paper, additional arbitrage-based tests of EMS credibility are considered but these tests do not explicitly rely on risk-neutral probabilities.

data on exchange traded real/US dollar options from July 1994 to July 1997. They regress risk-neutral minimum realignment intensities on various macro variables and find only monetary growth, the trade deficit, and central bank reserves to be significant in explaining minimum risk-neutral realignment intensities. They also compute risk-neutral probability density functions for the Real/US-Dollar exchange rate by fitting a spline function to the volatility smile and find evidence for increasing skewness and declining kurtosis. They show that the probability of a 2- or 5-percent devaluation declined over time, i.e. that the credibility of the exchange rate regime increased.

The data set considered in Campa, Chang, and Reider (1998) consists of weekly observations (April - December 1996) on OTC options on the exchange rates of Italian lira, British pound, French franc, Spanish peseta, Portugese escudo, Finnmark, Danish krona, and Swedish krona against the D-Mark with time to expiration of one, three, and six months. From these option prices the authors compute minimum risk-neutral realignment intensities for hypothetical exchange-rate bands. They do not rely on (7.8) but compute $R_t = e^{r(T-t)}C(S_t, K = \bar{S})$ from the risk-neutral probability density function constructed from a spline function fitted to the volatility smile. In addition to the minimum risk-neutral realignment intensities they compute the narrowest bands containing 90 or 95% probability mass of the risk-neutral density. They show that these bands are much wider for currencies that (re-) entered the EMS shortly before (lira and Finnmark) or that were still outside the EMS compared to those for the other EMS members. Inspection of these bands' behavior over time shows them to be relatively stable except for the British pound.

Söderlind (2000) estimates risk-neutral density functions for short- and long-term British interest rates, the Euromark rate and the British pound/D-Mark exchange rate using the bivariate lognormal mixture approach of Söderlind and Svensson (1998). He tracks the evolution of the 5% and 95% percentiles from June to November 1992 and investigates the evolution of market expectations during the EMS crises. The percentiles diverge steadily from the futures price from July to August 1992 indicating rising uncertainty among market participants. The expected values show that the market anticipated a devaluation of the pound and rising British interest rates. The author interpretes this result as showing that market participants expected a moderate exchange-rate realignment. The risk-neutral densities do not provide any evidence that the market anticipated the Pound's exit from the EMS. In fact, this event led to large increases in the percentile rangees (5% to 95%) for the pound and the interest rates indicating a sustained increase in uncertainty that was reversed only very slowly.

Malz (1996a, 1998c) estimates the parameters of a jump-diffusion model from OTC data on one-month risk-reversals and strangles on the British pound/D-Mark exchange rate (May - October 1992). He finds the product λk, i.e. the expected jump in the exchange rate to be close to zero at the beginning but to rise considerably at the end of August. Malz (1996a) computes the risk-neutral probability for the pound below the lower EMS band at the options' expiration by (5.135) and points to a rise in devaluation expectations beginning in August.[4]

Malz (1997) fits a quadratic function to implied volatilities (see section 5.3.1) obtained from prices of risk reversals and strangles on the exchange rates between US dollar, British pound, D-Mark and Japanese yen (March to June 1996). He computes skewness and kurtosis statistics and uses these variables in a regression analysis of the forward-bias puzzle. He shows skewness and excess kurtosis to contribute significantly to the explanation of exchange-rate excess returns.[5]. In a related paper, Malz (1996a) regresses the forward premium on the skewness variable in order to test whether the forward bias is related to a peso problem, i.e. to asymmetries in the risk-neutral density. Only for the US dollar/D-Mark exchange rate can some evidence be found for a statistically significant relationship between skewness and the forward premium.[6]

Galati and Melick (2002) use risk-neutral densities to study the effects of central-bank interventions in the foreign-exchange market. The risk-neutral density function is estimated as a mixture of two lognormal densities using daily OTC option data on the Japanese yen/US dollar exchange rate from September 1993 to April 1996. The authors regress moments computed from the risk-neutral probability density function on some control variables and a dummy variable indicating whether market participants perceived a central-bank intervention. The dummy variable is constructed from a probit model of the reaction functions of the Fed and the Bank of Japan. While the risk-neutral densities' expected value and skewness are unaffected by the intervention dummy, it has a significant positive effect on the density's variance, i.e. perceived interventions seem to increase uncertainty in the yen/US dollar market.

In addition to these studies that use risk-neutral probabilities as a starting point for detailed econometric investigations there are a number of event studies for exchange rates where changes in risk-neutral probabilities are tracked over short time periods at the occurrence of some important event. Since these studies require a much more careful interpretation and rely more strongly on subjective judgements on the part of the researcher we will only review some important examples.

---

[4] Malz (1996b) performs a similar analysis for the French Franc/German Mark exchange rate.

[5] See Malz (1997, p. 21) for details on the interpretation.

[6] Malz (1997) also finds the forward premium to be insufficient to compensate an investor for the jump risk implicit in risk-neutral expectations. See Malz (1997, p. 23).

Levin, McManus, and Watt (1998) study the evolution of expectations about the Canadian dollar/US dollar exchange rate using the mixture-of-lognormals approach. They focus on short time periods around the publication of the Bank of Canada's *Monetary Policy Report*, on some selected events during the Mexican peso crisis in 1995 and on the Asian financial crisis. Their results suggest that the information in the *Monetary Policy Report* has a greater impact on expectations if it signals a policy change. For the currency crises they obtain a similar result: market expectations react more strongly to unanticipated policy changes than to anticipated ones.
Leahy and Thomas (1996) investigate changes in market participants' expectations about the Canadian dollar exchange rate in the run up to the Quebec independence referendum in October 1995. Using the lognormal mixture technique they present some evidence for a high level of uncertainty about the referendum results and show that the risk-neutral density on the day immediately preceding the referendum can be interpreted as a combination of three different scenarios.
Cooper and Talbot (1998) apply the technique suggested by Malz (1998b) (fitting a quadratic function in *delta* to the volatility smile) to Japanese yen/US dollar options on selected dates in 1998. Their results indicate that the yen's appreciation was mostly unexpected and that interventions by the Fed and the Bank of Japan in April and June did not have significant effects on the risk-neutral probabilities for large changes in the yen/dollar exchange rate.
Jondeau and Rockinger (2000) study how market expectations about the French franc/D-Mark exchange rate reacted to selected political events in 1996 and 1997.

7.2 Interest Rates

Nakamura and Shiratsuka (1999) analyze changes in market expectations about Japanese government bond futures using the method of Neuhaus (1995). They study the evolution of distributional statistics over long time periods between 1989 and 1996 and set out to highlight specific characteristics in time series for various moments and look for systematic comovements between the risk-neutral densities of the government bond futures and the Nikkei 225.
In an event study, McManus (1999) uses various techniques to examine changes in market expectations with respect to future three-month Eurodollar rates at the time of Federal Open Market Committee meetings in September 1998. Bahra (1997) uses the lognormal mixture approach to study changes in interest-rate expectations related to the publication of the Bank of England's *Inflation Report* in May 1996, to the announcement of money growth figures by the Bundesbank on February, 23, 1996 and to the interest-rate decrease by the Bank of England on June, 06, 1996.
A variant of the Söderlind and Svensson (1998) bivariate lognormal mixture

approach is applied to Italian interest-rate options by Fornari and Violi (1998). They focus on the lira's exit from the EMS in 1992 and on some other events related to Italian monetary policy. In particular, they show that the EMS crisis coincides with rapidly and drastically changing risk-neutral expectations. Adão and Luís (1999) use risk-neutral probabilities on short-term interest rates to shed some light on the question of interest-rate convergence between Spain, Italy, and Germany in the run up to EMU. Their results indicate that market participants expected a faster convergence of Spanish to German rates than of Italian to German rates and that after June 1998 both Spanish and Italian interest rates were expected to converge further towards the German levels.

In another event study, Coutant, Jondeau, and Rockinger (2001) study the evolution of market expectations about French short (PIBOR) and long-term interest rates against the backdrop of snap elections in France in the summer of 1997. Using the Hermite polynomial approximation technique they find some evidence that market participants anticipated the calling of the snap election and that uncertainty increased after polls suggested a change in government.

7.3 Stock Indices

Gemmill and Saflekos (1999) model the risk-neutral density implicit in FTSE 100 index options as a mixture of two lognormal densities. They estimate risk-neutral probability density functions for some selected dates around the 1987 crash, the 1989 mini crash, the 1992 EMS crisis and the Asian financial crisis and cannot find any evidence for market participants anticipating these events. In addition, the inspection of skewness and kurtosis variables at times of crises does not convey any consistent impression. They also extract market expectations for some days just before British parliamentary elections in 1987, 1992 and 1997 and show that often bimodal risk-neutral densities appear shortly before election day.

Bates (1991) estimates the parameters of a jump-diffusion model from S&P index option prices observed in 1985 to 1987. The estimated jump parameters show that the risk-neutral expected value of a downward jump in the index level started to increase one year before the 1987 crash. However, these crash fears disappeared in the last two months preceding the crash only to return some time after the crash.

7.4 Risk Aversion

As discussed before (see Chapters 2 and 4) the risk-neutral density results from the interaction of the 'true' density and market participant's risk preferences. Aït-Sahalia and Lo (2000) discuss how this relationship can be used to obtain an empirical estimate of the market participants' risk-aversion. Their analysis is based on the dynamic equilibrium approach by Merton (1971) where a representative agent maximizes utility by deciding how much of his wealth W to invest in a risk-free bond and how much to invest in a risky stock where the stock price follows a geometric Brownian motion. The optimization problem is

$$\begin{aligned} \max_{\{x_S \mid t \le s \le T\}} \quad & \mathbf{E}[U(W_T)] \\ \text{s.t.} \quad & dW_s = \{rW_s + x_S\,(\mu(S_s, s) - r)\}\,ds + x_S\,\sigma(S_s, s)\,dB_s, \\ & W_s \ge 0, \qquad t \le s \le T, \end{aligned} \tag{7.9}$$

where μ and σ are the constant drift and volatility parameters of the stock-price process and x_S is the share of wealth in stocks. The first-order conditions are

$$\frac{\partial J(W_s, S_s, s)}{\partial W} = e^{-r(s-t)} \frac{\partial J(W_t, S_t, t)}{\partial W} \zeta_s, \tag{7.10}$$

where $J(W_s, S_s, s)$ is the representative agent's indirect utility function. The boundary condition is

$$U'(W_T) = e^{-r(T-t)} U'(W_t)\,\zeta_T, \tag{7.11}$$

where,

$$\zeta_s = \exp\left\{ \int_t^s \left(\frac{\mu(S_u, u) - r}{\sigma(S_u, u)} \right) dB_u - \frac{1}{2} \int_t^s \left(\frac{\mu(S_u, u) - r}{\sigma(S_u, u)} \right)^2 du \right\}. \tag{7.12}$$

The price of an asset with payoff $g(W_T)$ results in this model as

$$V_t = \mathbf{E}_t[g(W_T)\,M_{t,T}], \tag{7.13}$$

with $M_{t,T} = U'(W_T)/U'(W_t)$ as the stochastic discount factor or the marginal rate of substitution between t and T. Define the risk-neutral density (*state-price density*) as

$$q_t(S_T) = f_t(S_T) \cdot \mathbf{E}[\zeta_T | S_t, S_T] = f_t(S_T)\zeta_T, \tag{7.14}$$

it follows from (7.11)-(7.14) with $W_T = S_T$,[7]

[7] In equilibrium the representative agents' wealth consists entirely of stocks at each point in time so that consumption in T must be equal to S_T, i.e. $W_T = S_T = C_T$. See Aït-Sahalia and Lo (2000, p. 24).

$$\mathbf{E}_t[g(W_T)M_{t,T}] = \int_0^\infty g(W_T)\frac{U'(W_T)}{U'(W_t)} f_t(S_T), dW_T$$
$$= e^{-r(T-t)} \int_0^\infty g(W_T)\, q_t(S_T)\, dW_T \tag{7.15}$$
$$= e^{-r(T-t)} \mathbf{E}_Q[g(W_T)].$$

From (7.14) it can be seen that ζ_T is proportional to the agent's marginal rate of substitution,

$$\zeta_T \equiv \frac{q_t(S_T)}{f_t(S_T)} = e^{r(T-t)} \frac{U'(C_T)}{U'(C_t)} = e^{r(T-t)} M_{t,T}. \tag{7.16}$$

Since

$$\zeta_t'(S_T) = \lambda\, e^{-r(T-t)} \frac{U''(S_T)}{U'(S_t)}, \tag{7.17}$$

with a constant λ independent from the index level, the Arrow-Pratt measure of relative risk aversion $\rho_t(C_T)$ is equal to

$$\rho_t(C_T) \equiv -\frac{S_T\, U''(S_T)}{U'(S_T)} = -\frac{S_T\, \zeta_t'(S_T)}{\zeta_t(S_T)}. \tag{7.18}$$

Therefore, an estimate for the relative risk aversion can be derived from estimates for $f(S_T)$ and $q(S_T)$,

$$\hat{\rho}_t(S_T) = -\frac{S_T\, \hat{\zeta}_t'(S_T)}{\hat{\zeta}_t(S_T)} = \frac{S_T\, \hat{f}_t'(S_T)}{\hat{f}_t(S_T)} - \frac{S_T\, \hat{q}_t'(S_T)}{\hat{q}_t(S_T)}. \tag{7.19}$$

Aït-Sahalia and Lo (2000) estimate the risk-neutral and the 'true' density nonparametrically.[8] In their application S is represented by the S&P 500 index.
The estimated $\hat{\rho}$ function is U-shaped. For both very high and very low index values the representative agent appears to be very risk-averse. This indicates that models which assume constant relative risk aversion (CRRA) might be misspecified.

Jackwerth (2000) studies the agents' absolute risk aversion using S&P 500 index options observed from April 1986 to December 1995. From (7.19) the coefficient of absolute risk aversion is

[8] The risk-neutral density is estimated with the technique described in 5.3.2. For the estimation of the 'true' density, see Aït-Sahalia and Lo (2000, p. 23). As discussed in section 5.3.2 the nonparametric estimator implies aggregating observations over time.

$$RA_t(S_T) = -\frac{U''(S_T)}{U'(S_T)} = \frac{\rho_t(S_T)}{S_T} = \frac{f_t'(S_T)}{f_t(S_T)} - \frac{q_t'(S_T)}{q_t(S_T)}. \tag{7.20}$$

Jackwerth (2000) estimates the risk-neutral density from the volatility smile applying the maximum-smoothness criterion (see section 5.3.3) while the 'true' density f is estimated from historical index returns by a nonparametric kernel technique.[9] The resulting risk-aversion function undergoes significant changes over time. Prior to the 1987 crash the average absolute risk-aversion function is U-shaped. After the crash Jackwerth reports negative values for the coefficient of absolute risk aversion at the current index level.[10] Absolute risk aversion increases strongly with a rising index level. This general pattern remains intact across various modifications of the estimation procedure.[11]

Rosenberg and Engle (1999) estimate the ratio of marginal utilities ζ in (7.16) as the quotient of the risk neutral density (*state prices*) and the 'true' density (*state probabilities*). The risk-neutral density is constructed by spline interpolation of the volatility smile while the 'true' density results from an estimated asymmetric GARCH model.[12] The data set used consists of daily observations on S&P 500 index options from January 1991 to December 1995. The shape of the estimated ζ function is relatively constant over time but its level is very volatile. ζ declines with an increase in the index level and is always positive. Rosenberg and Engle (1999) compare an average of the ζ function to the ratio of marginal utilities derived from a CRRA specification and show that the latter drastically underestimates the ratio of marginal utilities at very low index levels.

Coutant (1999) investigates the behavior of absolute risk aversion using the Hermite polynomial approximation technique. Since she uses data on American-type CAC40 index options observed from January 1995 to June 1997, she follows Melick and Thomas (1997) in constructing the option prices as weighted averages of upper and lower bounds expressed in terms of European-type option prices. As in Abken, Madan, and Ramamurtie (1995) the expansion is truncated after the fourth order Hermite polynomial and the restrictions $b_0 = 1, b_1 = 0, b_2 = 0$, and $\mu = r$ are imposed. The parameters $\{\sigma_t, b_{3,t}, b_{4,t}, w_{C,t}, w_{P,t}\}$, where w_C, w_P are the weighting factors for the upper bounds for call and put options (see(5.16)-(5.17)), are estimated by

[9] See Jackwerth (2000) for details.

[10] Note that negative risk aversion is inconsistent with the representative agent's utility function being concave.

[11] Jackwerth (2000) discusses various potential reasons that can lead to a negative estimate for risk aversion if it is actually positive. By proving a trading strategy based on buying overpriced out-of-the money puts to be profitable he argues that after 1987 market participants overestimated the probability of a crash, so that the risk-neutral density is too positively skewed relative to the true density. Consequently, estimated risk aversion becomes negative.

[12] For details see Rosenberg and Engle (1999).

minimizing the sum of squared deviations of theoretical from observed implied volatilities.[13]
The 'true' density is also given by a fourth-order Hermite polynomial approximation around a lognormal density. Coutant (1999) assumes the parameters $\sigma_t, b_{3,t}, b_{4,t}$ to be equal under the risk-neutral and the 'true' probability measure so that only the drift under P has to be estimated,

$$\mu_t = \alpha_0 + \alpha_1 \mu_{t-1} + \beta_1 e_t, \tag{7.21}$$

where e_t is distributed as follows

$$\tilde{f}_t^{HER}(z) = \phi(z)\left[1 + \frac{3\hat{b}_{4,t}}{\sqrt{24}} - \frac{3\hat{b}_{3,t}}{\sqrt{6}}z - \frac{6\hat{b}_{4,t}}{\sqrt{24}}z^2 + \frac{\hat{b}_{3,t}}{\sqrt{6}}z^3 + \frac{\hat{b}_{4,t}}{\sqrt{24}}z^4\right]. \tag{7.22}$$

Using the estimated coefficients from the risk-neutral density and the estimate for the drift parameter, the 'true' density is

$$\begin{aligned}
\tilde{f}^{HER}(S_T)_t &= f(S, \hat{\sigma}_t, \hat{\mu}_t)_t^{BS}\left[1 + \frac{3\hat{b}_{4,t}}{\sqrt{24}} - \frac{3\hat{b}_{3,t}}{\sqrt{6}}\eta - \frac{6\hat{b}_{4,t}}{\sqrt{24}}\eta^2\right. \\
&\quad \left. + \frac{\hat{b}_{3,t}}{\sqrt{6}}\eta^3 + \frac{\hat{b}_{4,t}}{\sqrt{24}}\eta^4\right], \\
\eta &= \frac{\ln\frac{S_T}{S_t} - \left(\hat{\mu}_t - \frac{1}{2}\hat{\sigma}_t^2\right)(T-t)}{\hat{\sigma}_t\sqrt{T-t}}, \\
f(S, \hat{\sigma}_t, \hat{\mu}_t)_t^{BS} &= \frac{1}{\hat{\sigma}_t\sqrt{2\pi(T-t)}S_T}e^{-\frac{1}{2}\eta^2}.
\end{aligned} \tag{7.23}$$

Coutant (1999) assumes that the economic agents have CRRA preferences, $U(S_T) = \frac{S_T^{1-\gamma}}{1-\gamma}$, so that absolute risk aversion is

$$RA_t(S_T) = \frac{\tilde{f}_t^{HER\prime}(S_T)}{\tilde{f}_t^{HER}(S_T)} - \frac{\hat{q}_t^{HER\prime}(S_T)}{\hat{q}_t^{HER}(S_T)} = \frac{\lambda}{S_T}. \tag{7.24}$$

From this relationship she estimates a time series of risk aversion coefficients λ_t and studies their behavior at specific points in time. She finds the parameter undergoes pronounced changes and sometimes attains unrealistically high values.[14]

In all these studies risk aversion is implicitly defined by the relationship between the risk-neutral and the 'true' probability density function. In contrast, Aït-Sahalia, Wang, and Yared (2001) identify the risk-neutral density and the risk-neutral price process of the underlying separately and investigate whether

[13] (5.53) and (5.55) can be used to compute theoretical option prices from which implied volatilities are derived by the Black-Scholes formula.
[14] For details see Coutant (1999, p. 15).

observed prices for S&P 500 index options are consistent with the price process derived from a specific theoretical model. They estimate the risk-neutral density by the nonparametric approach suggested in Aït-Sahalia and Lo (1998) and assume the index value to follow a general Itô process,

$$dS_t = \mu(S_t)\,dt + \sigma(S_t)\,dB_t. \tag{7.25}$$

$\sigma(S_t)$ is estimated by a nonparametric variant of the minimum-contrast estimator (see Aït-Sahalia, Wang, and Yared (2001, p. 76)). Since they are interested in the risk-neutral process, the authors do not require an estimate for $\mu(S_t)$ but follow the Girsanov theorem in setting the drift equal to the difference of the risk-free interest rate and the dividend yield. From the estimated process the risk-neutral density of the underlying is computed by Monte Carlo integration.[15] They estimate the model from data on S&P 500 index options with a time to expiration of three months (sample period is 1986 to 1994) while the volatility process is estimated using data from a two-week period centered on the day of interest. They then compare the risk-neutral densities implied by option prices to those derived from the estimated risk-neutral process and regress the implied densities' moments on the corresponding moments of the time-series-based density. As a result, the implied density exhibits significantly more positive skewness and larger kurtosis. Testing for the equality of both density functions leads them to reject the null hypothesis. In addition, they show that the discrepancy between the implied and the time-series-based risk-neutral density could have been profitably exploited by an appropriately designed trading strategy (Aït-Sahalia, Wang, and Yared (2001, p. 89)). Taking into account the possibilities of a stochastic jump in the underlying's price that can be given an interpretation as representing a peso problem reduces the difference between the two densities but cannot make it disappear.[16] This shows that even such a flexible specification for the price process might be still too restrictive and the authors suggest also incorporating stochastic volatility into the model.

A related practical application for risk-neutral probabilities is discussed by Aït-Sahalia und Lo (2000) who consider including risk-neutral probabilities into value-at-risk (VaR) models. They contrast this approach with conventional VaR models that use probabilities computed from historical data (*statistical VaR*) whereas the implied risk-neutral probabilities refer explicitly to the future (*Economic VaR*). Comparing the risk-neutral density estimated from daily data on S&P 500 index options from 1993 to the historical density indicates considerable differences in both densities' skewness. They conclude that VaR models should not neglect potential information in option prices.

[15] See for details Aït-Sahalia, Wang, and Yared (2001, p. 77).

[16] For the modified model the identity of the two density functions cannot be tested statistically anymore because the jump-model requires an additional restriction which means that the model is no longer overidentified.

7.5 Summary

The applications reviewed in this chapter show that there is a variety of potential uses for risk-neutral probabilities extracted from option prices. In particular, these techniques have been applied to extract expectations about exchange rates, stock indices, and interest rates.
For example, risk-neutral realignment intensities derived from option prices as well as conditional risk-neutral probabilities are used to study the credibility of fixed-exchange-rate regimes. These studies show that macroeconomic variables appear to have a very limited role in explaining realignment expectations. Using various techniques many researchers have investigated changes in exchange-rate expecations for the 1992 EMS crisis. They show that in the run-up to the crisis devaluation expectations rose strongly for the Italian lira and to some extent for the British pound.
Other applications for exchange rates reconsider the forward-bias puzzle by using statistics derived from the risk-neutral density function or investigate market participant's reactions to perceived central-bank interventions in the foreign-exchange markt. There are also numerous event studies of changes of exchange-rate expectations.

For interest rates market expectations have been shown to react strongly to events related to monetary policy, such as releases of important information like monetary data or interest-rate changes by the central bank etc. In addition, many studies provide evidence for strong reactions in market expectations about interest rates and stock-index values to political events like general elections etc.

Some studies use the relationship between risk-neutral and 'true' probabilities to uncover market participants' risk preferences. They show unanimously that relative risk aversion is not a constant but depends strongly on wealth as approximated by some stock-market index. Furthermore, some evidence has been found indicating that risk-neutral expectations are inconsistent with the 'true' stochastic process of the S&P 500 index.

8

Central-Bank Council Meetings and Money Market Uncertainty

In this chapter we study the effects of central-bank council meetings on market expectations by extracting risk-neutral probability density functions from interest-rate options. Since monetary policy has the strongest impact on money-market rates our data set will consist of options on a short-term interbank interest rate.

If economic agents use all available information in forming their expectations, only new information (news) can cause expectations to be revised. This new information may be totally unexpected. Another possibility is that it is known that new information will be released at a specific point in the future but its content is uncertain. For example, the dates on which important statistical data are to be released or central-bank council meetings are to take place are usually known in advance. In this study we focus on the latter type of news. If the information released has been anticipated, expectations will not be revised because market participants will already have rebalanced their portfolios appropriately. However, if the information released does not conform to the expectations held by market participants they will adjust their expectations in the light of the new information, rebalance their portfolios and thereby cause changes in asset prices. After each central-bank council meeting important information on the future course of monetary policy and on the future development of interest rates might be revealed. Therefore, any important unanticipated information originating from the meeting should be reflected in changes in market expectations, i.e. changes in risk-neutral probabilities.

In this study we focus on changes in uncertainty in market expectations. It is shown in the literature that volatilities on financial markets increase in the days preceding central-bank council meetings while market participants adjust their portfolios according to their expectations about results of the meetings. Furthermore, volatilities have also been shown to rise if market participants receive unanticipated information (news) from council meetings.[1] However, instead of considering actual uncertainty manifesting itself in higher volatility levels we shall study uncertainties in expectations by investigating changes in statistics computed from the risk-neutral density at the time of central-bank council meetings.

As discussed in Chapter 6, the risk-neutral density function and its statistics are subject to substantial day-to-day fluctuations. We need to separate significant changes related to central bank council meetings from changes that are driven by 'noise'. Therefore, we compare the values of statistics on the days of interest, i.e. for each Wednesday before and for each Friday after a council meeting, to the values for Wednesdays and Fridays in weeks without a council meeting. Our approach is as follows: first, we compute for all Wednesdays and Fridays in our sample various statistics from the estimated risk-neutral densities. Then we construct two subsamples, one of which containing the statistics from the weeks in which a central-bank council meeting took place and the other containing statistics from weeks without a meeting. Finally, we use a homogeneity test to test for significant differences between both samples.

8.1 Estimation Method

We compute risk-neutral probability density functions using the approach suggested in Bliss and Panigirtzoglou (2002) and estimate a cubic-spline function in *delta*/volatility space. As discussed in Chapter 6, this technique has been well researched and is more robust with respect to measurement errors than the mixture of lognormals approach, particularly for comparatively short times to expiration. Furthermore, it is implemented easily and the optimization usually converges very well.

First, we compute *delta* values and implied volatilities from data on short-term interest-rate futures options using Black's (1976) formula. Then we fit a natural cubic spline to the m pairs of *delta* and implied volatility and impose the additional restriction that the volatility function should be linear outside the range of observed *delta* values (see 5.3.1). Following Bliss and Panigirtzoglou (2002) we do not force the spline function to fit exactly the observed *delta*/volatility pairs at the knot points and estimate the free parameters using an objective function that is based on the sum of squared deviations of estimated from observed volatilities as well as on the degree of smoothness of the estimated volatility smile.

Bliss und Panigirtzoglou (2002) weight the volatility deviations by *vega* and assume pricing errors to be homoskedastic (see section 5.3.1). In contrast, we put equal weights on all observations because *vega* weighting leads to an

[1] See, for example, Alexander (1998).

inferior fit for volatilities far out of or in the money. A less accurate estimation of the risk-neutral densities' tails would strongly affect some of the uncertainty statistics we want to compute. In our application all observations are therefore weighted equally,

$$\min_{\Theta} \sum_{i=1}^{m} \left(\sigma_i - f_i(\delta_i, \Theta)\right)^2 + \lambda \int_{-\infty}^{+\infty} f''(\delta; \Theta)^2 d\delta. \quad (8.1)$$

After some experimentation we set $\lambda = 0.01$. The integral can be solved analytically as a function of the estimated parameters in Θ.[2]

Having estimated the parameters in Θ we compute a large number of implied volatilities on the fitted spline function for equidistant strikes and also extrapolate outside the range of observed strikes. Note, that *delta* itself is a function of implied volatility so that estimated implied volatility and the corresponding *delta* have to be computed simultaneously (see Malz (1998b) and section 5.3.1.1).[3] Estimated implied volatilities are then converted back into option prices using Black's (1976) formula. The risk-neutral density is computed by differentiating the call-option prices numerically twice and multiplying by $e^{r(T-t)}$.

We then compute various statistics from the estimated risk-neutral probability density functions: expected value, standard deviation, the moments-based skewness and excess kurtosis statistics *sp*2 and *wp*3, relative intensity and various percentiles (10%, 25%, 75%, 90%) from which scaled interpercentile ranges are constructed by dividing the interpercentile range by the current futures price.

Our study aims at highlighting characteristic changes in the risk-neutral density functions related to central-bank council meetings. Empirical studies reviewed in Chapter 6 (e.g. Bliss und Panigirtzoglou (2002) and Cooper (1999)) show that statistics computed from estimated risk-neutral density functions are subject to pronounced day-to-day fluctuations. Therefore, we need to separate changes that are related to the information from central-bank council meetings from the 'noise' in the series. We divide the statistics into two subsamples, one for observations from weeks with a council meeting and one for

[2] Since the spline function is assumed to be linear outside the range of observed options these regions are irrelevant in computing the integral.

[3] Bliss and Panigirtzoglou (2002) compute implied volatilities for equidistant *delta* values so that estimated implied volatilities are more densely spaced at the money. Since we are also interested in the densities' tails the choice of equidistant strike prices is more appropriate. Furthermore, given *delta* values would have to be be tranformed into strike prices in order to compute the risk-neutral density. Therefore, the very closely spaced strike prices at the money would entail the risk that small numerical errors in the transformation might have large effects on the computed risk-neutral density function via computing the second-order difference quotient.

observations from weeks without. We then use the observations from weeks without a central-bank council meeting as a benchmark and compare them to those from the weeks in which a council meeting took place. Technically, we perform a homogeneity test to determine whether the statistics observed in weeks with and without council meetings are drawn from the same probability distribution, i.e. have the same distributional characteristics. Specifically, we use the Kolmogorov-Smirnov homogeneity test that is based on the difference between the empirical distribution functions in both subsamples (see, for example, Kendall and Stuart (1973), or Rinne (1997)).[4] Comparing Wednesdays to Wednesdays and Fridays to Fridays also avoids problems related to day-of-the-week effects.

Note that in our approach we implicitly assume that the only source of new information that might cause revisions in expectations is the central-bank council meeting.

8.2 Data

Our study uses data on a three-month Euribor (Euro Interbank Offered Rate) futures options contract, i.e. options on a futures contract on a short-term interbank interest rate. Both options and futures are traded on the London International Financial Futures and Options Exchange (LIFFE). Short-term interest-rate options at LIFFE are of the American type and can be exercised at any time up to the expiration date. However, the futures-style margining procedure applied to short-term interest-rate options at LIFFE leads to the result that they are actually priced like European-type options. Early exercise will not take place because the options are marked to the market daily causing variation margin flows so that there is no opportunity cost in holding a position in the option.[5]

For the options and the underlying futures contract we use settlement prices which are determined each day by the exchange at the close of trading. Both the options and the underlying futures contract expire simultaneously on the third Wednesday of March, June, September, and December.[6] Therefore, our results can be interpreted as referring to market expectations with respect to the Euribor rate although the underlying asset is the Euribor futures contract. Exercise prices are spaced by intervals of 0.125, i.e. 12.5 basis points.[7] Since

[4] An alternative is a χ^2 homogenity test. However, the Kolmogorov-Smirnov test is more appropriate for the small sample sizes in our application.

[5] See LIFFE (2000) for details. Chen and Scott (1993) provide a formal argument.

[6] This is the regular expiration cycle. Options and futures also exist that expire in the other two of the three nearest calendar months but these are not as liquid as the options on the regular cycle. For further details see LIFFE (2000).

[7] For seven weeks in 1999 there are only options available with strike prices spaced by 0.250.

the futures contract is quoted as 100.0 minus the interest rate, our results can be converted into interest-rate space by subtracting the futures price from 100. The minimum tick size, i.e. the minimum price movement recorded is 0.005.[8]

Starting with January 20, 1999, for each week we select the settlement prices from Wednesday and Friday. Our sample ends on Friday, December 15, 2000.[9] We always choose the option and futures contract on the regular cycle that have the shortest time to expiration provided it is not below one month.[10] For two weeks within this period there is no data available for Friday and in four other weeks the ECB Governing Council met on Wednesday instead of Thursday so that we had to drop these observations. This leaves a total of 92 weeks with 8894 observed option prices both for Wednesdays and Fridays with times to expiration between one and four months. In 43 out of these 92 weeks a meeting of the Governing Council of the ECB took place (see European Central Bank (2000, p. 181) and European Central Bank (2001a, p. 75)). Finally, all option prices were checked for monotonicity, convexity and violations of European put-call parity.
The range of strike prices to be used in the estimation was based on the options' time-adjusted moneyness (Dumas, Fleming, and Whaley (1998)) and only options with values between +1.35 and −1.35 percent were included. Using this criterion leads to a decline in the number of eligible options as their time to expiration shortens and trading activity concentrates in a smaller number of options close to or at the money.

From these options implied volatilities were computed using Black's (1976) formula for pricing futures options.[11] Since European put-call parity holds in our sample there is no difference to using put or call options. Therefore, we decided to construct the volatility smile from in-the-money call and in-the-money put options as in Aït-Sahalia, Wang, and Yared (2001).[12]

---

[8] However, the data on the CD-ROM "Financial Products: End of Day Data" distributed by LIFFE and used for this study is only recorded with an accuracy of 0.01.

[9] We did not include observations between December 20, 2000 and January, 3 2001 because of the holiday seasons.

[10] Compare the discussion in section 5.5.

[11] Apart from the exercise price and the current value of the underlying asset, calculating implied volatilities requires a risk-free interest rate with the same time to maturity as the option. We proxy for this interest rate by using interest rates interpolated linearly from Euribor rates with time to maturity of one to five months.

[12] This avoids problems with using out-of-the money options for which the ratio of minimum tick size to price is relatively large. Since the maximum error caused by discrete price quotation is equal to half the minimum tick size, these options are suspect to carry large measurement errors (e.g. Bliss and Panigirtzoglou (2002)).

In some cases inspection of the resulting *delta*/volatility pairs showed *delta* to be nonmonotonous in strike price. This problem was most severe for option prices from 1999 with only a short time to expiration.[13] In these cases we eliminated all *delta*/volatility combinations towards the outer edge of the strike-price spectrum beginning with the first observation violating monotonicity. Finally, we dropped all observations with delta below 0.025 or above 0.975 because *delta* is quite insensitive to changes in strike price when approaching zero or one and the volatility smile (in *delta* space) becomes so steep that it is no longer possible to fit the spline polynomials to the volatilities.

8.3 Results

The Kolmogorov-Smirnov test is based on the difference between the empirical distribution functions of the statistic in question in both subsamples. The empirical distribution function of the relevant statistic (or of its change) is calculated for each of the two subsamples and is denoted as $\hat{F}_{CM}$ for the weeks in which the Governing Council of the ECB met and $\hat{F}_{NCM}$ for the other weeks. The null hypothesis is that both samples of statistics are drawn from the same underlying distribution and that their distribution functions are therefore equal, $H_0 : F_{CM} = F_{NCM}$. Two alternative hypotheses are considered. In the first case $H_1 : F_{CM} > F_{NCM}$, i.e. the statistic is stochastically smaller in CM than in NCM. In the second case $H_1 : F_{CM} < F_{NCM}$, i.e. the statistic is stochastically larger in CM than in NCM. The test statistics are presented in table 8.1.[14]

The second column of table 8.1 shows whether or not the statistic was corrected for maturity dependence by a regression on time to expiration and the removal of the time trend.[15] We present results from the maturity-corrected

[13] Theoretically, *delta* should be monotonous in strike price. The observed nonmonotonicity probably results from measurement errors in option prices caused by the minimum tick size. Since the sensitivity of *delta* with respect to implied volatility is higher far out of or far in the money, even small errors in implied volatility can cause large deviations in *delta*.

[14] The 5 and 10 percent critical values for this sample size are 0.25283 and 0.22115, respectively. H_0 can be rejected in favour of H_1 in the center right column of table 1 if D+ exceeds the critical value. H_0 can be rejected in favour of H_1 in the right column of table 1 if D- is less than -1 times the critical value (e.g. Rinne (1997)).

[15] Compare section 4.3. Apart from a linear also a log-linear and a square-root specification for time to expiration were also considered all leading to very similar results.

samples only if time to expiration turned out to be significant in the regression.[16]

The results in the first three lines refer to the risk-neutral densities' expected value, i.e. the futures price.[17] First, the futures prices on Wednesdays in weeks with a council meeting are compared to the futures prices on Wednesdays in weeks without one. In the second line the comparison is made for futures prices observed on Fridays. In both cases no significant difference between the empirical distribution functions can be found. In the third line, we compare the *changes* in futures prices from Wednesday to Friday in both types of weeks. Again the null hypothesis cannot be rejected. Apparently, there is no systematic effect of central-bank council meetings on the expected level of the Euribor rate or on the change in the expected value.

In the next three lines the same tests are performed for the risk-neutral density's skewness statistic $sp2$. While the null hypothesis cannot be rejected for the levels of $sp2$ on Wednesdays and Fridays the change in $sp2$ is significantly stochastically larger in weeks with a council meeting than in the benchmark weeks. This implies that skewness either increased more or decreased less from Wednesday to Friday and that the relative probability of pronounced interest-rate rises increased more or decreased less when the ECB council met compared to the weeks without a council meeting. Noting the comparatively low (but insignificant) value of the (D-) statistic on Fridays it appears that in weeks in which a central-bank council meeting took place skewness was relatively high on Fridays.

Relative intensity is an alternative measure for asymmetry in the risk-neutral probability density function (compare section 4.3). The test results indicate a stochastically larger level of relative intensity on Fridays in weeks with a council meeting.[18] While the change from Wednesdays to Fridays does not differ significantly between the two subsamples, the (D-) statistic for the change is comparatively low so that these results support the conclusion from the $sp2$ statistic, in particular, that on Fridays after a council meeting market participants believe large interest-rate increases to be relatively more probable compared to the benchmark weeks than large interest-rate declines.

[16] Note that this correction procedure also eliminates any trend in the risk-neutral statistics caused by the continuous arrival of new information, e.g. a steady decline in uncertainty among market participants. We also experimented with different types of dummy variables for the various option contracts but neither turned out to be significant.

[17] The expected values computed from the risk-neutral density functions were always very close to the futures price.

[18] Relative intensity was computed with respect to thresholds one standard deviation above or below the futures price. Here, standard deviation refers to the futures price instead of its logarithm.

The lower part of table 8.1 contains the results for the statistics summarizing the degree of uncertainty in market expectations. From the theoretical point of view various hypotheses can be formulated:

a. (continuous flow of information/continuous information processing). If there is an almost continuous flow of information about the council meeting and if we assume that additional information tends to decrease uncertainty among market participants, uncertainty in expectations will not be systematically larger on Wednesdays in weeks with a council meeting compared to Wednesdays in weeks without a meeting.

b. (discontinuous flow of information/discontinuous information processing) Another possibility is that market participants receive more information about the council meeting on the days immediately preceeding the meeting than on other days. For example, the central bank or individual council members might make public statements about the upcoming meeting or there might be more intensive media coverage. Furthermore, it is possible that market participants do not continuously react to new information they receive. Portfolio adjustments are discontinuous and if they are delayed until shortly before the council meeting, information accumulated over the preceding days will only show up just one or a few days before the meeting takes place. Finally, market participants might react differently to some information if they receive it more shortly before the council meeting compared to some days before. Any of these effects should cause significant differences between the statistics in weeks with and without a council meeting.

c. (perfect anticipation). If the results of council meetings are generally well anticipated and if council meetings do not provide much new information changes in the statistics from Wednesdays to Fridays will not be different in the two subsamples.

d. (imperfect anticipation – new information). If council meetings provide market participants with news on the future course of monetary policy and cause revisions in expectations, uncertainty in expectations can rise or decline from Wednesday to Friday depending on the type of information revealed. Therefore, changes in the statistics should be different in the two subsamples.

e. (imperfect anticipation – uncertainty about the results of the meetings). If, in general, market participants are uncertain about the results of the next council meetings this uncertainty will disappear after the council's decisions have been announced. Therefore, uncertainty should decrease more strongly after council meetings than in the benchmark weeks.

While the first two hypotheses are about the levels of the statistics, the latter three refer to their changes from Wednesday to Friday. However, note that, for example, the last two hypotheses are not mutually exclusive. Generally, a council decision to change official interest rates or to leave them unchanged also contains some information on the future course of monetary policy so that the decline in uncertainty in expectations as described by hypothesis (e.) can coincide with a revision of expectations with respect to future council meetings (hypothesis d.).

For excess kurtosis (*wp*3) and standard deviation no significant differences in the levels or in the statistic's changes between both subsamples can be found.[19] For the scaled interpercentile ranges (*sipr*), i.e. the percentile differences divided by the futures price, we find high absolute but insignificant values of the (D+) and (D-) statistics for the change in the 90% to 10% scaled interpercentile range. However, statistically significant differences between both samples result for the change in the 75% to 25% scaled interpercentile range only. The change in the relative range from the 75% to the 25% was stochastically smaller in weeks with a council meeting, i.e. *sipr*7525 increased less or decreased more from Wednesdays to Fridays than in the benchmark weeks. Consequently, uncertainty increased less or decreased more in weeks in which a council meeting took place.

These results show some significant differences between the subsamples that are consistent with hypothesis b. and contradict hypothesis a. However, as far as hypotheses c. to e. are concerned, different interpretations of the results are possible. The large number of insignificant test statistics is consistent with hypothesis c., i.e. that central-bank council meetings do not convey much new information to market participants and that therefore uncertainty about the council meeting's results is almost negligible. On the other hand, these results could also be due to a combination of d. and e., where possibly small reductions in uncertainty in many cases are compensated by revisions of expectations caused by the council meeting. The significant (D+) statistic on *sipr*7525 and the comparatively high (D+) statistic on *sipr*9010 show that uncertainty appears to decline from Wednesday to Friday in council-meeting weeks relative to the benchmark weeks.

Additional information on how to interpret these results can be gained by looking at the correlations between selected statistics (table 8.2). Changes in standard deviation, volatility and the wider scaled interpercentile range (*sipr*9010) are highly correlated while correlations between any statistic from this group and the narrow scaled interpercentile range (*sipr*7525) are much smaller. This indicates that the first three statistics put more weight on changes in the tails of the risk-neutral density compared to *sipr*7525, i.e. these statistics convey information with a stronger focus on expectations about extreme outcomes for the Euribor whereas *sipr*7525 relates to uncertainty with respect to more moderate interest-rate changes.

[19] The standard deviation is computed for the logarithm of the Euribor rate.

Table 8.1. Kolmogorov-Smirnov tests for various statistics of implied density functions

statistic	trend	$D+$	$D-$
		$H_1 : F_{CM} > F_{NCM}$	$H_1 : F_{CM} < F_{NCM}$
futures (Wed)	n	0.04082	-0.07356
futures (Fr)	n	0.05505	-0.06170
Δfutures	n	0.09587	-0.14713
$sp2$ (Wed)	n	0.15045	-0.09492
$sp2$ (Fr)	n	0.04699	-0.21927
$\Delta sp2$	n	0.00000	-0.26673*
rel. int (Wed)	y	0.17086	-0.10441
rel. int (Fr)	y	0.04129	-0.23351**
Δrel. int	n	0.00759	-0.19174
$wp3$ (Wed)	n	0.18462	-0.05885
$wp3$ (Fr)	n	0.07167	-0.07897
$\Delta wp3$	n	0.06217	-0.13764
stddev (Wed)	y	0.06882	-0.07119
stddev (Fr)	y	0.16184	-0.06645
Δstddev	n	0.11011	-0.12957
vol (Wed)	y	0.06502	-0.08021
vol (Fr)	y	0.16184	-0.08685
Δvol	n	0.10916	-0.13052
sipr9010 (Wed)	y	0.10679	-0.06028
sipr9010 (Fr)	y	0.12008	-0.05078
Δsipr9010	n	0.21251	-0.17038
sipr7525 (Wed)	y	0.06217	-0.07784
sipr7525 (Fr)	y	0.09445	-0.03749
Δsipr7525	n	0.28714*	-0.04651
* (**) denotes significance at the 5% level (10%level).			

Table 8.2. Correlation coefficients for various statistics of implied density functions

	Δstddev	Δvol	$\Delta wp3$	Δsipr9010	Δsipr7525
Δstddev	1.00000				
Δvol	0.98319	1.00000			
$\Delta wp3$	0.18057	-0.18369	1.00000		
Δsipr9010	0.80281	0.78846	-0.25802	1.00000	
Δsipr7525	0.18720	0.19632	-0.67859	0.59594	1.00000

In the time period covered by our sample there were seven council meetings at which official rates were increased while there was only one decrease in official rates. This might affect our results, particularly those with respect to the skewness of the risk-neutral density. We therefore eliminated all observations for weeks in which the Governing Council decided to change official rates from the CM-subsample and repeated our tests (except for the futures price). The results in table 8.3 reveal some interesting differences from those in table 8.1.[20]

Neither for *sp*2 nor for relative intensity can any null hypothesis be rejected. Obviously, the significant results in table 8.1 were caused by the council meetings on which interest rates were changed. An economic interpretation of this result is that market participants expect the ECB to follow a policy of interest-rate smoothing, as is done by many central banks. An interest-rate-smoothing policy makes it more likely that after an interest rate increase official interest rates will be raised further than that they will lowered. Such a policy that changes interest rates in small steps makes market participants assign higher probabilities to significant future increases in interest rates than to future decreases following an interest-rate rise.[21] Since our observation period predominantly comprises interest-rate increases, interest-rate smoothing might have caused stochastically larger skewness in weeks with council meetings.

While the change in *sipr*7525 remains significantly stochastically smaller in weeks with ECB council meetings, changes in *sipr*9010, standard deviation, and volatility are now significantly stochastically larger in these weeks compared to the benchmark sample. In the light of the correlations presented in table 8.2 this indicates that central-bank council meetings appear to have increased uncertainty in market participants' expectations concerning extreme interest-rate movements in the future while at the same time uncertainty about more moderate interest rate movements has declined. Both results are consistent with hypothesis d. While the result for *sipr*7525 was robust with respect to the adjustments to the sample, the results for standard deviation, volatility and *sipr*9010 changed drastically. This provides some indirect evidence that uncertainty declined strongly for the observations eliminated.

Dropping council meetings on which interest rates were changed from the sample basically leaves two types of central-bank council meetings. First, council meetings where market participants' expectations of unchanged official interest rates turned out to be correct and second, council meetings where market participants expected interest rates to be changed but the council decided to leave rates untouched. It is possible that increases in uncertainty are mainly caused by council meetings of one of these types, most plausibly by those where the market participants' expectations about interest-rate changes were not fulfilled. In such a situation market participants might wonder about their ability to anticipate and understand central-bank actions so that uncertainty in their expectations rises. In contrast, if the market correctly anticipated the

[20] For this reduced sample size the critical values are 0.26743 (5%) and 0.23156 (10%), respectively.

[21] For interest-rate smoothing and the behaviour of money-market rates see Rudebusch (1995). Goodfriend (1991) discusses the implications of interest-rate smoothing for the behaviour of the central bank's operating target. See also Goodhart (1999).

Table 8.3. Kolmogorov-Smirnov tests for various statistics of implied density functions (no interest-rate changes)

statistic	trend	$D+$ $H_1 : F_{CM} > F_{NCM}$	$D-$ $H_1 : F_{CM} < F_{NCM}$
*sp*2 (Wed)	n	0.07347	-0.13878
*sp*2 (Fr)	n	0.07755	-0.20000
$\Delta sp2$	n	0.06531	-0.20408
rel.int (Wed)	y	0.11837	-0.14694
rel.int (Fr)	y	0.06122	-0.21244
Δrel.int	n	0.09796	-0.16327
*wp*3 (Wed)	n	0.19592	-0.04490
*wp*3 (Fr)	n	0.07347	-0.07347
$\Delta wp3$	n	0.05306	-0.17551
stddev (Wed)	y	0.12245	-0.09769
stddev (Fr)	y	0.07347	-0.11429
Δstddev	n	0.02041	-0.25714**
vol (Wed)	y	0.09388	-0.09796
vol (Fr)	y	0.09388	-0.13469
Δvol	n	0.04490	-0.24082**
sipr9010 (Wed)	y	0.19184	-0.05714
sipr9010 (Fr)	y	0.08571	-0.08980
Δsipr9010	n	0.09388	-0.24082**
sipr7525 (Mi)	y	0.07347	-0.08980
sipr7525 (Fr)	y	0.09388	-0.06939
Δperdiff7525	n	0.23265**	-0.05714

* (**) denotes significance at the 5% level (10% level).

council's decision not to change official interest rates, we should not expect to observe significant changes in uncertainty.

This raises the question of whether it is possible to find patterns in the changes of risk-neutral densities that are typical to specific situations described by various combinations of market expectations and council-meeting results. Obviously, the considerable heterogeneity within the sample makes it difficult to find more general effects of council meetings on the uncertainty in market expectations. Hence, a less aggregative approach seems to be appropriate.

8.4 Summary

Using LIFFE futures-options data from Wednesdays and Fridays in 1999 and 2000 we estimated risk-neutral density functions for the Euribor by fitting a cubic spline function to the volatility smile. We computed various statistics from the risk-neutral density functions and compared their levels and changes in their levels for the weeks in which a meeting of the ECB's governing council took place and weeks without a council meeting.

We found some evidence that the change in skewness from Wednesdays to Fridays was stochastically larger and that the level of skewness was stochastically larger on Fridays in the weeks with council meetings. We showed that these results were caused by the predominance of interest- rate increases among rate changes over the sample period. They reflect the market anticipating an interest-rate-smoothing policy by the ECB. Furthermore, our results indicate that uncertainty in market participants' expectations about moderate interest-rate changes decreases after council meetings relative to the weeks without a council meeting.

It was also shown that the results for changes in uncertainty with respect to more extreme changes in the Euribor rate were altered drastically if the council meetings on which official rates were changed were eliminated from the sample. While in the larger sample we found no significant effects of council meetings, in the smaller sample uncertainty about large deviations in the Euribor increased after council meetings relative to the benchmark sample. This effect is probably caused by the council meetings at which market participants' expectations about interest rate changes were not fulfilled.

The approach of splitting the sample into two parts and using one subsample as a benchmark in order to highlight important differences can be only used to study repeated events. Furthermore, we are only able to test for general differences between the characteristics of the statistics in the two subsamples without paying attention to the individual background of each council meeting. Since our results indicate some heterogeneity within the subsamples, a further partition with respect to different combinations of market expectations and council meeting results would be appropriate. However, this would lead to very small sample sizes so that it would be better to switch to event studies instead where a number of selected council meetings is studied individually.

9

Central-Bank Council Meetings - Event Studies

In this chapter we focus on the effects of individual ECB council meetings on market expectations. The results in Chapter 8 clearly show that all central-bank council meetings do not have identical effects on market expectations. A detailed investigation of individual episodes can potentially provide insights that cannot be gained from an aggregative point of view as in Chapter 8. Therefore, we present event studies in which we track the evolution of market expectations over short time periods centered on ten selected ECB council meetings.

As in the preceding chapter we compute statistics from the risk-neutral density functions and study their behaviour over time. First, we graph the risk-neutral density functions before and after each ECB council meeting. Second, we graph the statistics' time series and third, we use a regression technique to test for statistically significant effects of council meetings.

9.1 Methodology and Data

Again, we estimate risk-neutral density functions for the three-months Euribor by fitting a cubic spline function to implied volatilities in *delta* space.
We focus on ten-day time periods each centered on an ECB council meeting. As in the preceding chapter, we face the problem of separating changes in the statistics into the council meeting's effects and into the 'noise' component, i.e. the generally observed day-to-day fluctuations (e.g. Bliss and Panigirtzoglou (2002), Cooper (1999)). If market participants form rational expectations and quickly adjust their portfolios to new information, the effects of a council meeting are visible in the changes of the statistics from the observation just before to the one immediately after the meeting. However, the 'noise' in the time series and the potential presence of day-of-the-week effects complicate the interpretation of day-to-day changes.

Therefore, we look for more persistent changes. Assuming that the effects of important news can be detected in the data over some days we estimate regressions including a dummy variable that is set equal to one for *a number of trading days* after the council meeting. We interpret a significant coefficient on the dummy variable as evidence for a statistically significant effect of the council meeting on market expectations.

Looking only for these persistent effects causes the random fluctuations in the statistics to be smoothed by the additional observations. In deciding on how many additional trading days to include we face a trade-off: if we add too few observations, we will not be able to "average away" the 'noise' in the risk-neutral probability density functions. On the other hand, if we include too many trading days, the effects caused by the central-bank council meeting will be blurred by the additional information market participants learn during that extended period.

In this study we use periods of ten trading days and compare the final five days, i.e. the day on which the council meeting took place plus the next four trading days to the five trading days before the council meeting.[1] Choosing to compare five-day periods before and after the event to be considered has another benefit as well. Since both subsamples share an identical day-of-the-week composition, we effectively avoid problems related to day-of-the-week effects. On the other hand this leads to a low number of degrees of freedom in our regressions. However, extending the individual time windows in order to increase degrees of freedom would strain the assumptions required for our approach.

As events to be investigated we select among the meetings of the ECB-council between January 2000 and August 2001.[2] The selection was based on the following criteria: first, we wanted any of the potential combinations of market expectations and council-meeting results to be represented in our sample. These combinations are: correctly anticipated interest-rate increase, correctly anticipated interest-rate decrease, no change in official rates that was anticipated correctly, an unexpected interest-rate increase, an unexpected interest-rate decrease and a situation in which the market expects a change in offical rates which, however, does not occur. Second, for all business days within each ten-day period centered on the council meeting observed option prices had to be available, i.e. there should be no bank holidays etc. Even a single missing observation might lead to day-of-the-week effects no longer cancelling out between both subsamples so that the results might be distorted. Finally, we also required a clear picture of what market participants expected from the ECB council meeting. This information enables us to put each event into the appropriate category with respect to the combination of market expectations

[1] Trading in Euribor options at LIFFE closes at 16.10 so that the information from a council meeting is incorporated into the same day's settlement prices.

[2] Because of the differences in data quality (see below) observations for 2001 were not used for the homogenity tests.

and result of the meeting explained above and facilitates the interpretation of the results.[3]

By applying these criteria ten ECB council meetings were selected. Among these were two anticipated interest-rate increases, one anticipated interest-rate decrease, three council meetings where official interest rates were left unchanged as anticipated, one unanticipated interest-rate increase, two cases where an interest-rate step was expected but the council decided to leave official rates unchanged, and one unexpected interest-rate decrease.

As in Chapter 8 we use settlement prices for LIFFE options on the three-month Euribor futures contract. We select the options and futures contracts on the regular expiration cycle with the shortest time to expiration provided it is not below one month.[4] Again we used options with time-adjusted moneyness between +1.35 and −1.35 percent. Implied volatilities were computed from in-the-money options (see the discussion in Chapter 8) and *delta*/volatility pairs violating the monotonicity of *delta* in the exercise price were eliminated. After this procedure we were left with six to fourteen observations for each day to estimate the smile.[5]

The options' time to expiration generally extends over more central-bank council meetings than just the one considered in the event study. Therefore, we have to be careful in interpreting our results because the risk-neutral densities also involve market expectations about other council meetings further in the future. For example, market participants might expect a decrease in interest rates from the upcoming council meeting. If interest rates are kept constant and after the council meeting the market comes to expect that interest rates instead will be lowered at the next meeting, the risk-neutral statistics do not necessarily have to be affected by the refutation of the interest-rate change expectations.

---

[3] For the information on market sentiment we draw on reports in the Financial Markets section of the *Frankfurter Allgemeine Zeitung*. It should be emphasized that for our classification we require information on market expectations about the upcoming council meeting, not about expectations with respect to monetary policy further in the future.

[4] For one subperiod in January 2000 we used options expiring in June and not in March because we found considerable nonmonotonicities of delta with respect to strike price for the March contract.
The data for 2000 is from the CD-ROM "Financial Products: End of Day Data" distributed by LIFFE. There, option prices are only recorded with an accuracy of 0.01. However, for 2001 we used option prices obtained from the LIFFE website (*http://www.liffe.com*) with an accuracy of 0.005.

[5] The risk-free interest rate is interpolated linearly from observed Euribor rates.

9.2 Results

For each ECB council meeting considered we first graph the risk-neutral probability density functions (PDF) before and after the council meeting. Then, we discuss the evolution of market expectations within the ten-day period centered on the council meeting. Here, we study the evolution of various statistics computed from the risk-neutral densities. Finally, we present the results of our regression approach that highlights the significant and persistent effects of ECB council meetings on market expectations.

January 27 - February 9, 2000

On February 3, 2000 the ECB raised all official interest rates by 25 basis points, just a few days after the euro exchange rate had dropped below US dollar parity and just preceding an interest-rate increase by the Fed.[6] The rate increase was already expected by market participants at the beginning of the week.[7]

Figure 9.1 compares the risk-neutral density functions computed for the option contract expiring in June on February 2 and February 4, i.e. one day before and one day after the ECB council meeting. We do not find large differences between the densities but after the interest-rate increase the density seems to have a somewhat lower dispersion.[8]

In Figure 9.2 – showing the time series of the futures price (100 - interest rate) over the ten-day period – we do not find evidence for any effects of the council meeting. The next figure shows the standard deviation – computed for the logarithm of the interest rate – and the volatility implicit in market expectations. Volatility is computed by dividing the standard deviation by the square root of time to expiration and should not exhibit maturity dependence

[6] The euro exchange rate temporarily dropped below dollar parity on January 24, and the euro reference rate declined below dollar parity on January 27.

[7] "... and fears of increasing interest rates in the US and Europe led to a decline in German blue chips stock prices. The fact that the euro exchange rate appears to settle below dollar parity fuelled fears of interest-rate increases even further." (Angst vor einer Zinserhöhung belastet Aktienkurse, FAZ, February 1, 2000, p. 31). After the interest-rate increase it was noted that "The market anticipated the interest-rate increase. If the ECB had not raised rates at this time it would have had to do so at the next meeting." (Dax erreicht einen Rekord nach der Zinserhöhung, FAZ, February 4, 2000, p. 25.) Translations by the author.

[8] The small irregularities in the shape of the density functions are due to measurement errors in option prices, i.e. the minimum tick size, that cause a non-smooth volatility smile. It is possible to enforce a smoother shape for the densities by increasing the value for λ in the objective function but this makes the estimates more dependent on the technique than on the data.

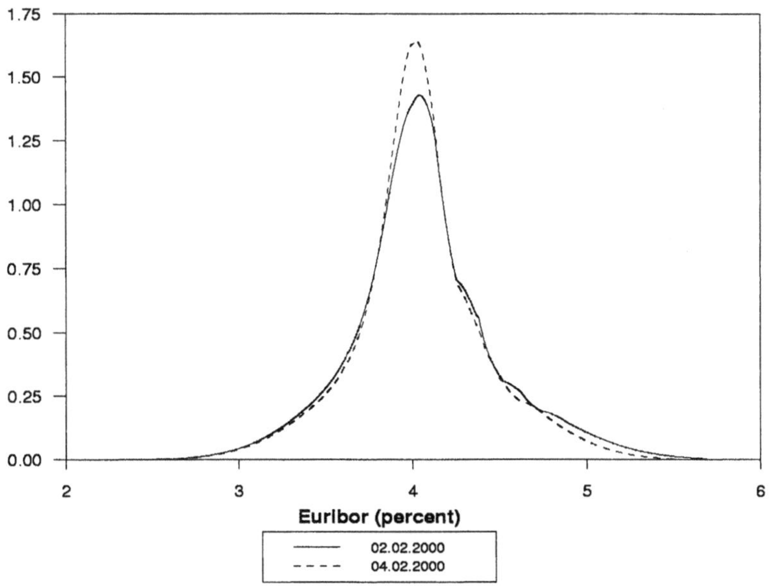

Fig. 9.1. Risk-neutral PDFs for three-month Euribor futures (June contract) on February 2 and February 4, 2000

because of this adjustment.[9] Both variables show a declining trend, an increase to a slightly higher level immediately before the council meeting and revert back to their previous trends after the meeting.

Figure 9.4 graphs the time series of the skewness statistic *sp*2, of the excess-kurtosis statistic *wp*3, and of relative intensity. Leptokurtosis increased before the council meeting but declined again on Friday. Since standard deviation also increased before the meeting, rising excess kurtosis should be interpreted as evidence for increasing uncertainty with respect to extreme interest-rate changes. Standard deviation and excess kurtosis declined after the council meeting so that uncertainty captured in the densities' tails decreased. Both skewness statistics do not show any strong effects of the council meeting. Most of the time, the risk-neutral density is negatively skewed. Obviously, the time series of relative intensity and *sp*2 are very similar.[10]

Figures 9.5 and 9.6. display the risk-neutral densities' percentiles together with the futures price and the scaled interpercentile ranges, i.e. the percentile

[9] However, in some of our regressions we still find volatility depends significantly on the time to expiration. This indicates that dividing standard deviation by the square root of the time to expiration is only a partial solution to the maturity dependence problem.

[10] The thresholds for which relative intensity is computed are set equal to the futures price ± one standard deviation.

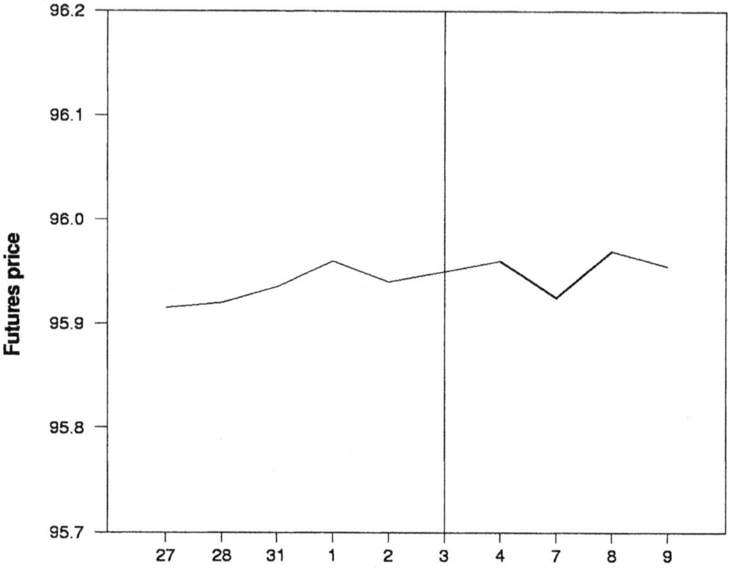

Fig. 9.2. Futures price 27.1.-9.2.2000

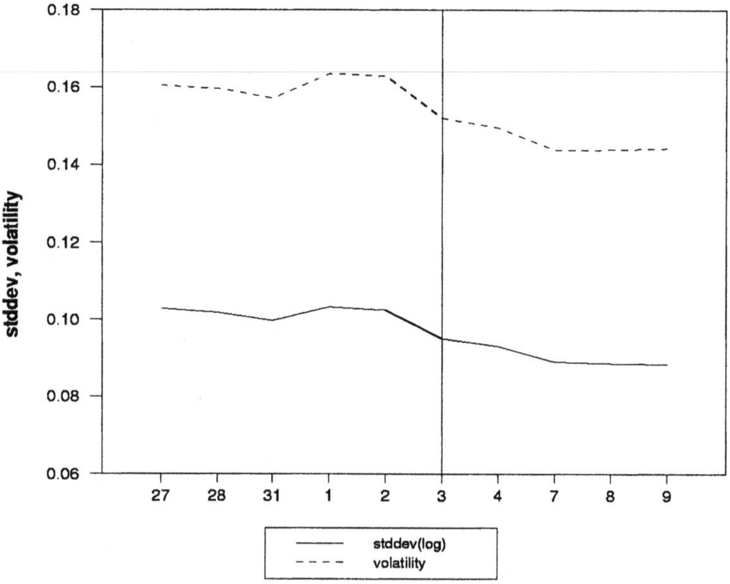

Fig. 9.3. Standard deviation and volatility 27.1.-9.2.2000

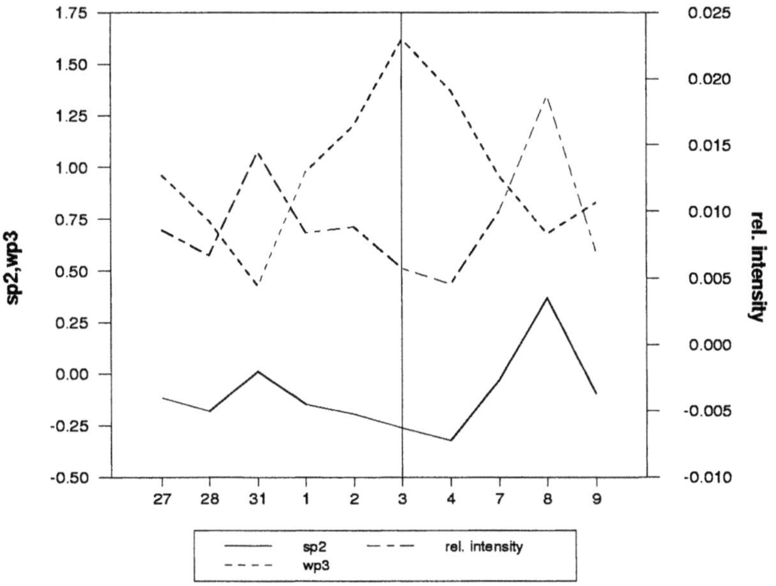

Fig. 9.4. Skewness and excess kurtosis 27.1.-9.2.2000

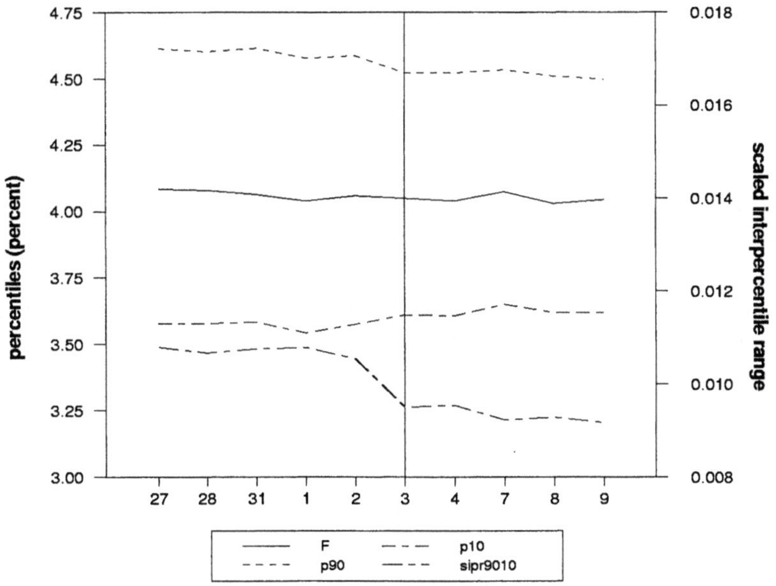

Fig. 9.5. 90% and 10% percentiles and scaled interpercentile range 27.1.-9.2.2000

range relative to the futures price. As expected, the percentiles slowly converge towards the futures price. The drop in both scaled interpercentile ranges (*sipr*9010) and (*sipr*7525) on February 3 indicates a decline in uncertainty after the council meeting.

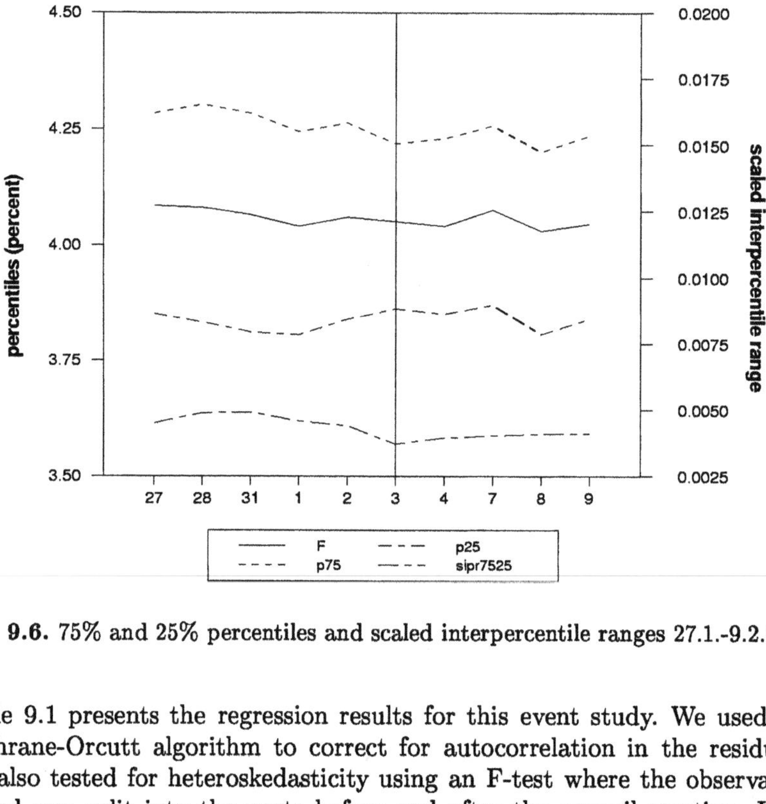

Fig. 9.6. 75% and 25% percentiles and scaled interpercentile ranges 27.1.-9.2.2000

Table 9.1 presents the regression results for this event study. We used the Cochrane-Orcutt algorithm to correct for autocorrelation in the residuals. We also tested for heteroskedasticity using an F-test where the observation period was split into the parts before and after the council meeting. If we found evidence for heteroskedasticity, we re-estimated the equation using the heteroskedasticity consistent covariance matrix of Hansen (1982) and White (1980) for the t-tests.

Only for standard deviation and the wider scaled interpercentile range (90% to 10%) do we find a significant dependence on the time to expiration.[11] The council-meeting dummy is significantly negative in the equations for standard deviation, volatility and both scaled interpercentile ranges indicating a significant decline in uncertainty in market expectations after the council meeting. These results correspond to those derived from visual inspection of the time

[11] Omitting the time to expiration from the regressions in most cases leaves signs and significance of the coefficients untouched.

Table 9.1. Regression results for implied PDFs 27.1.-9.2.2000

statistic	constant	dummy	time to expiration	$\bar{R}^2$
stddev(log)	-0.01198	-0.00625**	0.00113**	0.905
volatility	0.05401	-0.00991**	0.00107	0.848
*sp*2	4.32869	-0.16053	-0.04413	-0.275
*wp*3	-7.00032	0.61850	0.07783	0.013
rel. intensity	0.11049	-0.00528	-0.00100	-0.273
sipr9010	0.00378	-0.00103*	0.00007*	0.976
sipr7525	0.00703*	-0.00079*	-0.00002	0.749

* (**) denotes significance at the 5% level (10% level).

series. However, the regression approach is unable to capture the temporary increase in *wp*3.

February 24 - March 8, 2000

For the ECB council meeting on March 2 most market participants expected the announcement of the second interest-rate increase in 2000.[12] However, the ECB council decided to leave official rates unchanged.

As shown in Figure 9.7 the risk-neutral density shifts slightly to the right from Wednesday to Friday and contracts around the mean. However, these changes are only very small. As can be seen from Figure 9.8 the increase in the expectation for the Euribor already started at the beginning of the week.

Standard deviation and volatility on the days around the council meeting rise to slightly higher levels.

The time series of *wp*3 indicates a higher leptokurtosis on the days following the council meeting that cannot be clearly interpreted because of the absence of a clear trend in standard deviation. On most days, the risk-neutral density is positively skewed. It becomes temporarily negatively skewed on the day of the council meeting. The scaled interpercentile range *sipr*9010 is on a slightly higher level on the days close to the event indicating increased uncertainty among market participants.

The council-meeting dummy's coefficients are positive in the equations for standard deviation and volatility and negative in the equations for the scaled interpercentile ranges. Only one of these four statistics is negatively affected

[12] "One day before the members of the ECB council meet speculation has mounted that the ECB will raise interest rates once again. Analysts consider an interest rate hike of 25 basis points to be likely." (Eine Zinserhöhung der EZB ist wahrscheinlich, FAZ, March 2, 2000, p. 31.) Translation by the author.

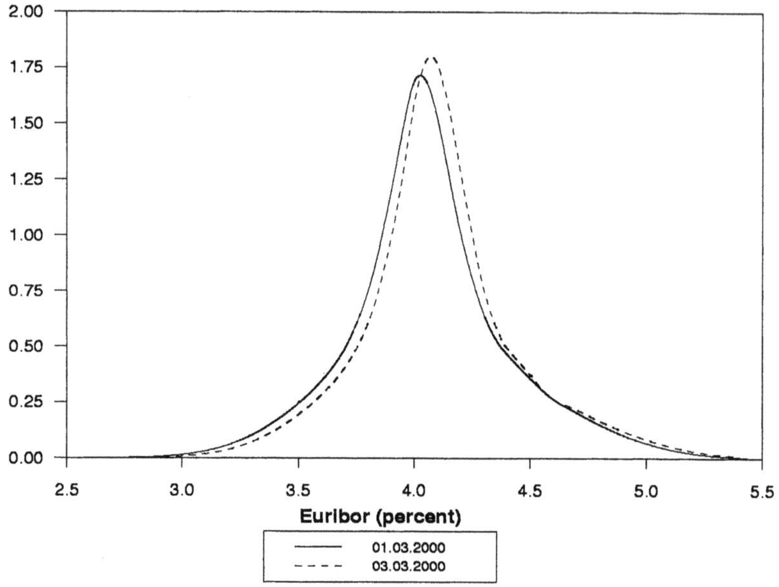

Fig. 9.7. Risk-neutral PDFs for three-month Euribor futures (June contract) on March 1 and March 3, 2000

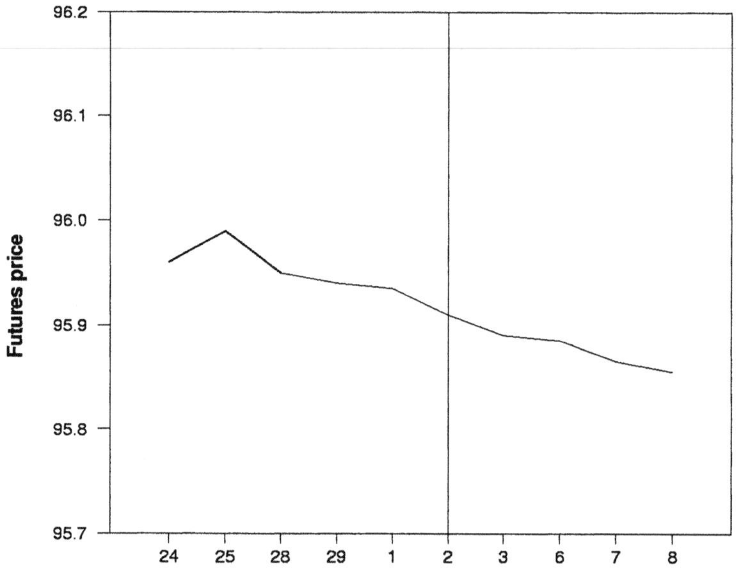

Fig. 9.8. Futures price 24.2.-8.3.2000

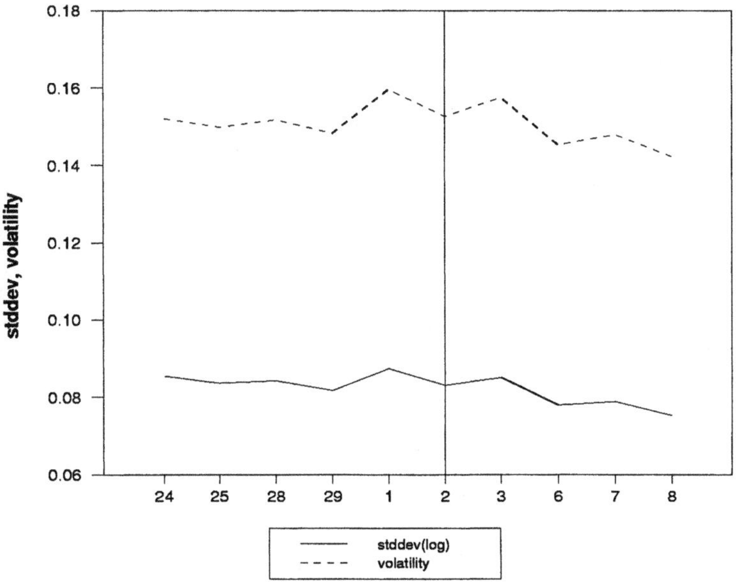

Fig. 9.9. Standard deviation and volatility 24.2.-8.3.2000

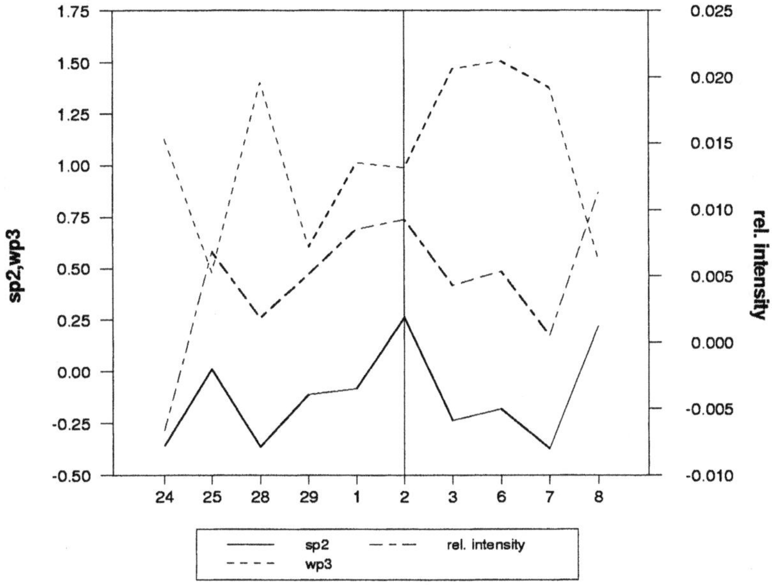

Fig. 9.10. Skewness and excess kurtosis 24.2.-8.3.2000

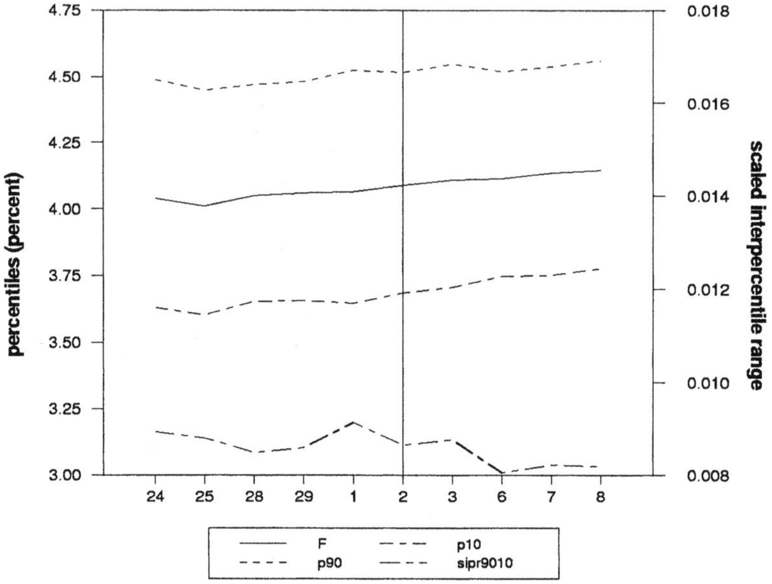

Fig. 9.11. 90% and 10% percentiles and scaled interpercentile range 24.2.-8.3.2000

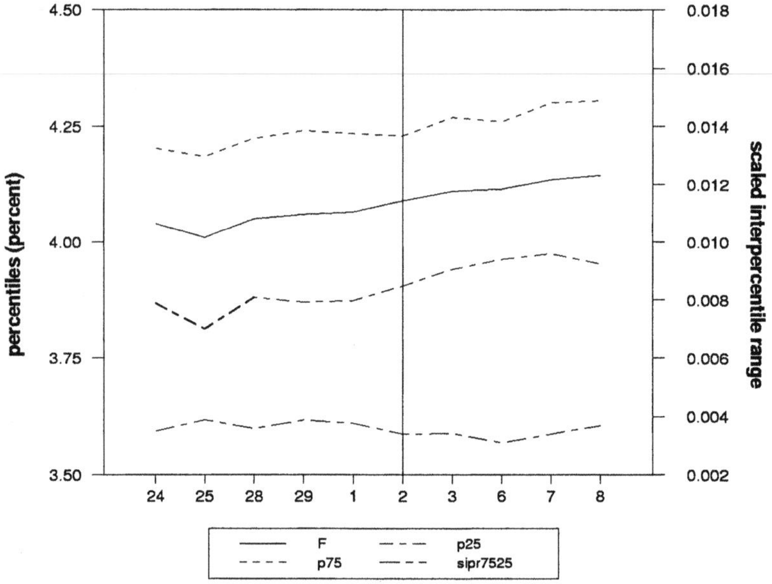

Fig. 9.12. 75% and 25% percentiles and scaled interpercentile range 24.2.-8.3.2000

Table 9.2. Regression results for implied PDFs 24.2.-8.3.2000

statistic	constant	dummy	time to expiration	$\bar{R}^2$
stddev(log)	0.00798	0.00052	0.00099	0.401
volatility	0.08755	0.00105	0.00084	-0.080
*sp*2	1.06802	-0.00554	-0.01601	-0.202
*wp*3	-2.85953	0.61860**	0.04861	0.218
rel. intensity	0.11028	-0.00469	-0.00139	0.106
sipr9010	0.00382	-0.00009	0.00006*	0.317
sipr7525	0.00689*	-0.00058*	-0.00041	0.558

* (**) denotes significance at the 5% level (10% level).

to a statistically significant degree by the council meeting (*sipr*7525), so that the evidence for a decline in uncertainty after the council meeting is much weaker for this event compared to the one before. Presumably, the significantly positive coefficient in the equation for *wp*3 is caused by the strong increase in excess kurtosis on the Friday following the council meeting. As before, in most cases there is significant maturity dependence.

June 1 - June 14, 2000

Most market participants were surprised by the size of the 50-basis point interest-rate increase on June 8, having expected the ECB to increase interest rates by only 25 basis points.[13]

Figure 9.13 compares the risk-neutral density functions for June 5, and June 9, and shows that the density shifts strongly to higher interest-rate levels and becomes more positively skewed after the council meeting. The jump of about 23.5 basis points in the futures price on Thursday underlines the surprise component in the council's decision.

Standard deviation and volatility do not exhibit any significant changes related to the council meeting. The risk-neutral density's skewness is very volatile and changes from positive to negative values, so that no clear interpretation is possible. *wp*3 first rises up to the day of the council meeting and then also becomes very volatile. Since there is no obvious trend in standard deviation the increase in excess kurtosis cannot be interpreted.

Figures 9.17 and 9.18 do not show pronounced changes in the scaled interpercentile ranges. The percentiles appear to shift parallel to the futures price.

[13] "Financial markets are sure that the ECB will increase interest rates on Thursday. Most bank economists expect the ECB to continue the policy of raising rates in »small steps«." (Finanzmärkte rechnen fest mit einer Zinserhöhung, FAZ, June 8, 2000, p. 31.) Translation by the author.

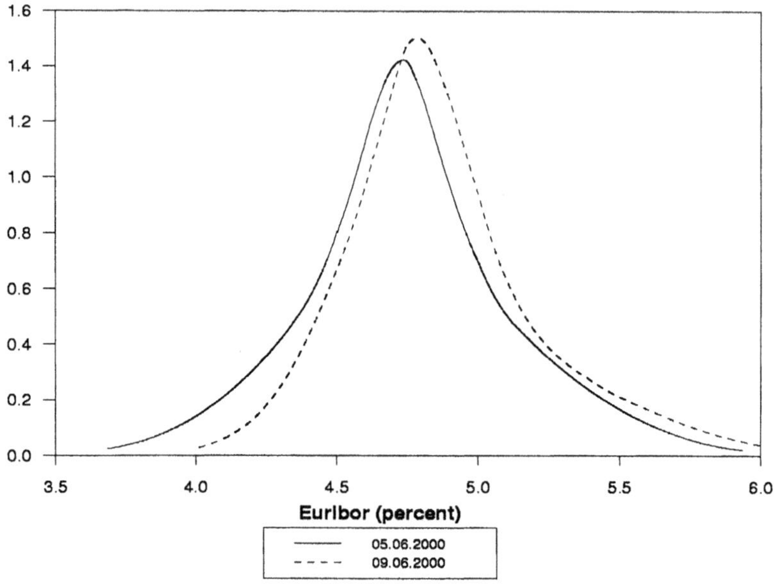

Fig. 9.13. Risk-neutral PDFs for three-month Euribor futures (September contract) on June 5 and June 9, 2000

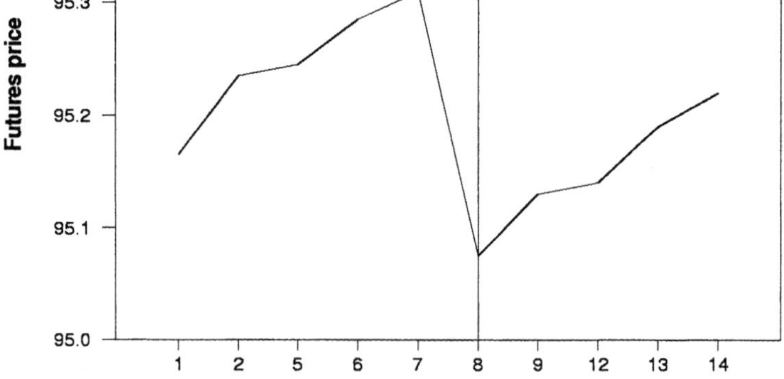

Fig. 9.14. Futures price 1.6.-14.6.2000

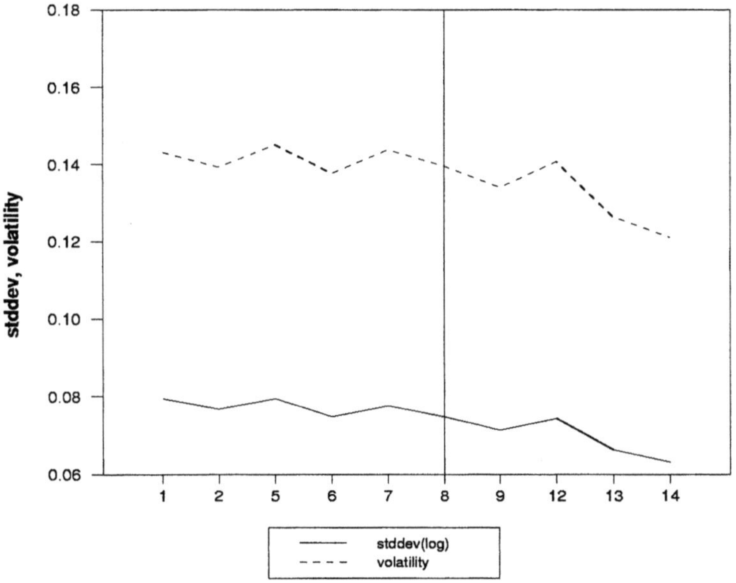

Fig. 9.15. Standard deviation and volatility 1.6.-14.6.2000

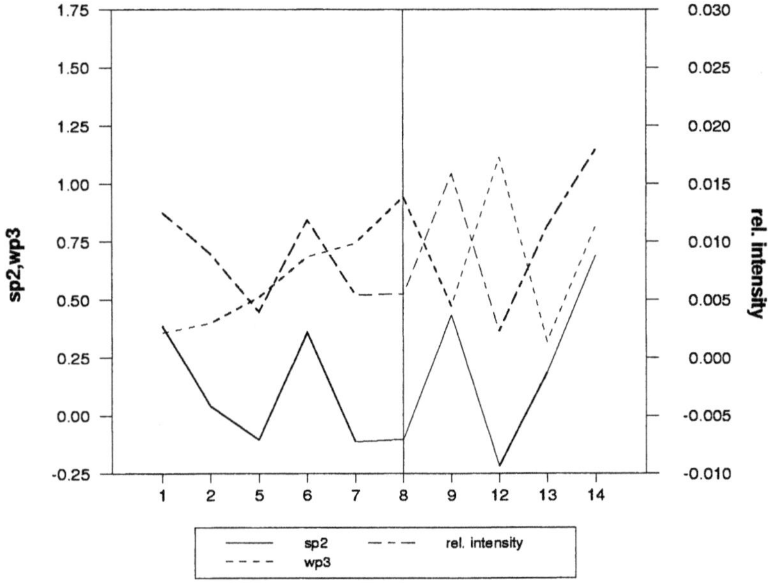

Fig. 9.16. Skewness and excess kurtosis 1.6.-14.6.2000

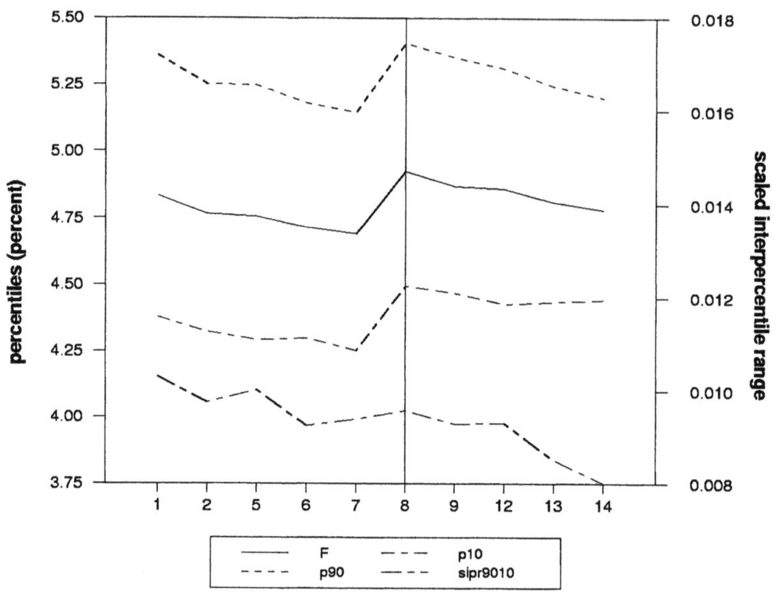

Fig. 9.17. 90% and 10% percentiles and scaled interpercentile range 1.6.-14.6.2000

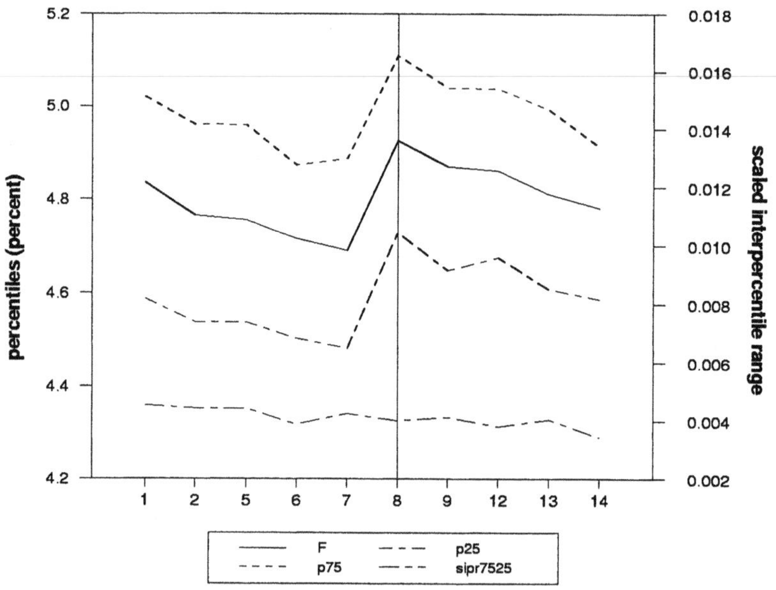

Fig. 9.18. 75%- and 25% percentiles and scaled interpercentile range 1.6.-14.6.2000

The regression results in table 9.3 show that after accounting for maturity dependence evidence can be found for a significant increase in uncertainty after the council meeting. The dummy variable's coefficients are positive in the equations for standard deviation and volatility and significantly positive for both scaled interpercentile ranges. Therefore, the larger-than-expected interest-rate increase seems to have raised uncertainty in market expectations. This effect is not as obvious in the time-series graphs because of the effects of decreasing time to expiration.

Table 9.3. Regression results for implied PDFs 1.6.-14.6.2000

statistic	constant	dummy	time to expiration	$\bar{R}^2$
stddev(log)	-0.05168	0.00116	0.00172*	0.652
volatility	-0.02977	0.00222	0.00229	0.395
*sp*2	1.04946	-0.00923	-0.01239	-0.324
*wp*3	3.93808	-0.04711	-0.04523	-0.060
rel. intensity	0.00928	0.00151	0.00001	-0.317
sipr9010	-0.01529*	0.00088*	0.00033*	0.852
sipr7525	-0.00669*	0.00035*	0.00015*	0.847

* (**) denotes significance at the 5% level (10% level).

July 13 - July 26, 2000

The ECB council decided on July 20, 2000 to leave official interest rates unchanged as anticipated by financial-market participants.[14]

While the expected value is almost unchanged the risk-neutral density strongly contracts from Wednesday to Friday (Figures 9.19 and 9.20) indicating a marked decline in uncertainty among market participants. Generally, the futures-price series is very smooth. Standard deviation and volatility first increase slightly and then decline again. A significant effect of the ECB council meeting is not visible.

The excess kurtosis statistic *wp*3 conveys little information because of its high volatility. The *sp*2 and relative intensity series are very volatile as well as the 75% percentile. This indicates that the erratic behaviour of *wp*3 and skewness is driven by the risk-neutral density's upper part. Some days before the council meeting the risk-neutral density becomes negatively skewed. After the meeting

[14] "The decision of the ECB to leave official interest rates for the euro zone unchanged had little effects on the bond market. Market participants said, »We expected this decision«." (Die Börsen reagieren freundlich auf Greenspan-Rede, FAZ, July 21, 2000, p. 25.) Translation by the author.

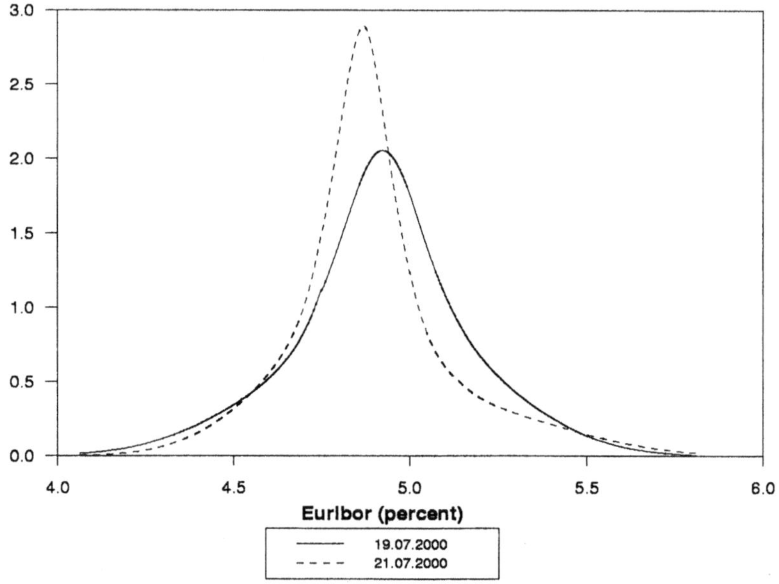

Fig. 9.19. Risk-neutral PDFs for three-month Euribor futures (September contract) on July 19 and July 21, 2000

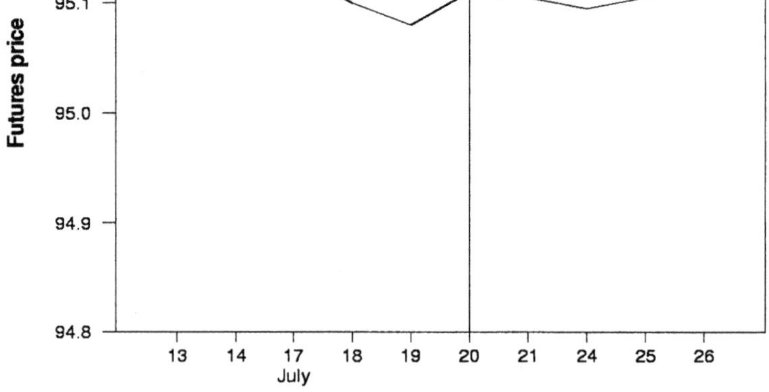

Fig. 9.20. Futures price 13.7.-26.7.2000

it oscillates between positive and negative skewness. The scaled interpercentile ranges indicate a slight decrease in uncertainty due to the council meeting.

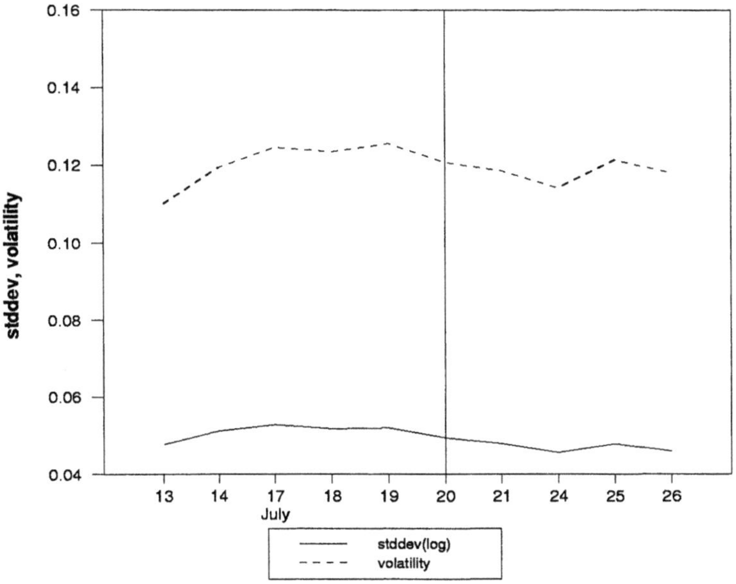

Fig. 9.21. Standard deviation and volatility 13.7.-26.7.2000

Table 9.4. Regression results for implied PDFs 13.7.-26.7.2000

statistic	constant	dummy	time to expiration	$\bar{R}^2$
stddev(log)	0.05272*	-0.00387	-0.00004	0.376
volatility	0.18917*	-0.00964	-0.00152	-0.026
*sp*2	-5.20488*	0.60838*	0.11733*	0.073
*wp*3	-2.08238	0.37039**	0.06811	-0.203
rel. intensity	-0.09186*	0.01061*	0.00215*	0.134
sipr9010	0.00607*	-0.00049**	0.00001	0.632
sipr7525	0.00475*	-0.00042**	-0.00005	0.272

* (**) denotes significance at the 5% level (10% level).

The significantly negative coefficients on the dummy variable in the equations for both scaled interpercentile ranges (table 9.4) show that the council meeting led to a decline in uncertainty in market participants' expectations. Another result is a significantly positive effect on *sp*2 and relative intensity, i.e. the council meeting caused a more positively skewed risk-neutral density, so that

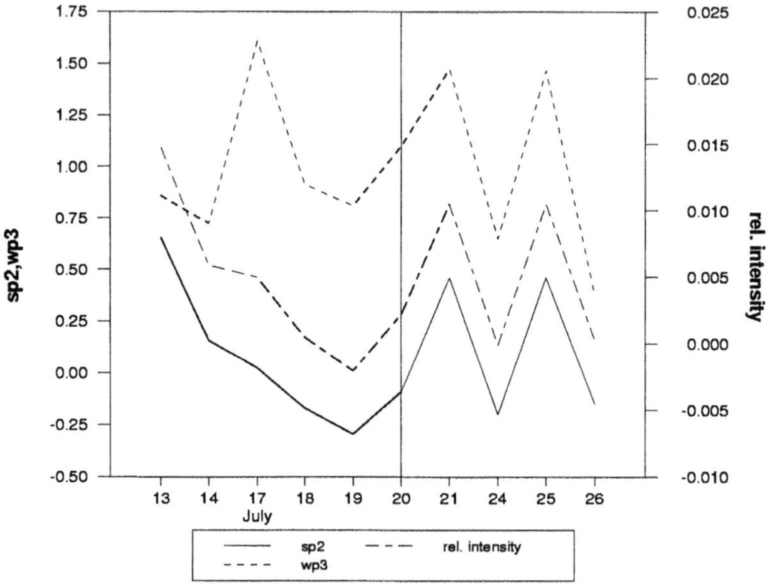

Fig. 9.22. Skewness and excess kurtosis 13.7.-26.7.2000

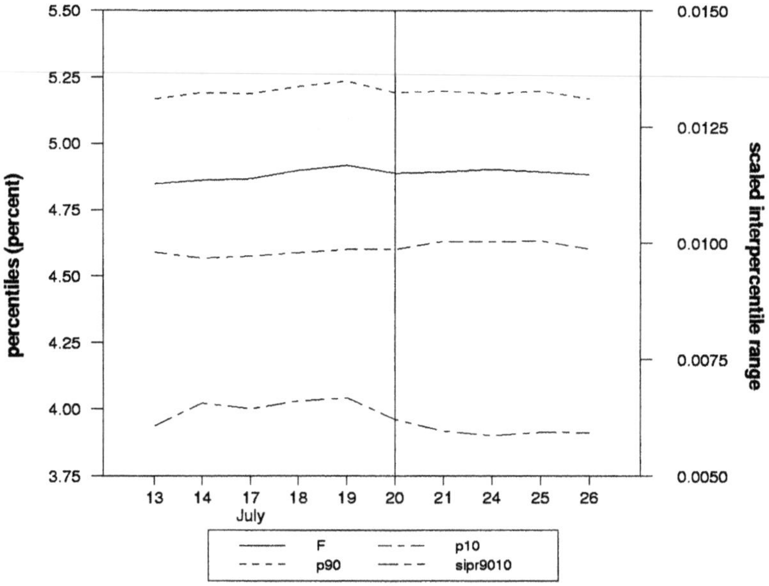

Fig. 9.23. 90% and 10% percentiles and scaled interpercentile range 13.7.-26.7.2000

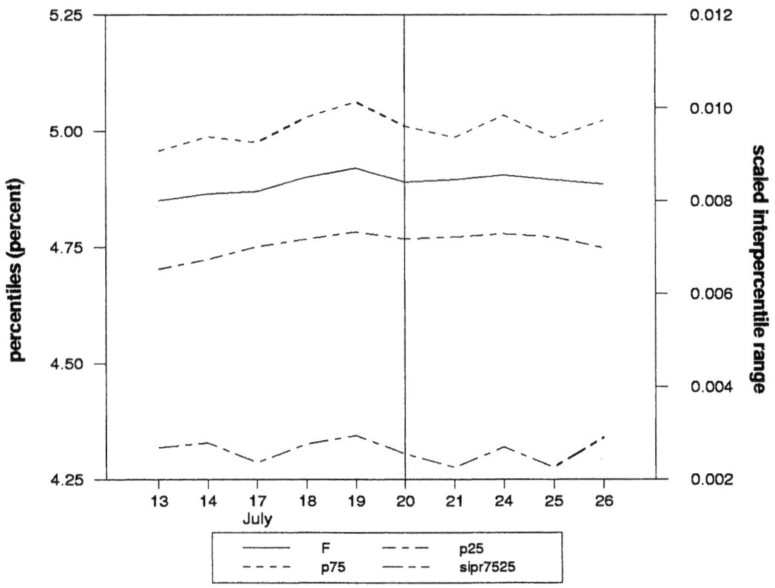

Fig. 9.24. 75% and 25% percentiles and scaled interpercentile range 13.7.-26.7.2000

the probability of large interest-rate increases rose relative to that of large interest rate declines. Note, however, that these equations, as well as that for *wp*3, exhibit very low values for $\bar{R}^2$.

August 24 - September 6, 2000

Market participants correctly anticipated the ECB council's decision on August 31 to increase official interest rates.[15]

From Wednesday to Friday the risk-neutral density shifted to the left and its dispersion decreased. The futures price did not move much. Standard deviation and volatility started to decrease well before the council meeting and were roughly constant afterwards.

Excess kurtosis exhibits a declining trend but was subject to an upward shift on Thursday. Since standard deviation at the same time declines this indicates increasing confidence in the current level of interest rates. The risk-neutral density was positively skewed on most days. Skewness increased on days close to the council meeting implying that market participants assigned increasing

[15] "... added to expectations that the ECB will raise official interest rates this Thursday." (Die Märkte rechnen fest mit einer Zinserhöhung, FAZ, August 31, 2000, p. 31.) Translation by the author.

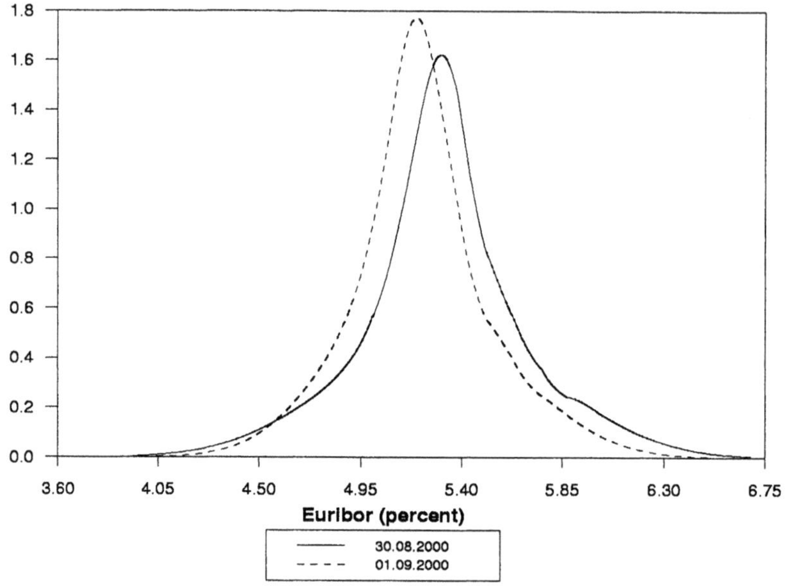

Fig. 9.25. Risk-neutral PDFs for three-month Euribor futures (December contract) on August 30 and September 1, 2000

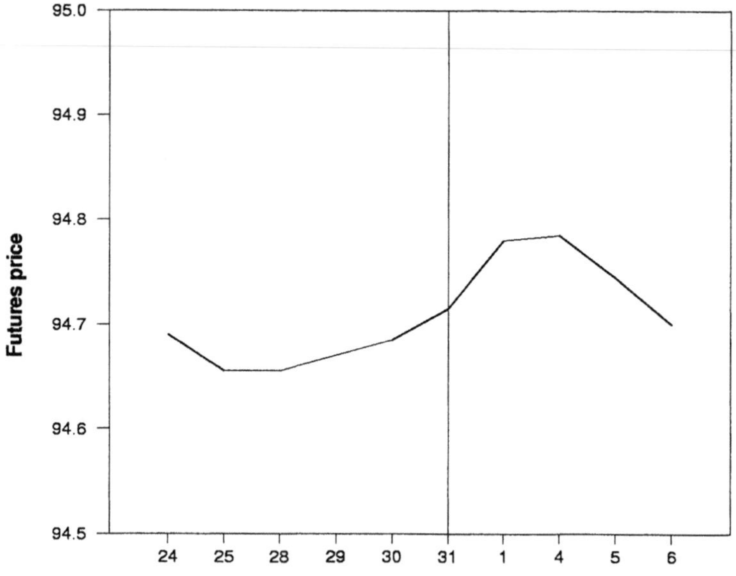

Fig. 9.26. Futures price 24.8.-6.9.2000

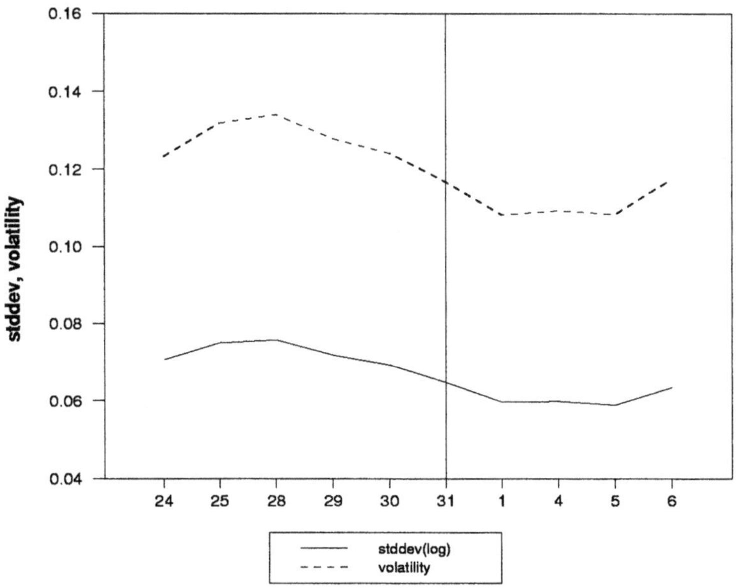

Fig. 9.27. Standard deviation and volatility 24.8.-6.9.2000

probabilities to significantly higher interest rates in the future. In the scaled interpercentile ranges' time series a negative effect of the council meeting can be observed. It seems to be most strongly related to the behaviour of the upper percentiles (75% and 90%) that converge much faster towards the futures price.

Table 9.5. Regression results for implied PDFs 24.8.-6.9.2000

statistic	constant	dummy	time to expiration	$\bar{R}^2$
stddev(log)	0.03624	-0.00889*	0.00045	0.813
volatility	0.12529**	-0.01598*	-0.00004	0.731
*sp*2	-1.06429	0.17399	0.00965	-0.275
*wp*3	2.79100	-0.32433	-0.01969	-0.160
rel. intensity	-0.04441	0.00408	0.00056	-0.445
sipr9010	0.00383	-0.00118*	0.00008	0.899
sipr7525	0.00193	-0.00039*	0.00003	0.574
* (**) denotes significance at the 5% level (10% level).				

The regression results provide evidence for significantly declining uncertainty as a consequence of the council meeting. The dummy variable's coefficients

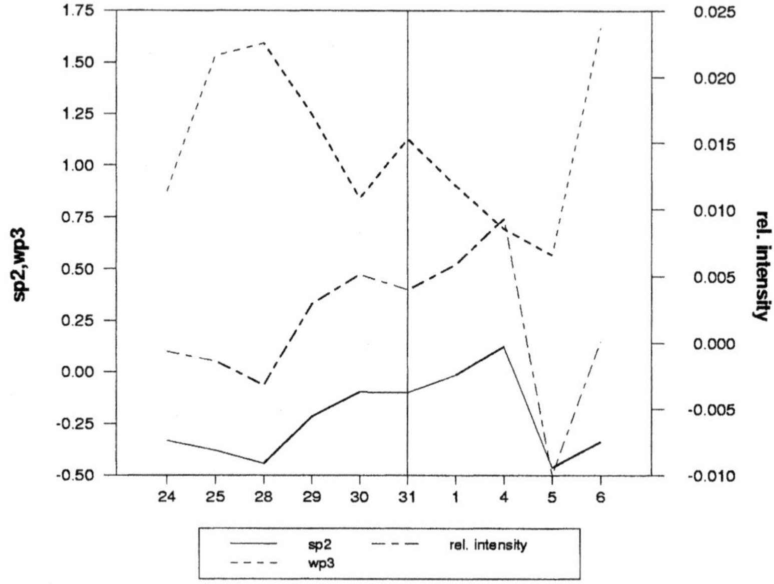

Fig. 9.28. Skewness and excess kurtosis 24.8.-6.9.2000

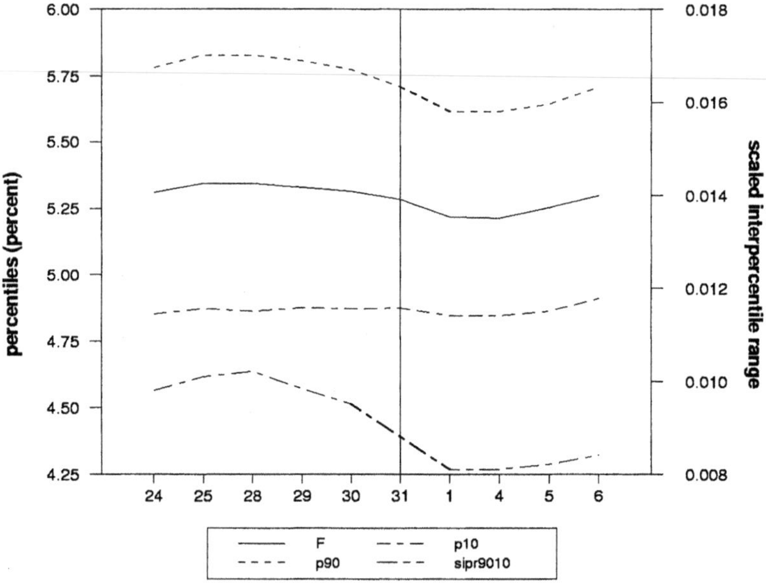

Fig. 9.29. 90% and 10% percentiles and scaled interpercentile range 24.8.-6.9.2000

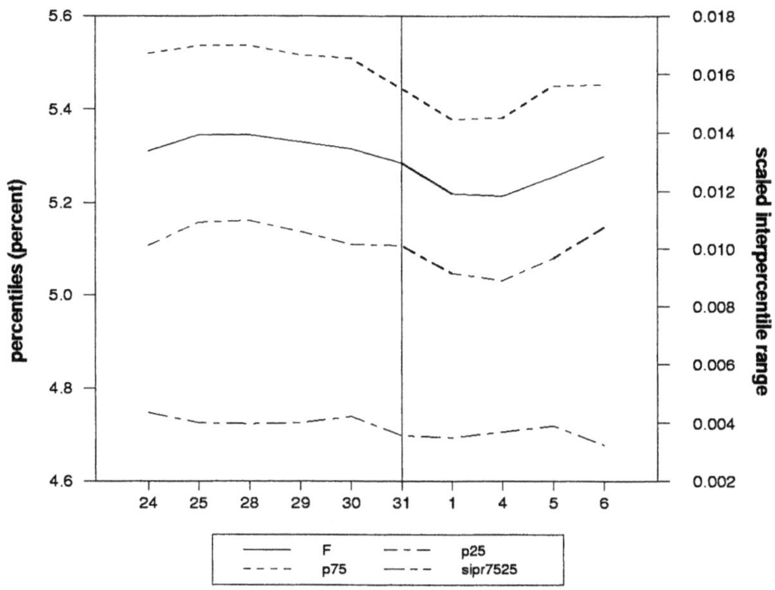

Fig. 9.30. 75% and 25% percentiles and scaled interpercentile range 24.8.-6.9.2000

are significantly negative in the equations for standard deviation, volatility, and both scaled interpercentile ranges.

January 11 - January 24, 2001

Most market participants did not expect the ECB council to change interest rates on its meeting on January, 18, 2001. However, many analysts expected a lowering of official interest rates to take place before March 2001. The expectations concerning the upcoming council meeting proved to be correct and the ECB left interest rates unchanged.[16]

The change in the risk-neutral density from Wednesday to Friday is difficult to interpret because on the one hand the density's tails contracted but on the other it's center became less concentrated. The futures price did not change much and standard deviation and volatility declined over the days preceding the council meeting but on Friday returned to their earlier levels.

[16] "The majority of analysts expect the ECB council to leave official interest rates unchanged at 4.75 percent at its regular meeting on Thursday . [...] Unaffected by this are speculations on the futures market that imply an interest-rate decrease

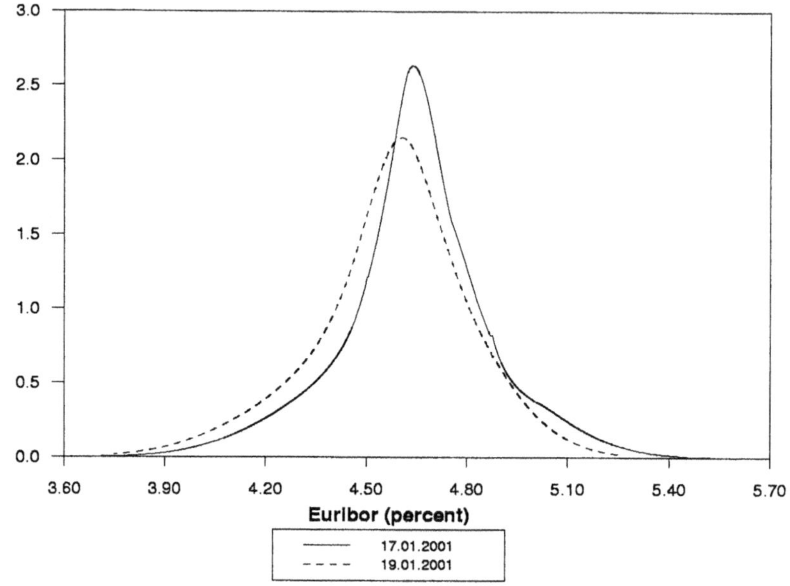

Fig. 9.31. Risk-neutral PDFs for three-month Euribor futures (March contract) on January 17 and January 19, 2001

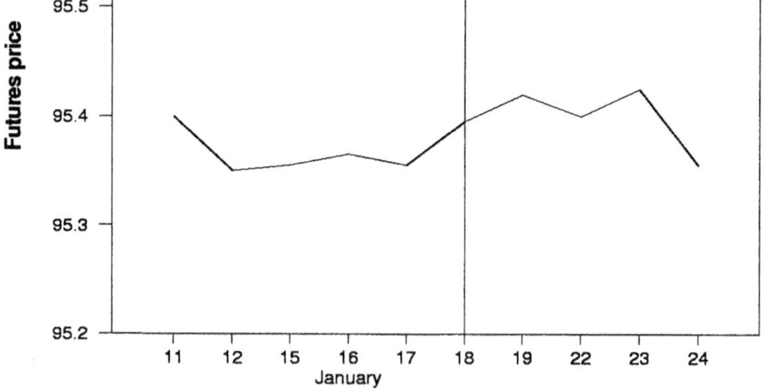

Fig. 9.32. Futures price 11.1.-24.1.2001

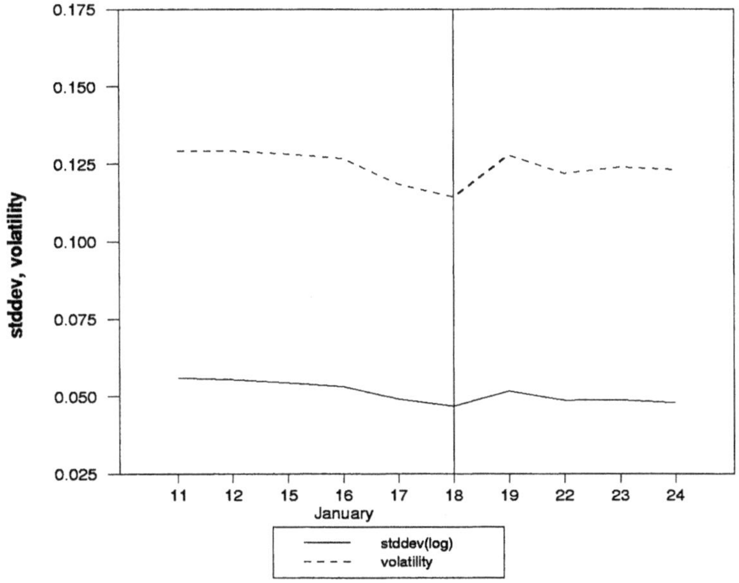

Fig. 9.33. Standard deviation and volatility 11.1.-24.1.2001

*wp*3 first increased and then declined considerably in the run-up to the council meeting while standard deviation also decreased. This indicates declining uncertainty with respect to extreme interest-rate changes in the future. On all days the risk-neutral density was negatively skewed.

*sipr*9010 attained its lowest value immediately after the council meeting, then rose again and continued on a falling trend. *sipr*7525 increased already on the day of the council meeting and stayed at a somewhat higher level for some days.

The significantly negative coefficient on the dummy in the equation for *wp*3 (Table 9.6) is probably caused by the 'hump' in excess kurtosis at the beginning of the sample. We do not find any evidence for a significantly negative effect of the council meeting on uncertainty in market expectations. In contrast, the coefficient in the equation for *sipr*7525 is significantly positive, indicating an increase in uncertainty. In interpreting these results we note that around the time of the council meeting important information on the US business cycle was also released suggesting that the downturn of the US economy was

by 25 basis points before March." (Die Märkte wittern eine Leitzinssenkung bis März, FAZ, January 17, 2001, p. 29.) Translation by the author.

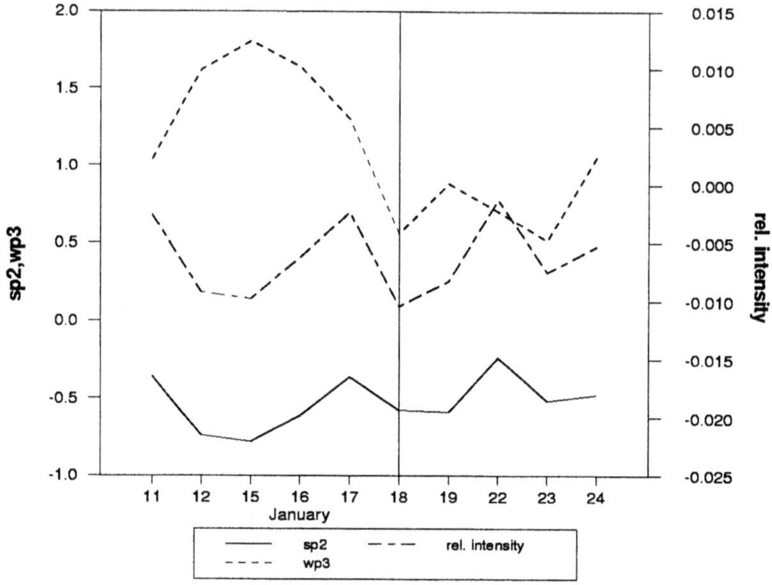

Fig. 9.34. Skewness and excess kurtosis 11.1.-24.1.2001

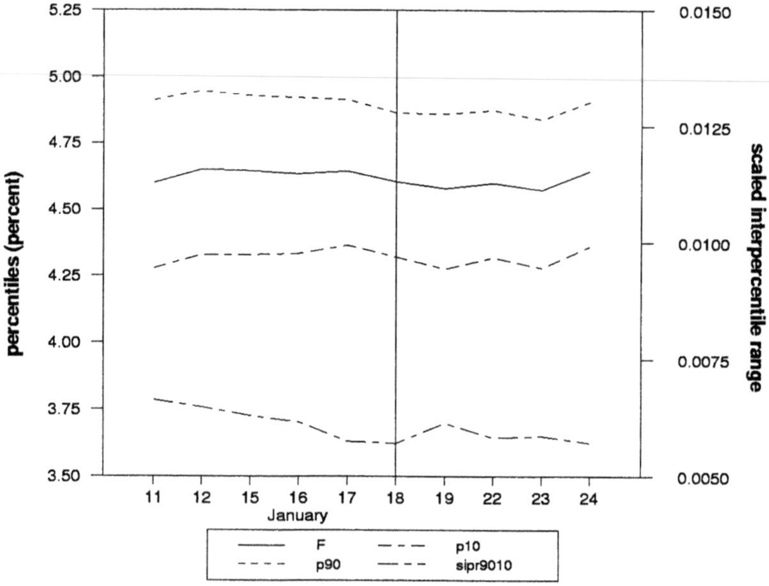

Fig. 9.35. 90% and 10% percentiles and scaled interpercentile range 11.1.-24.1.2001

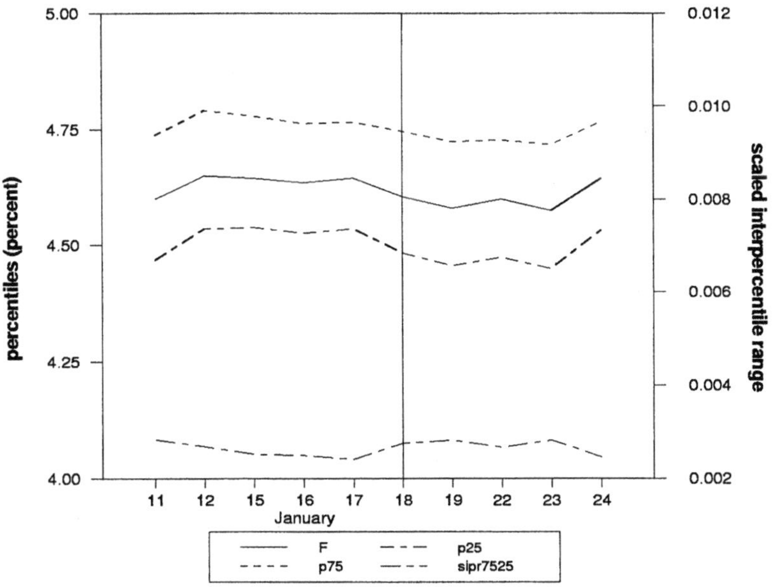

Fig. 9.36. 75% and 25% percentiles and scaled interpercentile range 11.1.-24.1.2001

much more severe than had been thought previously. It is possible that this information caused the increase in uncertainty shown in our results.[17]

Table 9.6. Regression results for implied PDFs 11.1.-24.1.2001

statistic	constant	dummy	time to expiration	$\bar{R}^2$
stddev(log)	0.02238	-0.00115	0.00069	0.584
volatility	0.11731**	-0.00284	0.00019	-0.121
*sp*2	1.27161	-0.11430	-0.04130	-0.271
*wp*3	4.10805*	-1.03002*	-0.05840	0.660
rel. intensity	0.02629	-0.00409	-0.00072	-0.142
sipr9010	0.00099	0.00017	0.00012*	0.608
sipr7525	-0.00071	0.00051*	0.00007*	0.697

* (**) denotes significance at the 5% level (10% level).

[17] See, for example, "Weiter warten auf den Start zur Frühjahrsrally", FAZ, January 19, 2001, p. 25.

March 22 - April 5, April 2001

Prior to the ECB council meeting on March 29 market participants expected the ECB to lower official interest rates. Consequently, market participants were disappointed by the ECB's announcement of its decision to keep interest rates at their then present level.[18]

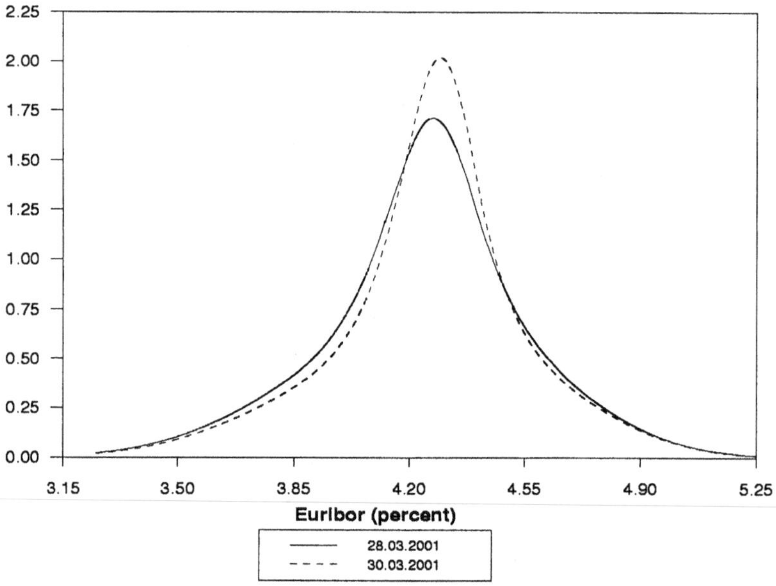

Fig. 9.37. Risk-neutral PDFs for three-month Euribor futures (June contract) on March 28, and March 30, 2001

By inspecting the risk-neutral densities only a slight contraction around the center is apparent while the densities' tails are very close to each other. The futures price series is without significant change,s while standard deviation and volatility exhibit a declining trend.

Skewness increased and peaked on the day of the council meeting when the risk-neutral density became positively skewed. However, it then became negatively skewed again. Relative intensity shows the same qualitative results. Excess kurtosis declined just before and after the council meeting indicating

[18] "... statements of ECB council members have fuelled hopes that the ECB will decrease official interest rates in the near future, perhaps as soon as the next council meeting on Thursday." (Hoffnung auf Zinssenkung hellt Stimmung auf, FAZ, March 24, p. 25.) See also "EZB-Entscheidung enttäuscht die Märkte", FAZ, March 30, 2001, p. 25. Translations by the author.

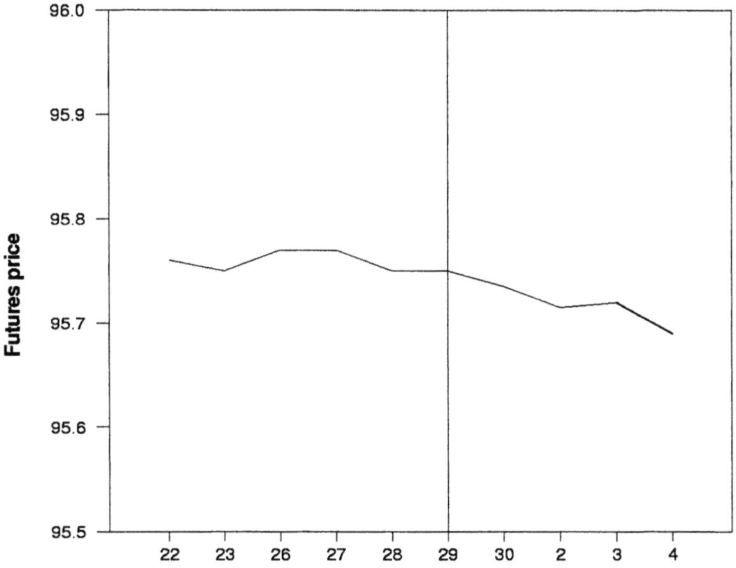

Fig. 9.38. Futures price 22.3.-4.4.2001

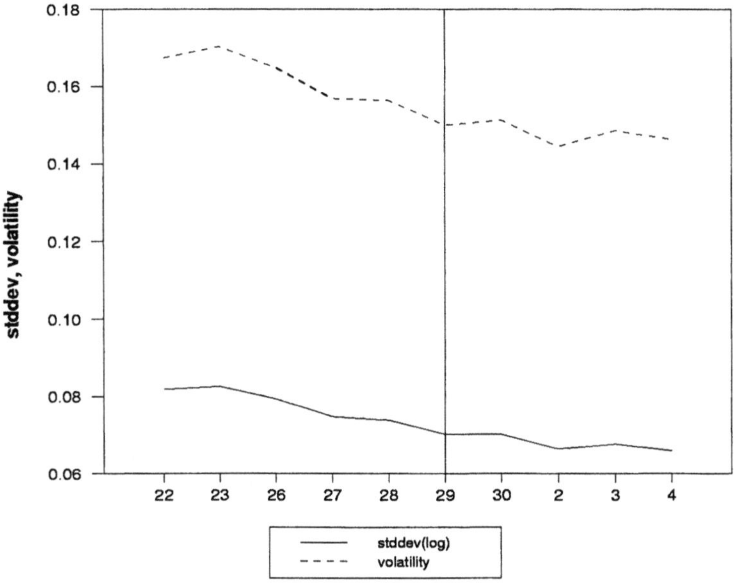

Fig. 9.39. Standard deviation and volatility 22.3.-4.4.2001

decreasing uncertainty about strong interest-rate changes in the future. Beginning on Friday after the council meeting, excess kurtosis rose again while standard deviation stayed roughly constant. For the scaled interpercentile ranges a declining trend is clearly visible.

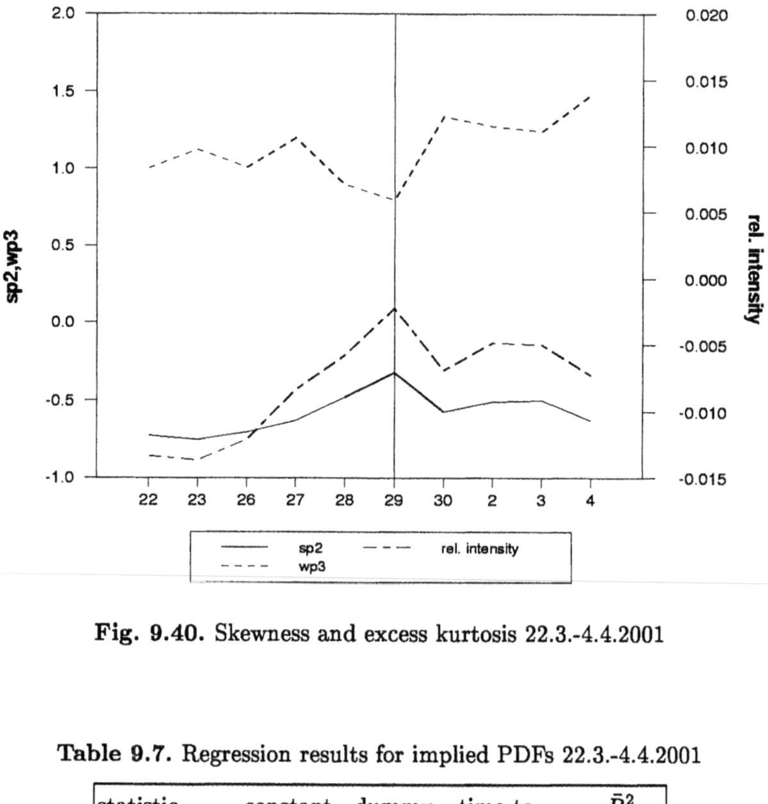

Fig. 9.40. Skewness and excess kurtosis 22.3.-4.4.2001

Table 9.7. Regression results for implied PDFs 22.3.-4.4.2001

statistic	constant	dummy	time to expiration	$\bar{R}^2$
stddev(log)	-0.02276	-0.00167	0.00175*	0.927
volatility	0.03075	-0.00362	0.00228*	0.854
*sp*2	-1.79572	0.18107	0.02062	0.249
*wp*3	4.93515	-0.13990	-0.06734	0.062
rel. intensity	-0.02620	0.00228	-0.00064	0.386
sipr9010	-0.00280	-0.00012	0.00019*	0.934
sipr7525	-0.00370**	-0.00008	0.00013*	0.901

* (**) denotes significance at the 5% level (10% level).

The regression results show standard deviation, volatility and scaled interpercentile ranges depend significantly on time to expiration. However, the council-meeting dummy has no significant effect on any of the variables. We

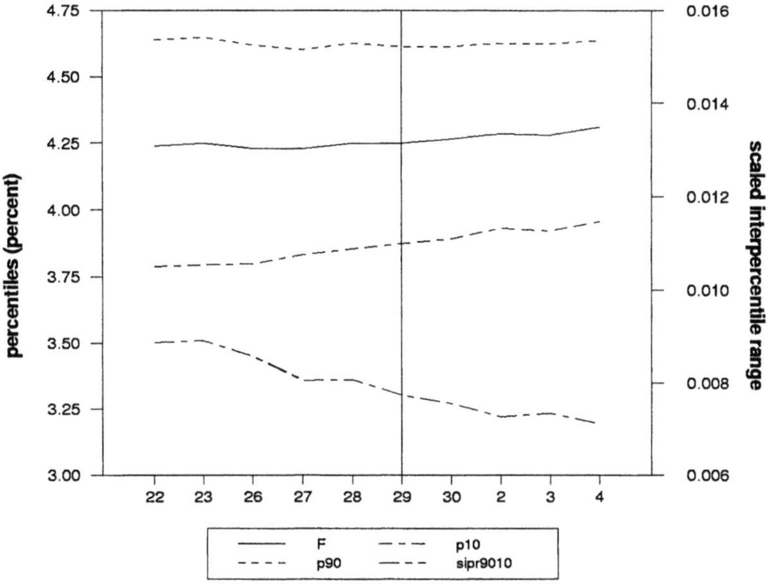

Fig. 9.41. 90% and 10% percentiles and scaled interpercentile range 22.3.-4.4.2001

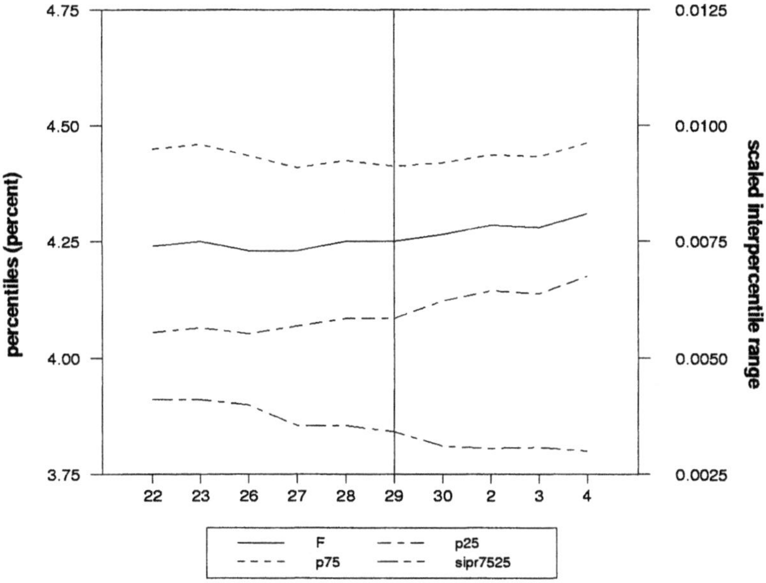

Fig. 9.42. 75% and 25% percentiles and scaled interpercentile range 22.3.-4.4.2001

find no evidence for decreasing uncertainty in expectations after the council meeting.

May 3 - May 16, 2001

Market participants were surprised by the lowering of interest rates announced after the council meeting on May 10, 2001. The ECB had left interest rates unchanged over the preceding weeks and inflation and money-growth figures were not suggesting an easing of monetary policy.[19] In order to justify the interest rate decrease the ECB released figures for an adjusted version of M3 with growth rates significantly below those of conventional M3. Some market participants criticized the ECB as behaving unpredictably others applauded its long overdue reaction to the deteriorating business cycle conditions.[20]

The surprise character of the interest rate decrease is clearly visible in the density's shift to the left and the jump in the futures price on May, 10. In addition, the risk-neutral density on Friday is more concentrated around the mean indicating a decline in uncertainty in expectations.

Figure 9.45 shows a decline in standard deviation and volatility on Thursday and Friday after the council meeting. Excess kurtosis increased strongly on May 10 indicating decreasing uncertainty in expectations about moderate interest-rate changes. Evidence for a decline in uncertainty in expectations is also provided by strongly decreasing scaled interpercentile ranges.

Table 9.8. Regression results for implied PDFs 3.5.-16.5.2001

statistic	constant	dummy	time to expiration	$\bar{R}^2$
stddev(log)	0.07379	-0.00749*	0.00035	0.803
volatility	0.20841*	-0.01261*	-0.00037	0.658
*sp*2	-0.11390	0.15720**	0.00773	0.060
*wp*3	-8.25700*	0.41774**	0.10588*	0.419
rel. intensity	-0.04670*	0.00958*	0.00033	0.197
sipr9010	0.00901*	-0.00143*	0.00003	0.963
sipr7525	0.01287*	-0.00111*	-0.00008**	0.781

* (**) denotes significance at the 5% level (10% level).

19 "In European financial markets hopes for lower official interest rates have been dashed. The majority of economists now expect the ECB at its meeting on Thursday to leave official interest rates unchanged at 4.75 percent." (Keine Hoffnung auf Zinssenkung der EZB, FAZ, May 8, 2001, p. 31.) Translation by the author.

20 See "EZB-Zinsbeschluß weckt Hoffnungen", FAZ, May 11, 2001, p. 25, and ECB (2001b).

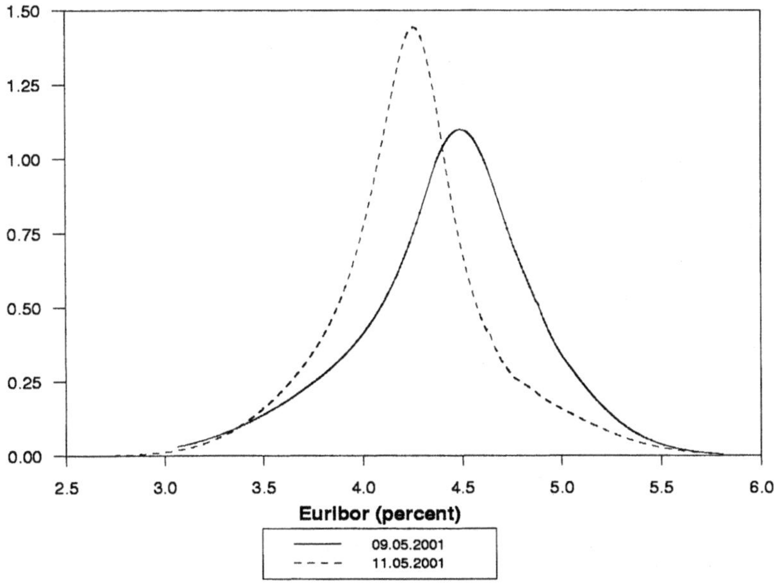

Fig. 9.43. Risk-neutral PDFs for three-month Euribor futures (September contract) on May 9 and May 11, 2001

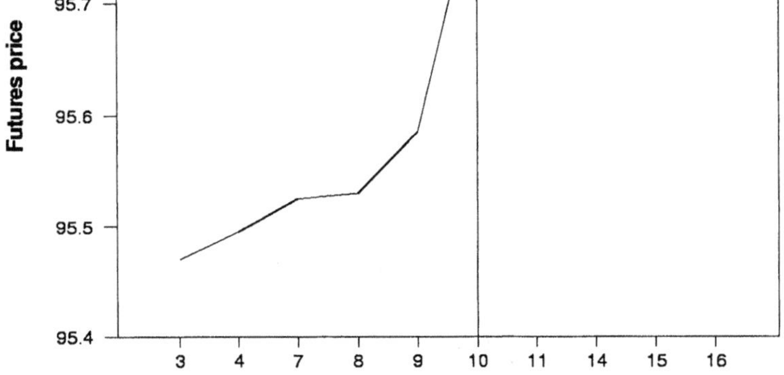

Fig. 9.44. Futures price 3.5.-16.5.2001

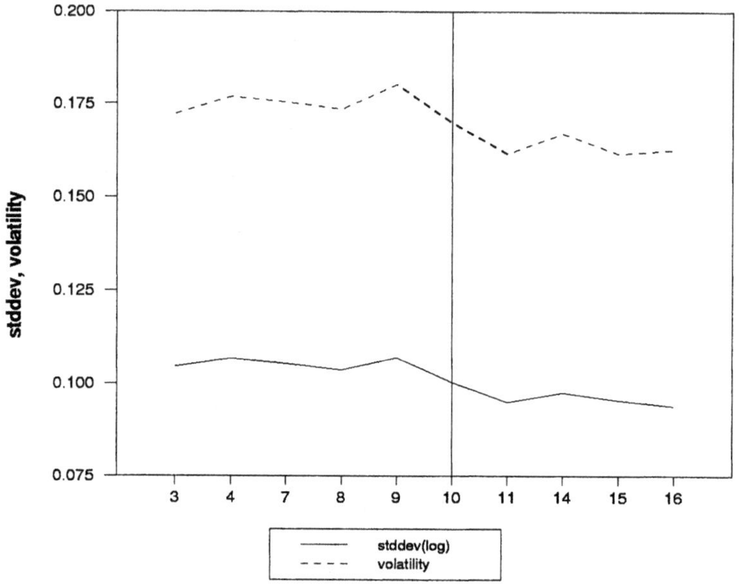

Fig. 9.45. Standard deviation and volatility 3.5.-16.5.2001

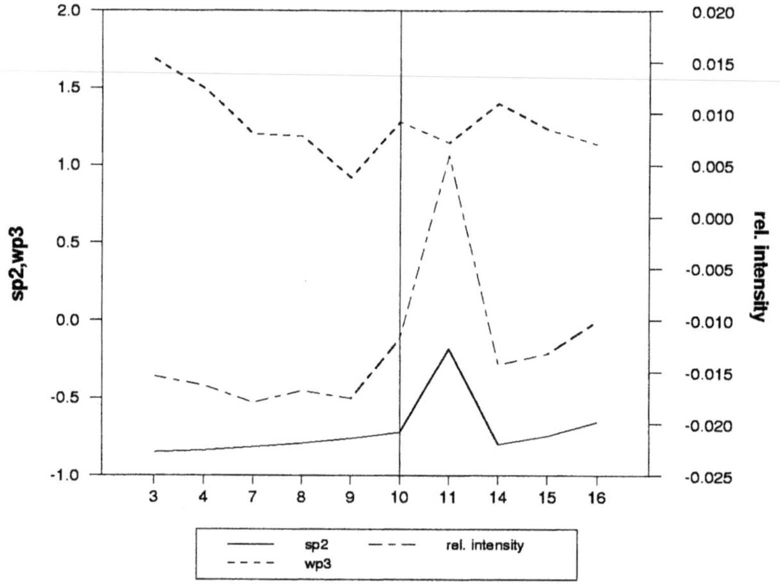

Fig. 9.46. Skewness and excess kurtosis 3.5.-16.5.2001

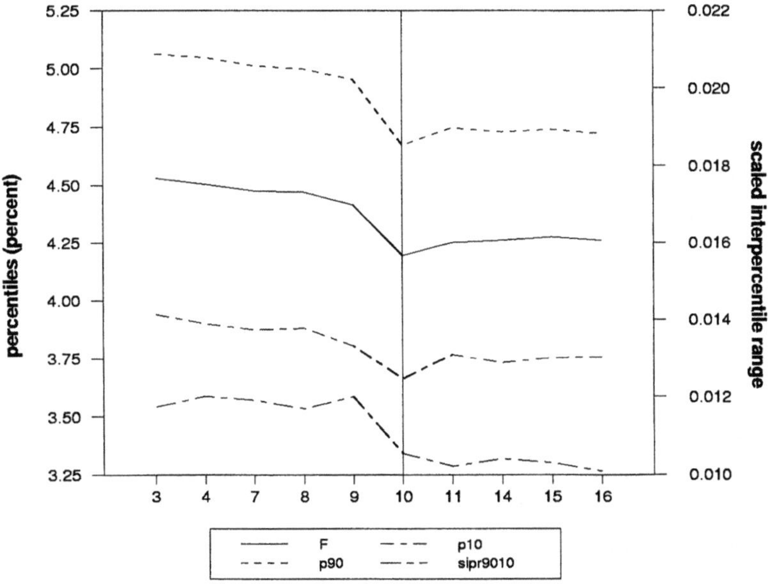

Fig. 9.47. 90% and 10% percentiles and scaled interpercentile range 3.5.-16.5.2001

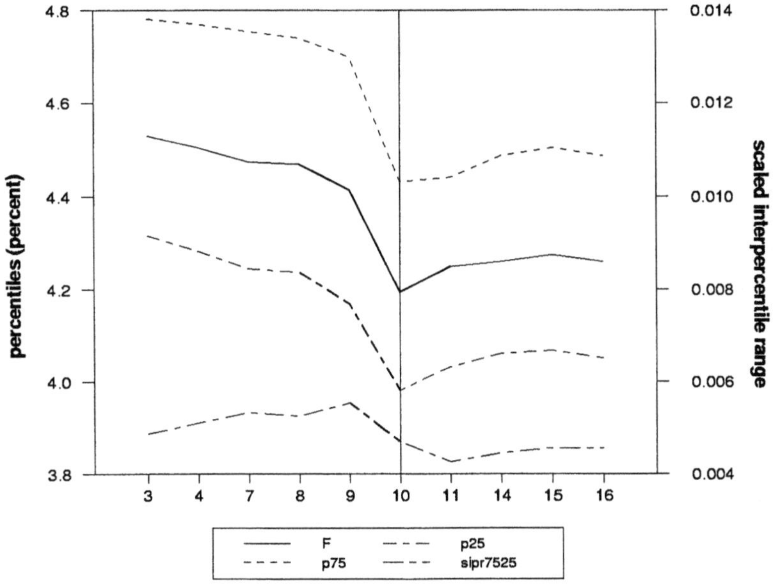

Fig. 9.48. 75% and 25% percentiles and scaled interpercentile range 3.5.-16.5.2001

The regression results support this interpretation. For all uncertainty-related statistics we find significantly negative coefficients on the dummy variable. Furthermore, we find evidence for increasing excess kurtosis and more negative skewness after the council meeting.[21] These results show that the ECB succeeded in reducing uncertainty in market participants' expectations despite the surprise character of the interest-rate decrease.

May 31 - June 13, 2001

As anticipated by the market, at its meeting on June, 7 the the ECB council decided to leave official interest rates unchanged.[22]
The risk-neutral densities before and after the council meeting are very close to each other. Some days before the council meeting the futures price began to decline. The futures price level indicates that market participants expected interest rates to fall further to about 4.25%.

Standard deviation and volatility declined slightly after the council meeting after having increased on Wednesday. Skewness and excess kurtosis patterns do not differ on the five days before and after the council meeting.

Both scaled interpercentile ranges were slightly lower after the council meeting. In addition, *sipr*7525 increased at the beginning of the council-meeting week and on Thursday returned to its previous level.

The regression results show evidence for a statistically significant decline in uncertainty in market expectations after the ECB-council meeting. The coefficient on the dummy variable is significanty negative in the equations for both scaled interpercentile ranges. In addition, the dummy has a negative but insignificant coefficient in the equations for standard deviation and volatility. Significant effects are also found for relative intensity and *wp*3 but with low values for $\bar{R}^2$.

---

[21] The latter result can be interpreted as showing that most market participants expected an additional small interest-rate decrease in the future. However, the regression results for *sp*2 are strongly influenced by the observation on May 11 so that they should be interpreted cautiously.

[22] "At the present time analysts do not expect a change in interest rates." (Die Börse heute, FAZ, June 7, 2001, p. 33.) "The ECB's decision to leave official interest rates unchanged was no surprise to financial markets." (Euro profitiert von Duisenbergs guten Worten, FAZ, June 8, 2001, p. 25.) Translation by the author.

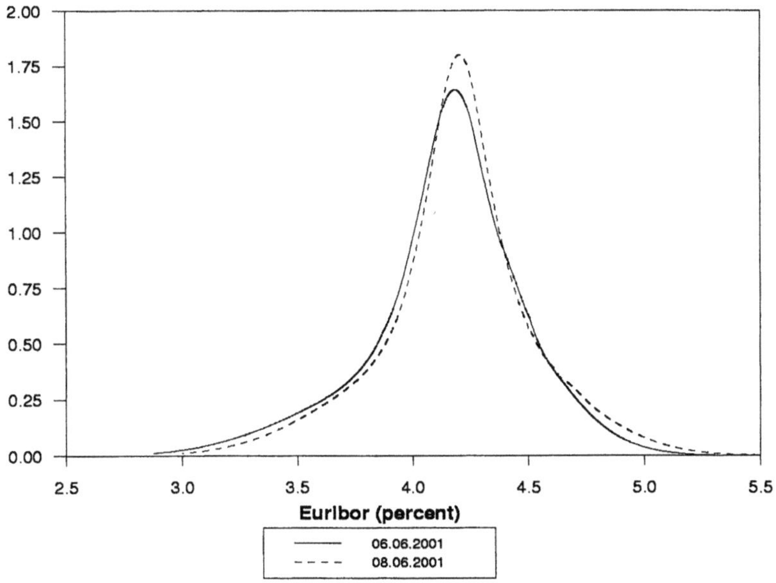

Fig. 9.49. Risk-neutral PDFs for three-month Euribor futures (September contract) on June 6 and June 8, 2001.

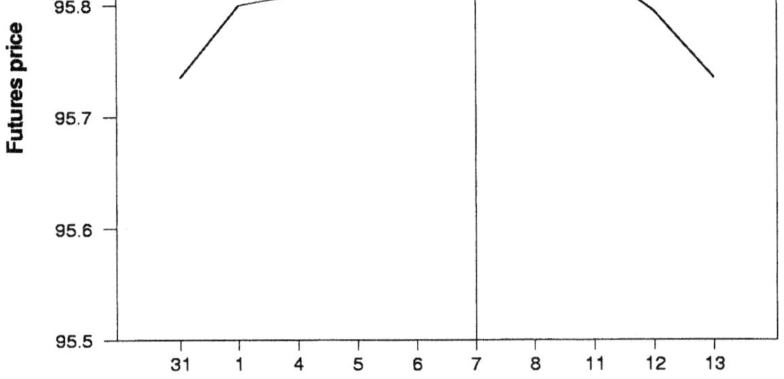

Fig. 9.50. Futures price 31.5.-13.6.2001

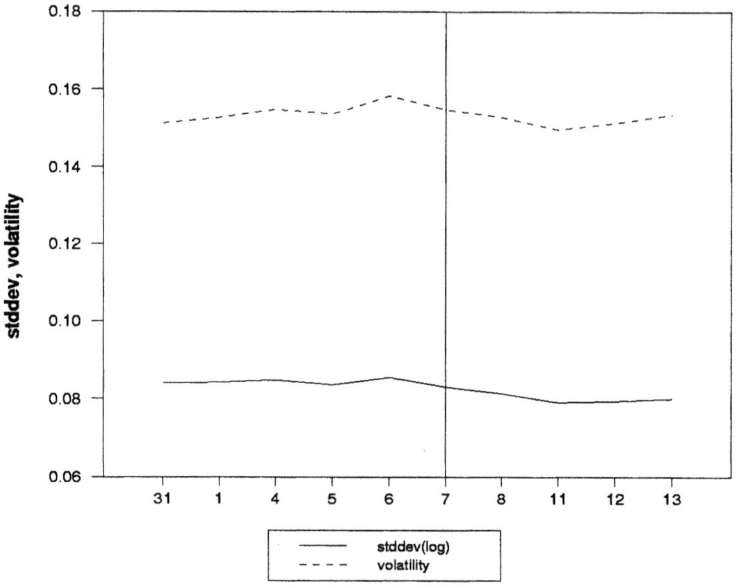

Fig. 9.51. Standard deviation and volatility 31.5.-13.6.2001

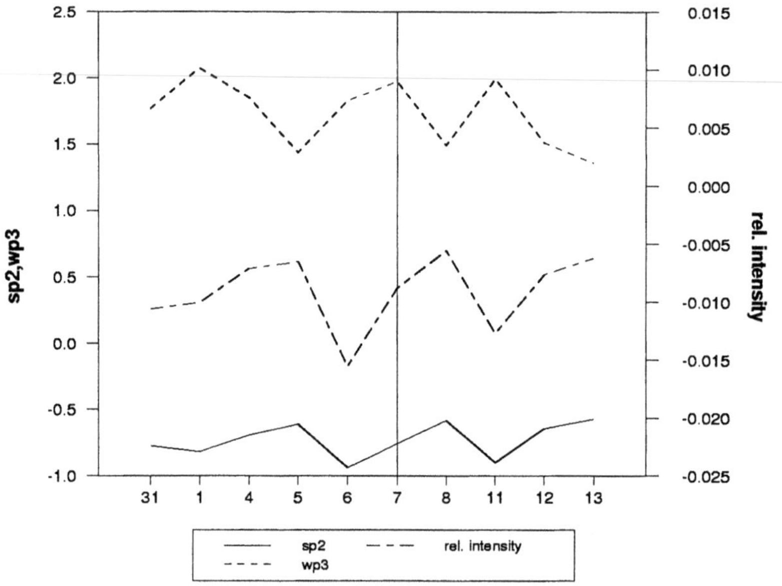

Fig. 9.52. Skewness and excess kurtosis 31.5.-13.6.2001

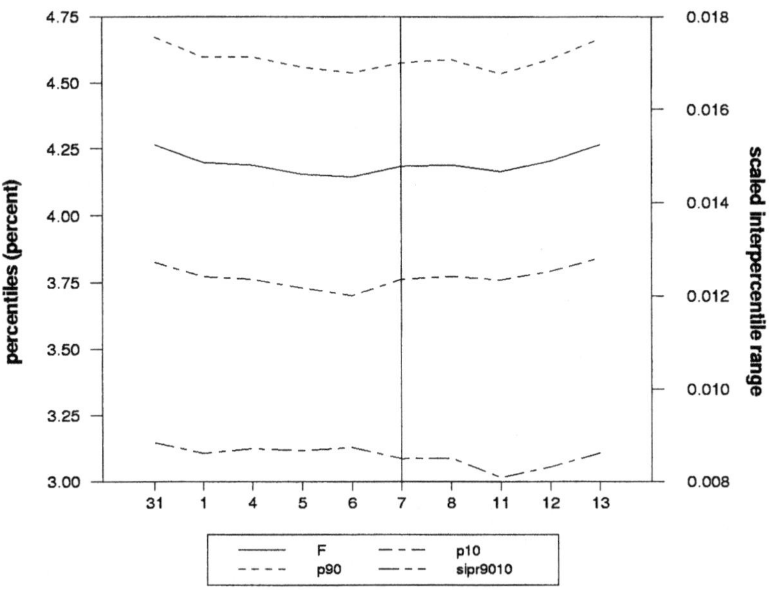

Fig. 9.53. 90% and 10% percentiles and scaled interpercentile range 31.5.-13.6.2001

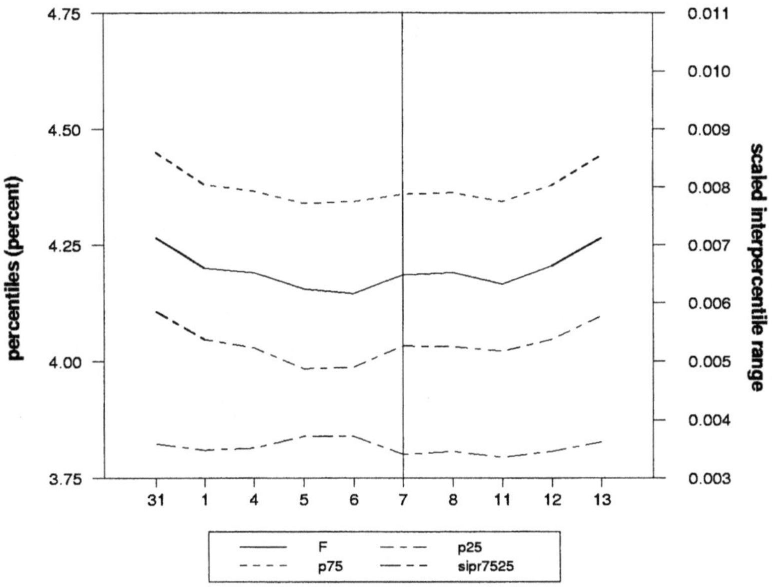

Fig. 9.54. 75% and 25% percentiles and scaled interpercentile range 31.5.-13.6.2001

Table 9.9. Regression results for implied PDFs 31.5.-13.6.2001

statistic	constant	dummy	time to expiration	$\bar{R}^2$
stddev(log)	0.05171	-0.00206	0.00044	0.742
volatility	0.17367*	-0.00383	-0.00025	0.156
*sp*2	-0.04021	0.02830	-0.00968	-0.147
*wp*3	-4.66458*	0.30475*	0.08609*	0.117
rel. intensity	-0.02179	0.00258*	0.00016	-0.165
sipr9010	0.00826*	-0.00028*	0.00001	0.409
sipr7525	0.00705*	-0.00037*	0.00005*	0.576

* (**) denotes significance at the 5% level (10% level).

August 23 - September 5, 2001

Against the background of deteriorating business-cycle conditions and falling inflation in Europe, market participants expected interest rates to be lowered at the ECB council meeting on August 30, 2001.[23] The ECB council decided to decrease official interest rates by 25 basis points. At the press conference ECB-president Duisenberg made some very pessimistic remarks concerning European business cycle conditions that prompted some market participants to expect further interest-rate decreases.[24]

The risk-neutral density did not change much over the council meeting while standard deviation and volatility show no obvious reactions.

Skewness and kurtosis do not exhibit drastic changes apart from a small positive trend in excess kurtosis beginning on Friday, August 31. For the scaled interpercentile ranges we observe a negative time trend in *sipr*9010 but no obvious effects of time to expiration on *sipr*7525.

The coefficients on the dummy variable are negative but insignificant in the equations for standard deviation, volatility, and *sipr*9010. We find a significantly positive effect on *sipr*7525 indicating that uncertainty did not unambigiously decline after the council meeting. The significantly negative coefficient in the *wp*3-equation ignores the positive trend shown at the right-hand side of Figure 9.58 and cannot be interpreted without a significant result for standard deviation.

From all these event studies it is clear that graphical comparisons of risk-neutral probability density functions provide only limited information about changes in market expectations. Only pronounced changes in market expec-

[23] "On European bond markets it is expected that the ECB will certainly lower official interest rates on Thursday." (Leitzinssenkung wird erwartet, FAZ, August 29, 2001, p. 13.) Translation by the author.

[24] See, for example, "Die EZB senkt den Leitzins auf 4,25 Prozent", FAZ, August 31, 2001, p. 23.

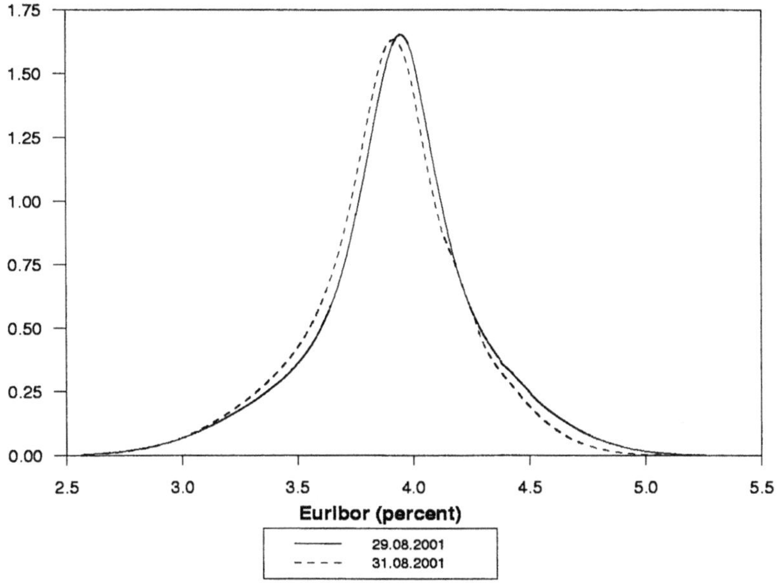

Fig. 9.55. Risk-neutral PDFs for three-month Euribor futures (December contract) on August 29 and August 31, 2001

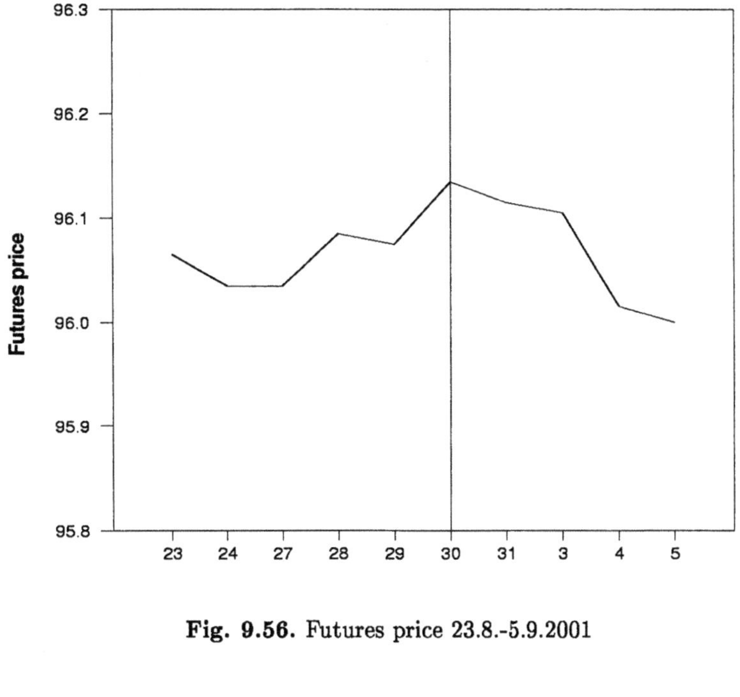

Fig. 9.56. Futures price 23.8.-5.9.2001

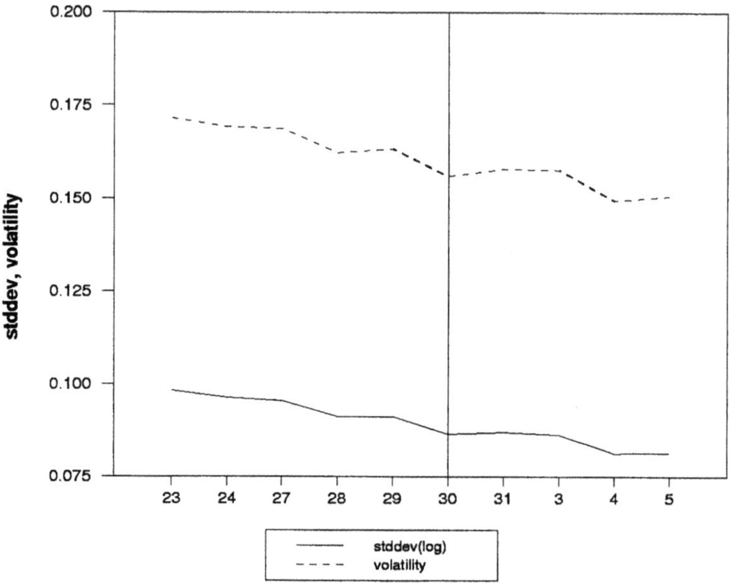

Fig. 9.57. Standard deviation and volatility 23.8.-5.9.2001

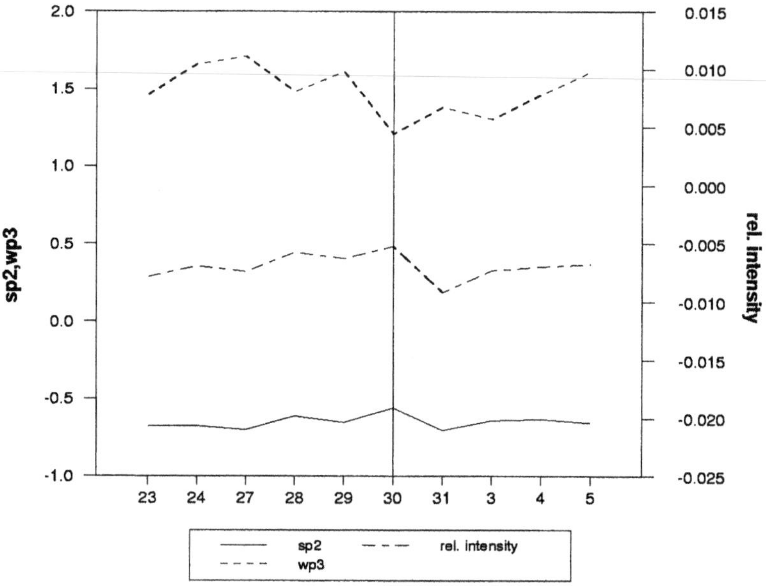

Fig. 9.58. Skewness and excess kurtosis 23.8.-5.9.2001

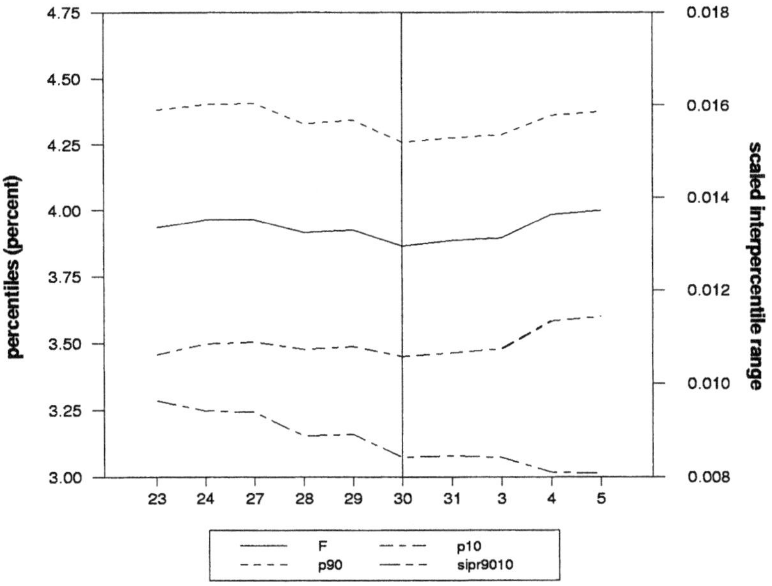

Fig. 9.59. 90% and 10% percentiles and scaled interpercentile range 23.8.-5.9.2001

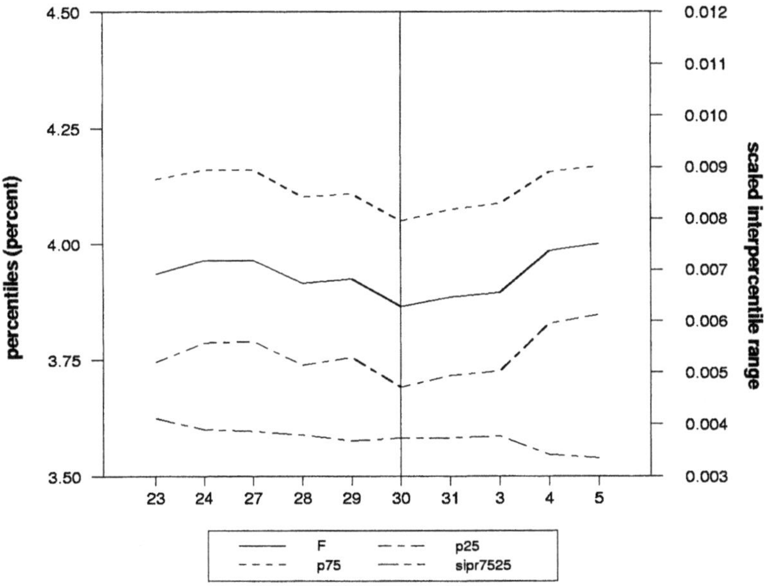

Fig. 9.60. 75% and 25% percentiles and scaled interpercentile range 23.8.-5.9.2001

Table 9.10. Regression results for implied PDFs 23.8.-5.9.2001

statistic	constant	dummy	time to expiration	$\bar{R}^2$
stddev(log)	-0.05538*	-0.00034	0.00187	0.958
volatility	-0.01813	-0.00067	0.00231*	0.917
*sp*2	-0.32808	-0.00534	-0.00408	-0.132
*wp*3	5.60633*	-0.44266*	-0.05027*	0.498
rel. intensity	0.00307	-0.00090	-0.00012	-0.387
sipr9010	-0.00356	-0.00014	0.00016*	0.932
sipr7525	-0.00437*	0.00025*	0.00010*	0.852

* (**) denotes significance at the 5% level (10% level).

tations are clearly visible, in particular large shifts in the density caused by changes in the expected value and considerable changes in the density's dispersion, i.e. of standard deviation/volatility and percentile ranges. Smaller changes in standard deviation, volatility, skewness, excess kurtosis and percentile ranges are more difficult to detect. It is also clear that inspecting risk-neutral probability density functions has considerable advantages compared to only studying changes in futures prices. For example, around July 20, 2000 the density functions show large differences while the futures price is almost unchanged.

In many cases important changes in standard deviation/volatility and in the scaled interpercentile ranges can be highlighted by visual inspection of the statistic's time series. One advantage of this approach is that it allows us to place the statistics' changes over the council meeting in a broader context. For example, some observed changes might turn out to be part of an ongoing trend that is probably not very closely related to the council meeting in question. Furthermore, by looking at the time series we can also identify transitory changes in the statistics that take place shortly before the council meeting (e.g. standard deviation and volatility in June 2001). In many cases the time series graphs suggest that the statistics might depend on the time to expiration. However, only in one case (June 2000) is maturity dependence strong enough to hide the effects of the council meeting on the statistics.
It is also important not to put too much weight on temporary changes in the risk-neutral density functions. These changes might be caused by 'noise' due to measurement errors or numerical difficulties in the estimation process. In particular *sp*2 and *wp*3, which are based on moments of order three and four, show substantial day to day fluctuations. These statistics appear to be quite sensitive to small changes in the risk-neutral densities and are more strongly affected by problems like measurement errors in option prices and difficulties with the optimization algorithm.[25] The changes in relative intensity are very

[25] Note that for the more accurate 2001 data these statistics are much less volatile.

closely related to those in *sp*2, so that relative intensity does not appear to be a more robust skewness statistic.

Very short-lived changes are much less important for the regression approach, where we focus on more persistent effects of ECB-council meetings on market expectations. In interpreting the regression results we have to bear in mind that they are based on a very limited number of observations (see the discussion in section 9.1).[26] The regression results indicate that maturity dependence is not important for the short time periods considered here.[27]

The various event studies suggest that market participants' expectations react differently to each council meeting. Nevertheless, some general conclucions can be drawn. First, if the council's decision was anticipated correctly by the market, uncertainty in expectations declined more often than in cases where market expectations turned out to be incorrect. In four out of six cases where market expectations proved to be correct both scaled interpercentile ranges declined. For the two remaining episodes the negative results might be attributed to the release of new information coinciding with the council meeting. This information led to a revision in business-cycle expectations for the US (January 2001) or the euro area (August 2001). On the other hand, if the results of council meetings were not anticipated correctly by the market, both scaled interpercentile ragnes declined in only one out of four cases. In addition, the only significant increase in both scaled interpercentile ranges occurred in May 2000 after the unexpected large increase in official interest rates.
Second, the decrease in uncertainty in market expectations is particularly strong for both correctly anticipated interest-rate increases. Here, both scaled interpercentile ranges decline significantly, as well as standard deviation and volatility. This suggests that it might be more important to market participants to correctly anticipate interest-rate *changes* than constant official interest rates. A similar result can be found for cases of expectational errors. More significant results are found for unanticipated interest-rate changes than for events where interest rates were left at their current levels while the market expected them to be changed.
For the skewness and excess-kurtosis statistics such strong effects of ECB-council meetings cannot be established. In contrast, these statistics appear to depend more heavily on the specific circumstances of the event in question. The regression approach turns out to be less suitable for these statistics because temporary changes play a more prominent role, there.

[26] The statistically significant coefficients on the dummy variable in the equations for standard deviation, volatility and the scaled interpercentile ranges are generally robust with respect to omitting or adding a single observation.
In addition, the absolute value of these coefficients is non-negligible. In most cases it is about 6% to more than 20% relative to the statistics' average value.

[27] However, if specific option contracts are studied over longer time periods as in Chapter 8, time to expiration has significant effects on most statistics.

How do these results relate to those presented in Chapter 8? Note that the observation periods are different and overlap only partially. In particular, the time of interest-rate decreases in 2001 is not covered by the homogeneity tests. As in Chapter 8, our results provide some evidence for central-bank-council meetings conveying important news to financial markets. This news causes revisions in expectations leading to changes in uncertainty in market participants' expectations (hypothesis d). In particular, uncertainty in expectations is more likely to decline if market participants correctly anticipate interest-rate changes by the ECB council than if they are surprised by the council's decision. This is in support of hypothesis e.
Furthermore, we can indirectly conclude that most interest rate changes that were eliminated from the sample in table 8.3 were correctly anticipated by market participants because uncertainty in expectations generally decreased among the dropped observations. We did not find evidence for significantly increasing uncertainty in expectations in cases where interest-rate change expectations failed to realize. This suggests that the evidence for significantly increasing uncertainty after ECB-council meetings shown in table 8.3 might be due to some outliers. No general effects of council meetings' on skewness and excess kurtosis were found. Probably this is caused by the event studies being more balanced than the sample for the homogeneity test that was dominated by a regime of increasing interest rates.

Our results show that the reactions of market participants' expectations to ECB-council meetings depend on the (economic) background that shapes how the market interprets the council meeting's results. Furthermore, the implicit assumption that the central-bank-council meeting is the only source of information affecting market expectations is not always satisfied. Both aspects make it difficult to establish general results about the effects of central-bank-council meetings on market expectations so that the event study approach appears more promising than an aggregate perspective.

9.3 Summary

In event studies of ten selected ECB-council meetings in 2000 and 2001 the effects of central-bank-council meetings on market expectations were investigated in some detail. Risk-neutral density functions were extracted from Euribor futures options prices by fitting a cubic spline function to the implied volatility smile with respect to *delta* and various techniques were used to present and discuss the results.
Graphical comparisons of risk-neutral density functions before and after an ECB-council meeting provide information only on very pronounced changes in market expectations. Smaller changes in the risk-neutral densities are less easily discernible. Inspecting the time series of various statistics computed from

implied risk-neutral density functions allows us to put day-to-day changes in the statistics into the context of more general trends. In order to deal with the well known problem of considerable 'noise' in the statistic's day-to-day changes, we used a regression technique to test for significant and persistent effects of ECB-council meetings on market expectations. While we are forced to use only a very limited number of observations in the regressions, this technique nevertheless is capable of providing some information on the statistical significance of changes in the statistics - information that cannot be derived from the graphical presentations alone.

We showed reactions in market expectations depend on the context of each ECB-council meeting and demonstrated the importance of checking for coincident releases of other important information, e.g. business cycle forecasts, that might also have significant effects on market expectations.

Our results indicate that decisions of the ECB council that are anticipated by financial markets lead to declining uncertainty in market participants' expectations. The reduction in uncertainty is particularly strong if market participants correctly anticipate increases in official interest rates. On the other hand, if market participants are surprised by the council's decision, significant declines in uncertainties are observed less often and uncertainty in expectations might even rise.

10

Summary and Conclusions

In this book we first reviewed techniques to extract implied probabilities from option prices and presented some empirical applications. We discussed how implied probabilities can be interpreted as representing the expectations of a risk-neutral agent with respect to the underlying's price in the future. We then explained various methods used for the presentation and interpretation of risk-neutral probabilities. In Chapter 5, we reviewed in some detail the most important techniques for extracting implied probabilities from option prices that in turn were compared with respect to robustness and issues related to their implementation in Chapter 6.
While the risk-neutral density functions extracted by different techniques are similar in shape, moments of higher order often differ widely. Robustness studies compare selected techniques' sensititivities with respect to measurement errors in option prices. Their results show the approach of fitting a spline function to the volatility smile to be affected less by small errors in option prices than the mixture of lognormals approach.

We used the spline-based technique to study the effects of ECB-council meetings on uncertainty in expectations on the money market. We estimated risk-neutral probability density functions from LIFFE Euribor futures options and computed various distributional statistics. Since statistics computed from risk-neutral density functions have been shown to be subject to substantial day-to-day fluctuations, we developed a methodology to separate economically significant changes from those caused by 'noise'.
Our results show that uncertainty in money-market expectations is obviously affected by monetary-policy decisions, as represented by ECB-council meetings. In Chapter 8 we used homogeneity tests to study the differences between risk-neutral statistics from weeks in which a ECB-council meeting took place to those from weeks without a council meeting. Using the observations from weeks without a council meeting controls for the 'noise' in the statistics and enables us to test for substantial deviations in the statistics computed for the council-meeting weeks. The results showed stochastically larger changes

in the risk-neutral density's skewness over the ECB-council meetings. By adjusting our sample we showed that this result might be evidence for the market expecting the ECB to follow an interest rate smoothing policy. In addition, our results indicate that uncertainty in expectations with respect to moderate interest-rate changes declines relatively over the ECB-council meeting. However, we also found some evidence for considerable heterogeneity in expectations' reactions to council meetings. For example, deleting from the sample the council meetings on which official interest rates were changed made the significant differences in the skewness statistics disappear. Furthermore, the results from the smaller sample indicate arelative increase in uncertainty with respect to extreme interest-rate changes over council meetings.
For a more detailed study of the effects of ECB-council meetings on uncertainty in market expectations we turned to event studies of ten selected ECB-council meetings. Using graphical and regression-based techniques, we showed that uncertainty in expectations is more likely to decrease after a council meeting if the market has correctly anticipated the ECB council's decisions. In particular, significant reductions in uncertainty are found for central-bank-council meetings where market participants correctly anticipated interest-rate changes, especially increases in official interest rates. Furthermore, we showed that it is important to consider the context of an individual council meeting very carefully, if changes in the risk-neutral density are to be correctly interpreted.

Future research will have to re-examine our results thoroughly using a larger data set. Since LIFFE Euribor-futures options have only been traded since the beginning of 1999, only about two and a half year of observations were available for our research.

Other interesting questions for future theoretical and empirical research relate to the implications our results have for the operation of monetary policy. For example, should central banks change interest rates gradually, i.e. change rates in small steps, or should they go for the "big leap" and adjust interest rates to their desired level at once? Our results show that the market is quite capable of incorporating an interest-rate smoothing policy into its expectation formation. Furthermore, we showed that if a policy is anticipated correctly, uncertainty in market expectations tends to decline. Therefore, there is a trade-off: a single "big leap" might be more difficult for market participants to anticipate – in particular with respect to its size, while a number of consecutive interest-rate changes might be easier to anticipate individually. However, it is not clear which strategy is superior with respect to overall uncertainty since for the latter strategy uncertainty might be slightly higher than normal before each council meeting.
This issue is closely related to the transparency discussion in monetary policy. Our results suggest that a central bank that wants to avoid increasing uncertainty in the money market should aim for transparency in the con-

duct of monetary policy so that market participants will be able to correctly anticipate the central bank's actions.[1]

Another interesting application might be to compare how different operating procedures and monetary policy strategies employed by central banks affect money-market expectations. For example, the Fed announces its target for the Federal Funds rate, while the ECB leaves market participants uncertain about the implicit target rate. Further research might investigate how these different approaches affect the reactions of market expectations.

[1] An interesting point is that such a policy might actually cause our results to vanish. If monetary policy is very predictable there will be very little uncertainty concerning the council meeting's results so that hypothesis c) from Chapter 8 might hold.

List of Figures

List of Tables

Bibliography

Abadir, Karim M. and Michael Rockinger (1997), Density-Embedding Functions, *Discussion Papers in Economics* 97/16, University of York.

Abken, Peter A., Dilip B. Madan, and Sailesh Ramamurtie (1996), Estimation of Risk-Neutral and Statistical Densities by Hermite Polynomial Approximation: With an Application to Eurodollar Futures Options, Working Paper, Federal Reserve Bank of Atlanta, WP 96-5.

Adão, Bernardino and Jorge Barros Luís (1999), Interest Rate Spreads Implicit in Options: Spain and Italy against Germany, in: Estimating and Interpreting Probability Density Functions – Proceedings of a Workshop held at the BIS on 14 June 1999, Bank for International Settlements.

Aït-Sahalia, Yacine and Andrew W. Lo (1998), Nonparametric Estimation of State-Price Densities Implicit in Financial Asset Prices, *Journal of Finance* 53, 499-547.

Aït-Sahalia, Yacine and Andrew W. Lo (2000), Nonparametric Risk Management and Implied Risk Aversion, *Journal of Econometrics* 94, 9-51.

Aït-Sahalia, Yacine, Yubo Wang, and Francis Yared (2001), Do Option Markets Correctly Price the Probabilities of Movement in the Underlying Asset?, *Journal of Econometrics* 102, 67-110.

Alexander, Volbert (1998), Geldpolitik und Volatilitäten auf Finanzmärkten, in: Baltensperger, Ernst (ed.) (1998), *Spekulation, Preisbildung und Volatilität auf Finanzmärkten*, Duncker & Humblodt, Berlin, 95-128.

Aparicio, Silio D. and Stewart Hodges (1998), Implied Risk-Neutral Distributions: A Comparison of Estimation Methods, Working Paper, Financial Option Research Centre, Warwick Business School.

Avellaneda, Marco, Craig Friedman, Richard Holmes, and Dominick Samperi (1997), Calibrating Volatility Surfaces Via Relative Entropy Minimization, *Applied Mathematical Finance*, 4, 5-37.

Bahra, Bupinder (1997), Implied Risk-Neutral Probability Density Functions from Option Prices: Theory and Application, Working Paper, Bank of England.

Ball, Clifford A. and Walter N. Torous (1983), A Simplified Jump Process for Common Stock Returns, *Journal of Financial and Quantitative Analysis* 18, 53-65.

Ball, Clifford A. and Walter N. Torous (1985), On Jumps in Common Stock Prices and their Impact on Call Option Pricing, *Journal of Finance* 40, 155-73.

Ball, Clifford A. and Walter N. Torous (1999), The Stochastic Volatility of Short-Term Interest Rates: Some International Evidence, *Journal of Finance* 54, 2339-59.

Bank of Japan (1995), Empirical Analyses of the Information Content of Implied Volatilities, *Quarterly Bulletin*, February, 63-88.

Banz, Rolf W. and Merton H. Miller (1978), Prices for State-contingent Claims: Some Estimates and Applications, *Journal of Business* 51, 653-72.

Barle, Stanko and Nusret Cakici (1995), Growing a Smiling Tree, *RISK Magazine* 8, 76-81.

Barle, Stanko and Nusret Cakici (1998), How to Grow a Smiling Tree, *Journal of Financial Engineering* 7, 127-46.

Barro, Robert J. (1977), Unanticipated Money Growth and Unemployment in the United States, *American Economic Review* 67, 101-15.

Bates, David S. (1991), The Crash of '87: Was It Expected? The Evidence from Options Markets, *Journal of Finance* 44, 1009-44.

Bates, David S. (1996a), Testing Option Pricing Models, in: G.S. Maddala and C.R. Rao (eds.), *Handbook of Statistics, Vol. 14*, Elsevier, North Holland 1996, 567-611.

Bates, David S. (1996b), Dollar Jump Fears 1984-1992: Distributional Abnormalities Implicit in Currency Futures Options, *Journal of International Money and Finance* 15, 65-93

Bates, David S. (1996c), Jumps and Stochastic Volatility: Exchange Rate Processes Implicit in Deutsche Mark Options, *Review of Financial Studies* 9, 69-105.

Bates, David S. (1997), The Skewness Premium: Option Pricing under Asymmetric Processes, *Advances in Futures and Options Research* 9, 51-82.

Bates, David S. (2000), Post '87 Crash Fears in the S&P 500 Futures Option Market, *Journal of Econometrics* 94, 181-238.

Baxter, Martin and Andrew Rennie (1996), *Financial Calculus — An Introduction to Derivative Pricing*, Cambridge University Press, Cambridge.

Beckers, Stan (1981), Standard Deviations Implied in Option Prices as Predictors of Future Stock Price Variability, *Journal of Banking and Finance* 5, 363-81.

Bertola, Guiseppe and Lars E.O. Svensson (1993), Stochastic Devaluation Risk and the Empirical Fit of Target-Zone Models, *Review of Economic Studies* 60, 689-712.

Bick, Avi (1982), Comments on the Valuation of Derivative Assets, *Journal of Financial Economics* 10, 331-45.

Bjørk, Tomas (1998), *Arbitrage Theory in Continuous Time*, Oxford University Press, Oxford.

Black, Fischer (1976a), The Pricing of Commodity Contracts, *Journal of Financial Economics* 3, 167-79.

Black, Fischer (1976b), Studies of stock price volatility changes. *Proceedings of the American Statistical Association*, 177-81.

Black, Fischer and Myron S. Scholes (1972), The Valuation of Option Contracts and a Test of Market Efficiency, *Journal of Finance* 27, 399-417.

Black, Fischer and Myron S. Scholes (1973), The Pricing of Options and Corporate Liabilities, *Journal of Political Economy* 81, 637-54.

Bliss, Robert B. and Nicolaos Panigirtzoglou (2002), Testing the Stability of Implied Probability Density Functions, *Journal of Banking and Finance* 26, 381-422.

Bodurtha, James N., Jr. and Georges R. Courtadon (1987), Tests of an American Option Pricing Model on the Foreign Currency Options Market, *Journal of Financial and Quantitative Analysis* 22, 153-67.

Bodurtha, James N., Jr. and Martin Jermakyan (1999), Non-Parametric Estimation of an Implied Volatility Surface, *Journal of Computational Finance* 2, 29-60.

Bodurtha, James N., Jr. and Qi Shen (1999), Historical and Implied Measures of "Value at Risk": The DM and Yen Case, Working Paper, Georgetown University, October.

Bollen, Nicolas P. B., Stephen F. Gray, and Robert E. Whaley (2000), Regime Switching in Foreign Exchange Rates: Evidence from Currency Option Prices, *Journal of Econometrics* 94, 239-76.

Bollerslev, Tim (1986), Generalized Autoregressive Conditional Heteroskedasticity, *Journal of Econometrics* 31, 307-27.

Bollerslev, Tim, Robert F. Engle, and Daniel B. Nelson (1994), ARCH Models, in: Robert Engle and Daniel F. McFadden (eds.), *Handbook of Econometrics Vol. IV*, 2059-3038.

Bollerslev, Tim, Robert F. Engle, and Jeffrey M. Wooldridge (1988), A Capital Asset Pricing Model with Time-Varying Covariances, *Journal of Political Economy* 96, 116-31.

Breeden, Douglas and Robert H. Litzenberger (1978), Prices of State-contingent Claims Implicit in Option Prices, *Journal of Business* 51, 621-51.

Britten-Jones, Mark and Anthony Neuberger (2000), Option Prices, Implied Price Processes, and Stochastic Volatility, *Journal of Finance* 60, 839-66.

Brown, Gregory and Klaus Bjerre Toft (1999), Constructing Binomial Trees from Multiple Implied Probability Distributions, *Journal of Derivatives* 7, 83-100.

Buchen, Peter W. and Michael Kelly (1996), The Maximum Entropy Distribution of an Asset Inferred from Option Prices, *Journal of Financial and Quantitative Analysis* 31, 143-59.

Butler, Creon and Neil Cooper (1997), Implied Exchange Rate Correlations and Market Perceptions of European Monetary Union, *Bank of England Quarterly Bulletin*, November, 413-23.

Butler, Creon and H. Davies (1998), Assessing Market Views on Monetary Policy: The Use of Implied Risk Neutral Probability Distributions, Working Paper, Bank of England.

Campa, José M. and P.H. Kevin Chang (1995), Testing the Expectations Hypothesis on the Term Structure of Volatilities in Foreign Exchange Options, *Journal of Finance* 50, 529-47.

Campa, José M. and P.H. Kevin Chang (1996), Arbitrage-Based Tests of Target-Zone Credibility: Evidence from ERM Cross-Rate Options, *American Economic Review* 86, 726-740.

Campa, José M. and P.H. Kevin Chang (1998a), The Forecasting Ability of Correlations Implied in Foreign Exchange Options, *Journal of International Money and Finance* 17, 855-80.

Campa, José M. and P.H. Kevin Chang (1998b), Learning from the Term Structure of Implied Volatilities in Foreign Currency Options, in: Chen, Zhaohui (ed.) (1998), *Currency Options and Exchange Rate Economics*, World Scientific, Singapore, 73-93.

Campa, José M. and P.H. Kevin Chang (1998c), ERM Realignment Risk and its Economic Determinants as Reflected in Cross-Rate Options, *Economic Journal* 108, 1046-66.

Campa, José M. and P.H. Kevin Chang (1998d), Options on Exchange Rates in Target Zones, in: Chen, Zhaohui (ed.) (1998), *Currency Options and Exchange Rate Economics*, World Scientific, Singapore, 157-82.

Campa, José M., P.H. Kevin Chang, and Robert L. Reider (1997), EMS Credibility: Exchange Rate Expectations Implied by Derivatives Prices, *Economic Policy* 12, 53-89.

Campa, José M., P.H. Kevin Chang, and Robert L. Reider (1998), Implied Exchange Rate Distributions: Evidence from OTC Option Markets, *Journal of International Money and Finance* 17, 117-60.

Campa, José M., P.H. Kevin Chang, and James F. Refalo (2002), An Option-Based Analysis of Emerging Market Exchange Rate Expectations: Brazil's *Real*-Plan 1994-97, forthcoming, *Journal of Development Economics.*

Campbell, John Y., Andrew W. Lo, and A. Craig MacKinlay (1997), *The Econometrics of Financial Markets*, Princeton University Press, Princeton.

Campbell, John Y. and Robert J. Shiller (1984), A Simple Account of the Behavior of Long-Term Interest Rates, *American Economic Review Papers and Proceedings* 74, 44-48.

Canina, Linda and Stephen Figlewski (1993), The Informational Content of Implied Volatility, *Review of Financial Studies* 6, 659-81.

Capozza, Dennis R. and Bradford Cornell (1979), Treasury Bill Pricing in the Spot and Futures Market, *Review of Economics and Statistics* 61, 513-20.

Carlson, John A. (1977), A Study of Price Forecasts, *Annals of Economic and Social Measurement* 6, 27-56.

Carr, Peter and Dilip B. Madan (1998), Determining Volatility Surfaces and Option Values from an Implied Volatility Smile, Working Paper, University of Maryland.

Chang, Carolyn W. and Jack S. K. Chang (1990), Forward and Futures Prices: Evidence from the Foreign Exchange Market, *Journal of Finance* 45, 1333-36.

Chang, P.H. Kevin and William R. Melick (1999), Background Note, in: Estimating and Interpreting Probability Density Functions – Proceedings of a Workshop held at the BIS on 14 June 1999, Bank for International Settlements.

Chaudhury, Mohammed M. and Jason Wei (1994), Upper Bounds for American Futures Options: A Note, *Journal of Futures Markets* 14, 111-16.

Chen, Ren-Raw and Louis O. Scott (1993), Pricing Interest Rate Futures Options with Futures-Style Margining Procedures, *Journal of Futures Markets* 13, 15-22.

Chiras, Donald P. and Steven Manaster (1978), The Information Content of Option Prices and a Test of Market Efficiency, *Journal of Financial Economics* 5, 213-34.

Chriss, Neil A. (1996), Transatlantic Trees, *RISK Magazine* 9, 45-48.

Chriss, Neil A. (1997), *Black-Scholes and Beyond - Option Pricing Models*, McGraw-Hill, New York etc.

Christie, Andrew A. (1982), The Stochastic Behavior of Common Stock Variances: Value, Leverage and Interest Rate Effects, *Journal of Financial Economics* 10, 407-32.

Clement, E., C. Gourieroux, and A. Montfort (2000), Econometric Specification of the Risk-Neutral Valuation Model, *Journal of Econometrics* 94, 117-43.

Coleman, Thomas F., Yuying Li, and Arun Verma (1999), Reconstructing the Unknown Local Volatility Function, *Journal of Computational Finance* 2,77-102.

Cont, Rama (1999), Beyond Implied Volatility, in: Kertesz, J. and I. Kondor (eds.), *Econophysics*, Kluwer, Amsterdam.

Cooper, Neil (1999), Testing Techniques for Estimating Implied RNDs from the prices of European-Style Options, in: Estimating and Interpreting Probability Density Functions – Proceedings of a Workshop held at the BIS on 14 June 1999, Bank for International Settlements.

Cooper, Neil and James Talbot (1999), The Yen/Dollar Exchange Rate in 1998: Views from Options Markets, *Bank of England Quarterly Bulletin*, Februar, 68-77.

Cornell, Bradford and Marc E. Reinganum (1981), Forward and Futures Prices: Evidence from the Foreign Exchange Markets, *Journal of Finance* 36, 1035-45.

Corrado, Charles J. and Tie Su (1996a), S&P Index Option Tests of Jarrow and Rudd's Approximate Option Valuation Formula, *Journal of Futures Markets* 16, 611-29.

Corrado, Charles J. and Tie Su (1996b), Skewness and Kurtosis in S&P 500 Index Returns Implied by Option Prices, *Journal of Financial Research* 19, 175-92.

Corrado, Charles J. and Tie Su (1997), Implied Volatility Skews and Stock Index Skewness and Kurtosis Implied by S&P 500 Index Option Prices, *Journal of Derivatives* 4, 8-19.

Coutant, Sophie (1999), Implied Risk Aversion in Option Prices Using Hermite Polynomials, in: Estimating and Interpreting Probability Density Functions – Proceedings of a Workshop held at the BIS on 14 June 1999, Bank for International Settlements.

Coutant, Sophie, Eric Jondeau, and Michael Rockinger (2001), Reading Interest Rate and Bond Futures Options' Smiles: How PIBOR and Notional Operators Appreciated the 1997 French Snap Election, *Journal of Banking and Finance*, 25, 1957-87.

Cox, John C., Jonathan E. Ingersoll, and Stephen A. Ross (1981), The Relation between Forward Prices and Futures Prices, *Journal of Financial Economics* 9, 321-46.

Cox, John C., Jonathan E. Ingersoll, and Stephen A. Ross (1985), An Intertemporal General Equilibrium Model of Asset Prices, *Econometrica*, 53, 363-84.

Cox, John C. and Stephen A. Ross (1976), The Valuation of Options for Alternative Stochastic Processes, *Journal of Financial Economics* 3, 145-66.

Cox, John C., Stephen A. Ross, and Mark Rubinstein (1979), Option Pricing: A Simplified Approach, *Journal of Financial Economics* 7, 229-63.

Cuthbertson, Keith (1996), *Quantitative Financial Economics. Stocks, Bonds and Foreign Exchange*, Wiley, Chichester etc.

Das, Sanjiv R. and Rangarajan K. Sundaram (1999), Of Smiles and Smirks: A Term Structure Perspective, *Journal of Financial and Quantitative Analysis* 34, 211-40.

Davidson, James (1994), *Stochastic Limit Theory*, Oxford University Press, Oxford.

Day, Theodore E. and Craig M. Lewis (1988), The Behavior of the Volatility Implicit in the Prices of Stock Index Options, *Journal of Financial Economics* 22, 103-22.

Day, Theodore E. and Craig M. Lewis (1992), Stock Market Volatility and the Information Content of Stock Index Options, *Journal of Econometrics* 52, 267-87.

DeBondt, Werner F. M. and Mary M. Bange (1992), Inflation Forecast Errors and Time Variation in Term Premia, *Journal of Financial and Quantitative Analysis* 27, 479-96.

Derman, Emanuel (1999), Regimes of Volatility - Some Observations on the Variation of S&P 500 Implied Volatilities, *Goldman Sachs Quantitative Strategies Research Notes.*

Derman, Emanuel and Iraj Kani (1994), Riding on a Smile, *RISK Magazine* 7, 32-39.

Derman, Emanuel and Iraj Kani (1998), Stochastic Implied Trees: Arbitrage Pricing with Stochastic Term and Strike Structure of Volatility, *International Journal of Theoretical and Applied Finance* 1, 61-110.

Derman, Emanuel, Iraj Kani, and Neil A. Chriss (1996), Implied Trinomial Trees of the Volatility Smile, *Journal of Derivatives* 3, 7-22.

Dezhbakhsh, Hashem (1994), Foreign Exchange Forward and Futures Prices: Are They Equal?, *Journal of Financial and Quantitative Analysis* 29, 75-87.

Diebold, Francis X. and Roberto S. Mariano (1995), Comparing Predictive Accuracy, *Journal of Business and Economic Statistics* 13, 253-63.

Diz, Fernando and Thomas J. Finucane (1993), Do the Options Markets Really Overreact?, *Journal of Futures Markets* 13, 299-312.

Dominguez, Kathryn M. (1986), Are Foreign Exchange Forecasts Rational?, *Economics Letters* 21, 277-81.

Duffie, Darrell (1988), *Security Markets — Stochastic Models*, Academic Press, San Diego etc.

Duffie, Darrell (1996), *Dynamic Asset Pricing Theory*, 2nd ed., Princeton University Press, Princeton.

Duffie, Darrell and Kenneth Singleton (1993), Simulated Method of Moments Estimation of Markov Models of Asset Prices, *Econometrica* 61, 929-952.

Dumas, Bernard, Jeff Fleming, and Robert E. Whaley (1998), Implied Volatility Functions: Empirical Tests, *Journal of Finance* 53, 2059-2106.

Dupire, Bruno (1994), Pricing with a Smile, *RISK Magazine* 7, 18-20.

Emanuel, David C. and James D. MacBeth (1982), Further Results on the Constant Elastiticity of Variance Call Option Pricing Model, *Journal of Futures Markets* 17, 533-54.

Engle, Robert F. (1982), Autoregressive Conditional Heteroskedasticity with Estimates of the Variance of United Kingdom Inflation, *Econometrica* 50, 987-1006.

Engle, Robert F., Alex Kane, and Jaesun Noh (1994), Forecasting Volatility and Option Prices of the S&P 500 Index, *Journal of Derivatives* 2, 17-30.

Engle, Robert F. and Kenneth F. Kroner (1995), Multivariate Simultaneous Generalized ARCH, *Econometric Theory* 11, 122-50.

European Central Bank (2000), Annual Report 1999.

European Central Bank (2001a), Monthly Report, January.

European Central Bank (2001b), Monthly Report, June.

Evans, George W. and Seppo Honkapohja (2001), *Learning and Expectations in Macroeconomics*, Princeton University Press, Princeton.

Fair, Ray C. and Robert J. Shiller (1990), Comparing Information in Forecasts from Econometric Models, *American Economic Review* 80, 375-89.

Fama, Eugene F. (1984a), The Information in the Term Structure, *Journal of Financial Economics* 13, 509-28.

Fama, Eugene F. (1984b), Forward and Spot Exchange Rates, *Journal of Monetary Economics* 14, 319-38.

Fama, Eugene F. and Robert R. Bliss (1987), The Information in Long-Maturity Forward Rates, *American Economic Review* 77, 680-92.

Feinstein, Steven P. (1989), The Black-Scholes Formula is Nearly Linear in σ for At-The-Money Options; Therefore Implied Volatilities from At-The-Money Options are Virtually Unbiased, Working Paper, Federal Reserve Bank of Atlanta.

Fleming, Jeff (1998), The Quality of Market Volatility Forecasts Implied by S&P 100 Index Option Prices, *Journal of Empirical Finance* 5, 317-45.

Fleming, Jeff (1999), The Economic Significance of the Forecast Bias of S&P 100 Index Option Implied Volatility, *Advances in Futures and Options Research* 10, 219-51.

Fleming, Jeff, Barbara Ostdiek, and Robert E. Whaley (1995), Predicting Stock Market Volatility: A New Measure, *Journal of Futures Markets* 3, 265-302.

Fleming, Jeff and Robert Whaley (1994), The Value of Wildcard Options, *Journal of Finance* 49, 215-36.

Fornari, Fabio and Roberto Violi (1998), The Probability Density Function of Interest Rates Implied in the Price of Options, *Temi di Discussione del Servizio Studi* 339, Banca D'Italia.

Frankel, Jeffrey A. (1980), Tests of Rational Expectations in the Forward Exchange Market, *Southern Economic Journal* 46,1083-1101.

Frankel, Jeffrey A. and Kenneth A. Froot (1987), Using Survey Data to Test Standard Propositions Regarding Exchange Rate Expectations, *American Economic Review* 77, 133-53.

French, Kenneth R. (1983), A Comparison of Futures and Forward Prices, *Journal of Financial Economics* 12, 311-42.

Friedman, Benjamin (1980), Survey Evidence on the 'Rationality' of Interest Rate Expectations, *Journal of Monetary Economics* 6, 453-65.

Galati, Gabriele and William R. Melick (2002), Perceived Central Bank Intervention and Market Expectations: An Empirical Study of the Yen/Dollar Exchange Rate 1993-96, Working Paper No. 77, Bank for International Settlements.

Garcia, René and Éric Renault (1998), Risk Aversion, Intertemporal Substitution, and Option Pricing, *CIRANO Scientific Series* 98s-02, Montréal.

Gay, Gerald. D. and Steven Manaster (1984), The Quality Variation Option Implicit in Futures Contracts, *Journal of Financial Economics* 13, 353-70.

Gemmill, Gordon (1996), Did Option Traders Anticipate the Crash? Evidence from Volatility Smiles in the U.K. with U.S. Comparisons, *Journal of Futures Markets* 16, 881-97.

Gemmill, Gordon and Apostolos Saflekos (1999), How Useful are Implied Distributions? Evidence from Stock-Index Options, in: Estimating and Interpreting Probability Density Functions – Proceedings of a Workshop held at the BIS on 14 June 1999, Bank for International Settlements.

Ghysels, Eric, Valentin Patilea, Éric Renault, and Olivier Torrès (1997), Nonparametric Methods and Option Pricing, *CIRANO Scientific Series* 97s-19, Montréal.

Goodfriend, Marvin (1991), Interest Rates and the Conduct of Monetary Policy, *Carnegie-Rochester Conference Series on Public Policy* 34, 7-30.

Goodhart, Charles E. A. (1999), Central Bankers and Uncertainty, *Quarterly Bulletin*, February, 102-121, Bank of England.

Granger, Clive W. J. and Paul Newbold (1976), Spurious Regressions in Econometrics, *Journal of Econometrics* 2, 111-20.

Grossman, Sanford J. (1988), An Analysis of the Implications for Stock and Futures Price Volatility of Program Trading and Dynamic Hedging Strategies, *Journal of Business* 61, 275-98.

Grossman, Sanford J. and Zhongquan Zhou (1996), Equilibrium Analysis of Portfolio Insurance, *Econometrica* 51, 1379-1403.

Härdle, Wolfgang (1990), *Applied Nonparametric Regression*, Cambridge University Press, Cambridge.

Härdle, Wolfgang and O. Linton (1994), Applied Nonparametric Methods, in: Engle, Robert. F. and David L. McFadden (eds.), *Handbook of Econometrics Vol. 4*, North Holland, Amsterdam, 2297-2308.

Härtter, Erich (1978), Splinefunktionen: Darstellung ihrer elementaren Eigenschaften, in: Schäffer, Karl-August (ed): *Splinefunktionen in der Statistik, Sonderheft zum Allgemeinen Statistischen Archiv*, Heft 14, 7-23.

Hansen, Lars P. (1982), Large Sample Properties of Generalized Method of Moments Estimators, *Econometrica* 50, 1029-54.

Hansen, Lars P. and Robert J. Hodrick (1980), Forward Exchange Rates as Optimal Predictors of Future Spot Rates: An Econometric Analysis, *Journal of Political Economy* 88, 829-53.

Hardouvelis, Gikas A. (1988), The Predictive Power of the Term-Structure during Recent Monetary Regimes, *Journal of Finance* 43, 339-56.

Harrison, J. Michael and David M. Kreps (1979), Martingales and Arbitrage in Multiperiod Securities Markets, *Journal of Economic Theory* 20, 381-408.

Harrison, J. Michael and Stanley R. Pliska (1981), Martingales and Stochastic Integrals in the Theory of Continuous Trading, *Stochastic Processes and their Applications* 11, 215-60.

Hegde, Shantaram P. and Bill McDonald (1986), On the Informational Role of Treasury Bill Futures, *Journal of Futures Markets* 6, 629-43.

Heston, Steven L. (1993), A Closed-Form Solution for Options with Stochastic Volatility with Applications to Bond and Currency Options, *Review of Financial Studies* 6, 327-43.

Heynen, Ronald (1994), An Empirical Investigation of Observed Smile Patterns, *Review of Futures Markets* 13, 317-51.

Heynen, Ronald, Angelien Kemna, and Ton Vorst (1994), Analysis of the Term Structure of Implied Volatilities, *Journal of Financial and Quantitative Analysis* 29, 31-56.

Hodges, Hardy M. (1996), Arbitrage Bounds on the Implied Volatility Strike and Term Structures of European-Style Options, *Journal of Derivatives* 3, 23-35.

Hodrick, Robert J. (1987), *The Empirical Evidence on the Efficiency of Forward and Futures Foreign Exchange Markets*, Harwood, Chur etc.

Horowitz, Joel L. (2001), The Bootstrap, in: Heckman, J.J. and Edward E. Leamer (eds.), *Handbook of Econometrics Vol. 5*, Amsterdam.

Howard, Charles T. (1982), Are T-Bill Futures Good Forecasters of Interest Rates?, *Journal of Futures Markets* 1, 305-15.

Hull, John C. (1997), *Options, Futures, and Other Derivatives*, 3rd ed., Prentice Hall, London etc.

Hull, John C. and Alan White (1987), The Pricing of Options on Assets with Stochastic Volatilities, *Journal of Finance* 42, 281-300.

Jackwerth, Jens C. (1997), Generalized Binomial Trees, *Journal of Derivatives* 5, 7-17.

Jackwerth, Jens C. (1999), Option-Implied Risk-Neutral Distributions and Implied Binomial Trees: A Literature Review, *Journal of Derivatives* 7, 66-82.

Jackwerth, Jens C. (2000), Recovering Risk Aversion from Option Prices and Realized Returns, Review of Financial Studies 13, 433-51.

Jackwerth, Jens C. and Mark Rubinstein (1996), Recovering Probability Distributions from Option Prices, *Journal of Finance* 51, 1611-31.

Jackwerth, Jens C. and Mark Rubinstein (1998), Recovering Stochastic Processes from Option Prices, Working Paper, Haas School of Business.

Jarrow, Robert A. and George S. Oldfield (1981), Forward Contracts and Futures Contracts, *Journal of Financial Economics* 9, 373-82.

Jarrow, Robert A. and Andrew Rudd (1982), Approximate Option Valuation for Arbitrary Stochastic Processes, *Journal of Financial Economics* 10, 347-69.

Jaynes, E. T. (1979), Where Do We Stand on Maximum Entropy?, in: Levine, R. D. and M Tribus (eds.), *The Maximum Entropy Formalism*, MIT Press, Cambridge, MA.

Jaynes, E. T. (1982), On the Rationale of Maximum-Entropy Methods, *Proceedings of the IEEE* 70, 939-52.

Johnson, Norman .L. (1949), Systems of Frequency Curves Generated by Methods of Translation, *Biometrika* 36, 149-76.

Jondeau, Eric and Michael Rockinger (2000), Reading the Smile: The Message Conveyed by Methods Which Infer Risk Neutral Densities, *Journal of International Money and Finance.* 19, 885-915.

Jondeau, Eric and Michael Rockinger (2001), Estimating Gram-Charlier Expansions under Positivity Constraints, Working Paper, HEC School of Management, *Journal of Economic Dynamics & Control*, 25, 1457-1483.

Jorion, Phillipe (1995), Predicting Volatility in the Foreign Exchange Market, *Journal of Finance* 50, 507-29.

Jorion, Phillipe (1997), Value at Risk: The New Benchmark for Controlling Derivatives Risk, McGraw-Hill, New York etc.

Karatzas, Ioannis and Steven E. Shreve (1991), *Brownian Motion and Stochastic Calculus*, 2nd ed., Springer, New York etc.

Kendall, Maurice and Alan Stuart (1973), The Advanced Theory of Statistics, Vol. II, 3rd ed., Charles Griffin & Company, London.

Kendall, Maurice and Alan Stuart (1977), The Advanced Theory of Statistics, Vol. I, 4th ed., Charles Griffin & Company, London.

Kumar, Manmohan S. (1992), The Forecasting Accuracy of Crude Oil Futures Prices, *IMF Staff Papers* 39, 432-61.

Lagnado, Ronald and Stanley Osher (1997), Reconciling Differences, *RISK Magazine*, 10, 79-83.

Lamoureux, Christopher G. and William D. Lastrapes (1993), Forecasting Stock-Return Variance: Toward an Understanding of Stochastic Implied Volatilities, *Review of Financial Studies* 6, 293-325.

Latané, Henry A. and Richard J. Rendleman Jr. (1976), Standard Deviations of Stock Price Ratios Implied in Option Prices, *Journal of Finance* 31, 369-81.

Laurent, Jean-Paul and Dietmar P.J. Leisen (1998), Building a Consistent Pricing Model from Observed Option Prices, Working Paper, Universität Bonn.

Leahy, Michael P. and Charles P. Thomas (1996), The Sovereignty Option: The Quebec Referendum and Market Views on the Canadian Dollar, *International Finance Discussion Paper* 555, Board of Governors of the Federal Reserve System.

Ledoit, Olivier and Pedro Santa-Clara (1999), Relative Pricing of Options with Stochastic Volatilitiy, Working Paper, UCLA.

Levin, Alexander, Des McManus, and David Watt (1998), The Information Content of Canadian Dollar Futures Options, in: *Information in Financial Asset Prices*, Proceedings of a Conference held by the Bank of Canada, May 1998, 229-75.

Lewis, Karen K. (1995), Puzzles in International Financial Markets, in: Grossman, Gene and Kenneth Rogoff (eds.)(1995), *Handbook of International Economics, Vol III*, Elsevier, Amsterdam, 1913-71.

LIFFE (2000), Short Term Interest Rate Futures Options, London International Financial Futures and Options Exchange, London.

Longstaff, Francis (1995), Option Pricing and the Martingale Restriction, *Review of Financial Studies* 8, 1091-1124.

Lucas, Robert E. Jr. (1972), Expectations and the Neutrality of Money, *Journal of Economic Theory* 4, 103-24.

Lucas, Robert E. Jr. (1973), Some International Evidence on the Output-Inflation Tradeoff, *American Economic Review* 63, 326-34.

Lyons, Richard K. (1988), Tests of the Foreign Exchange Risk Premium Using the Expected Second Moments Implied by Option Pricing, *Journal of International Money and Finance* 7, 91-108.

Lyons, Richard K. (1998), Options and the Currency Risk Premium, in: Chen, Zhaohui (ed.) (1998), *Currency Options and Exchange Rate Economics*, World Scientific, Singapore, 33-46.

Macbeth, James D. and Larry J. Merville (1979), An Empirical Examination of the Black-Scholes Call Option Pricing Model, *Journal of Finance* 34, 1173-86.

MacDonald, Robert (1983), Some Tests of the Rational Expectations Hypothesis in the Foreign Exchange Market, *Scottish Journal of Political Economy* 30, 235-50.

MacDonald S. Scott and Scott E. Hein (1989), Futures Rates and Forward Rates as Predictors of Near-Term Treasury Bill Rates, *Journal of Futures Markets* 9, 249-62.

Madan, Dilip B. and Frank Milne (1994), Contingent Claims Valued and Hedged by Pricing and Investing in a Basis, *Mathematical Finance* 4, 224-45.

Malz, Allan M. (1996a), Using Option Prices to Estimate Realignment Probabilities in the European Monetary System: The Case of Sterling-Mark, *Journal of International Money and Finance* 15, 717-48.

Malz, Allan M. (1996b), Using Option Prices to Estimate Realignment Probabilities in the European Monetary System, *Federal Reserve Bank of New York, Staff Report.*

Malz, Allan M. (1997), Option-Implied Probability Distributions and Currency Excess Returns, *Federal Reserve Bank of New York Staff Reports* 32/1997.

Malz, Allan M. (1998a), An Introduction to Currency Option Markets, in: Chen, Zhaohui (ed.) (1998), *Currency Options and Exchange Rate Economics*, World Scientific, Singapore, 33-46.

Malz, Allan M. (1998b), Option Prices and the Probability Distribution of Exchange Rates, in: Chen, Zhaohui (ed.) (1998), *Currency Options and Exchange Rate Economics*, World Scientific, Singapore, 108-37.

Malz, Allan M. (1998c), The ERM Realignment Probabilities: Estimates Using Option Prices, in: Chen, Zhaohui (ed.) (1998), *Currency Options and Exchange Rate Economics*, World Scientific, Singapore, 138-56.

Mandler, Martin (2002), Extracting Market Expectations from Option Prices: Two Case Studies in Market Perception's of the ECB's Monetary Policy 1999/2000, *Swiss Journal of Economics and Statistics*, 138, 165-89.

Mankiw, N. Gregory and Jeffrey A. Miron (1986), The Changing Behavior of the Term Structure of Interest Rates, *Quarterly Journal of Economics* 51, 211-28.

Mankiw, N. Gregory and Lawrence H. Summers (1984), Do Long-Term Interest Rates Overreact to Short-Term Interest Rates?, *Brookings Papers on Economic Activity* 1:1984, 223-47.

Mayhew, Stewart (1995), On Estimating the Risk-Neutral Probability Distribution Implied by Option Prices, Working Paper, Haas School of Business, University of California, Berkeley.

McCollough, B.D. and H.D. Vinod (1999), The Numerical Reliability of Econometric Software, *Journal of Economic Literature* 37, 633-65.

McManus, Des (1999), The Information Content of Interest Rate Futures Options, in: Estimating and Interpreting Probability Density Functions – Proceedings of a Workshop held at the BIS on 14 June 1999, Bank for International Settlements.

Meese, Richard A. and Kenneth Rogoff (1983), Empirical Exchange Rate Models of the Seventies: Do They Fit Out of Sample?, *Journal of International Economics* 14, 3-24.

Melick, William R. (1999), Results of the Estimation of Implied PDFs from a Common Dataset, in: Estimating and Interpreting Probability Density Functions – Proceedings of a Workshop held at the BIS on 14 June 1999, Bank for International Settlements.

Melick, William R. and Charles P. Thomas (1997), Recovering an Asset's Implied PDF from Option Prices: An Application to Crude Oil during the Gulf Crisis, *Journal of Financial and Quantitative Analysis* 32, 91-115.

Melick, William R. and Charles P. Thomas (1998), Confidence Intervals and Constant-Maturity Series for Probability Measures Extracted from Options Prices, in: *Information in Financial Asset Prices*, Proceedings of a Conference held by the Bank of Canada, May 1998, 293-320.

Merton, Robert C. (1971), Optimum Consumption and Portfolio Rules in a Continuous-Time Model, *Journal of Economic Theory* 3, 373-413. reprinted in: Merton, Robert C. (1990), *Continuous Time Finance*, Blackwell, Oxford, 120-65.

Merton, Robert C. (1973), Theory of Rational Option Pricing, *Bell Journal of Economics and Management Science* 4, 141-83, reprinted in: Merton, Robert C. (1990), *Continuous Time Finance*, Blackwell, Oxford, 255-308.

Merton, Robert C. (1976), Option Pricing when Underlying Stock Returns are Discontinuous, *Journal of Financial Economics* 3, 125-44, reprinted in:

Merton, Robert C. (1990), *Continuous Time Finance*, Blackwell, Oxford, 309-29.

Merton, Robert C. (1990), *Continuous Time Finance*, Blackwell, Oxford.

Mishkin, Frederic S. (1988), The Information in the Term Structure: Some Further Results, *Journal of Applied Econometrics* 3, 307-14.

Mizrach, Bruce (1996), Did Option Prices Predict the ERM Crisis?, Working Paper, Rutgers University.

Moles, Peter and Nicholas Terry (1997), *The Handbook of International Financial Terms*, Oxford University Press, Oxford.

Nakamura, Hisashi and Shigenori Shiratsuka (1999), Extracting Market Expectations from Option Prices: Case Studies in Japanese Option Markets, Working Paper, Bank of Japan.

Neuhaus, Holger (1995), Der Informationsgehalt von Derivaten für die Geldpolitik: Implizite Volatilitäten und Wahrscheinlichkeiten, Diskussionspapier der Volkswirtschaftlichen Arbeitsgruppe der Deutschen Bundesbank 3/95.

Neuhaus, Holger (1999), Discussion of Neil Cooper's Paper: Testing Techniques for Estimating Implied RNDs from the prices of European-Style Options, in: Estimating and Interpreting Probability Density Functions – Proceedings of a Workshop held at the BIS on 14 June 1999, Bank for International Settlements.

Neftci, Salih N. (1996), *An Introduction to the Mathematics of Financial Derivatives*, Academic Press, San Diego etc.

Nelson, Daniel B. (1991), Conditional Heteroskedasticity in Asset Returns: A New Approach, *Econometrica* 59, 347-70.

Øksendal, Bernt (1998), *Stochastic Differential Equations — An Introduction with Applications*, 5th ed., Springer, Berlin etc.

Pesando, James E. (1975), A Note on the Rationality of the Livingston Price Expectations, *Journal of Political Economy* 83, 849-58.

Phillips, Peter C. B. (1986), Understanding Spurious Regressions in Econometrics, *Journal of Econometrics* 33, 311-40.

Platen, Eckhard and Martin Schweizer (1994), On Smile and Skewness, Diskussionspapier B-302, SFB 303 Universität Bonn.

Polakoff, Michael A. and Paul C. Grier (1991), A Comparison of Foreign Exchange Forward and Futures Prices, *Journal of Banking and Finance* 15, 1057-80.

Posner, Steven E. and Moshe A. Milevsky (1998), Valuing Exotic Options by Approximating the SPD with Higher Moments, *Journal of Financial Engineering* 7, 109-25.

Poterba, James M. and Lawrence H. Summers (1986), The Persistence of Volatility and Stock Market Fluctuations, *American Economic Review* 76, 1142-51.

Potters, M., Rama Cont, and J.-P. Bouchaud (1998), Financial Markets as Adaptive Systems, *Europhysics Letters* 41, 239-44.

Rendleman, Richard J. Jr., and Christopher F. Carabini (1979), The Efficiency of the Treasury Bill Futures Market, *Journal of Finance* 34, 895-914.

Rinne, Horst (1997), *Taschenbuch der Statistik*, 2.A., Verlag H. Deutsch, Frankfurt/Main-Thun.

Ritchey, Robert J. (1990), Call Option Valuation for Discrete Normal Mixtures, *Journal of Financial Research* 13, 285-296.

Rookley, Cameron (1997), Fully Exploiting the Information Content of Intra-Day Option Quotes: Applications in Option Pricing and Risk Management, Working Paper, University of Arizona.

Rose, Andrew K. and Lars E.O. Svensson (1994), Exchange Rate Credibility before the Fall, *European Economic Review* 38, 1185-216.

Rosenberg, Joshua V. (1998), Pricing Multivariate Contingent Claims Using Estimated Risk-Neutral Density Functions, *Journal of International Money and Finance* 17, 229-47.

Rosenberg, Joshua V. (2000), Implied Volatility Functions: A Reprise, *Journal of Derivatives* 7,51-64.

Rosenberg, Joshua V. and Robert F. Engle (1999), Empirical Pricing Kernels, Working Paper, New York University.

Ross, Stephen A. (1976), Options and Efficiency, *Quarterly Journal of Economics* 90, 75-89.

Rubinstein, Mark (1985), Nonparametric Tests of Alternative Option Pricing Models Using All Reported Trades and Quotes on the 30 Most Active CBOE Option Classes from August, 23, 1976 through August, 31, 1978, *Journal of Finance* 40, 455-80.

Rubinstein, Mark (1994), Implied Binomial Trees, *Journal of Finance* 49, 771-818.

Rudebusch, Glenn D. (1995), Federal Reserve Interest Rate Targeting, Rational Expectations, and the Term Structure, *Journal of Monetary Economics* 35, 245-74.

Schmalensee, Richard and Robert R. Trippi (1978), Common Stock Volatility Expectations Implied by Option Premia, *Journal of Finance* 33, 129-147.

Scott, Louis O. (1987), Option Pricing When the Variance Changes Randomly: Theory, Estimation and an Application, *Journal of Financial and Quantitative Analysis* 22, 419-38.

Scott, Louis O. (1992), The Information Content of Prices in Derivative Security Markets, *IMF Staff Papers* 39, 596-625.

Scott, Louis O. (1998), The Implied Volatility in Prices of Foreign Currency Options, in: Chen, Zhaohui (ed.) (1998), *Currency Options and Exchange Rate Economics*, World Scientific, Singapore, 49-72.

Sheikh, Amir M. (1991), Transaction Data Tests of S&P 100 Call Option Pricing, *Journal of Financial and Quantitative Analysis* 26, 459-475.

Sherrick, Bruce J., Philip Garcia and Viswanath Tirupattur (1996), Recovering Probabilistic Information from Options Markets: Tests of Distributional Assumptions, *Journal of Futures Markets* 16, 545-60.

Sherrick, Bruce J., Scott H. Irwin and D. Lynn Forster (1992), Option-based Evidence of the Nonstationarity of Expected S&P 500 Futures Price Distributions, *Journal of Futures Markets* 12, 275-90.

Shiller, Robert J., John Y. Campbell, and Kermit L. Schoenholtz (1983), Forward Rates and Future Policy: Interpreting the Term Structure of Interest Rates, *Brookings Papers on Economic Acitivity* 1:1983, 173-223.

Shimko, David (1993), Bounds of Probability, *RISK Magazine* 6, 33-37.

Shiratsuka, Shigenori (1999), Discussion of Gemmill and Saflekos' Paper "How Useful are Implied Distributions? Evidence from Stock-Index Options", in: Estimating and Interpreting Probability Density Functions – Proceedings of a Workshop held at the BIS on 14 June 1999, Bank for International Settlements.

Shreve, Steven E. (1997), *Stochastic Calculus and Finance*, Manuscript, Carnegie Mellon University.

Silverman , B. W. (1986), *Density Estimation for Statistics and Data Analysis*, Chapman & Hall, London.

Söderlind, Paul (2000), Market Expectations in the UK before and After the ERM Crisis, *Economica* 67, 1-18.

Söderlind, Paul and Lars E.O. Svensson (1998), New Techniques to Extract Market Expectations from Financial Instruments, *Journal of Monetary Economics* 40, 383-429.

Stein, Jeremy (1989), Overreactions in the Options Market, *Journal of Finance* 44, 1011-1023.

Stutzer, Michael (1996), A Simple Nonparametric Approach to Derivative Security Valuation, *Journal of Finance* 51, 1633-52.

Svensson, Lars E.O. (1993), Assessing Target Zone Credibility: Mean Reversion and Devaluation Expectations in the ERM, 1979-1992, *European Economic Review* 37, 763-93.

Tobin, James (1958), Liquidity Preference as Behavior Towards Risk, *Review of Economic Studies* 25, 65-86.

Toft, Klaus Bjerre and Brian Prucyk (1997), Options on Leveraged Equity: Theory and Empirical Tests, *Journal of Finance* 52, 1151-80.

Tucker, Alan L., David R. Peterson, and Elton Scott (1988), Tests of the Black-Scholes and Constant Elasticity of Variance Currency Call Option Valuation Models, *Journal of Financial Research* 11, 201-13.

Walter, Christian and José A. Lopez (2000), Is Implied Correlation Worth Calculating? Evidence from Foreign Exchange Options and Historical Data, Working Paper, Federal Reserve Bank of San Francisco, March.

Whaley, Robert E. (1982), Valuation of American Call Options on Dividend-Paying Stocks: Empirical Tests, *Journal of Financial Economics* 10, 29-58.

Whaley, Robert E. (1986), Valuation of American Futures Options: Theory and Empirical Tests, *Journal of Finance* 41, 127-50.

White, Halbert (1980), A Heteroskedasticity-Consistent Covariance Matrix Estimator and Direct Test for Heteroskedasticity, *Econometrica* 48, 817-38.

Xu, Xinzhong and Stephen J. Taylor (1994), The Term Structure of Volatility Implied by Foreign Exchange Options, *Journal of Financial and Quantitative Analysis* 29, 57-74.

Yatchew, Adonis (1998), Nonparametric Regression Techniques for Economists, *Journal of Economic Literature* 36, 669-721.

GPSR Compliance

The European Union's (EU) General Product Safety Regulation (GPSR) is a set of rules that requires consumer products to be safe and our obligations to ensure this.

If you have any concerns about our products, you can contact us on ProductSafety@springernature.com

In case Publisher is established outside the EU, the EU authorized representative is:

Springer Nature Customer Service Center GmbH
Europaplatz 3
69115 Heidelberg, Germany

Batch number: 10725973

Printed by Printforce, the Netherlands